The **Bedside Guardian** *37*

STAR WARS

2 December 1987

The **Bedside Guardian** *37*

A selection from *The Guardian* 1987–88
Edited by
Hugh Hebert

With an introduction by
Fay Weldon

Cartoons by
Gibbard
Bryan McAllister
Steve Bell

COLLINS
8 Grafton Street, London W1
1988

William Collins Sons & Co Ltd
London · Glasgow · Sydney · Auckland
Toronto · Johannesburg

BRITISH LIBRARY CATALOGUING IN PUBLICATION DATA

The Bedside Guardian – 37
1. English essays – Periodicals
I. The Guardian
082'.05   PR1361

ISBN 0-00-215091-3

First published 1988
© Guardian Newspapers 1988

Photoset in Linotron Century Schoolbook
by Rowland Phototypesetting Ltd, Bury St Edmunds, Suffolk
Printed and bound in Great Britain
by Hartnolls Ltd, Bodmin, Cornwall

Introduction

Time for *The Bedside Guardian* yet again. The seasons race by, alas, as if we were all on H. G. Wells's Time Machine, bucking and galloping through the centuries, faster and faster. A flash of thigh for Miss World, a hint of a bark for Cruft's, a gleam and a crash for Christmas – and another year gone! Others say, of course, it's to do with oneself getting older and policemen getting younger – but I'm not so sure any more. For these days the young feel it too. 'Can't be time for the Cup Final *again*,' protests the ten-year-old. 'It's the Flower Show already,' laments the girl (child) behind the new thief-proof grille at the bank, '– and we've only just finished January. What's *happening*?'

So I've come to believe this disagreeable phenomenon, this increasing speed of time, has something to do with the soap opera that TV and newspapers make of the reality of our lives: the way they punctuate our year. News stories unfold, episode by episode, and we live in expectation of tomorrow, rather than living in today. The Hijack (will they live, won't they?), Irangate (did they, didn't they?), the Seamen's Strike (who's the baddie, who's the goodie?), and so on – terrifying and terrible for those who live through them, fascinating for the rest of us as we wait, cliffhanger by cliffhanger, for the resolution, the verdict, the consensus of opinion to be reached. We are not allowed to be *bored*, in fact. (Perhaps that's all it is? Those long golden days of remembered childhood – were we just plain *bored*?)

Nothing is for nothing. As the technology of communications gets more and more efficient (what is seen out of a window in Karachi races round the world in seconds) so time itself goes faster: our lives whip by.

How pleasant, then, to be allowed *The Bedside Guardian*, this eloquent retrospective of a year; to be given a little space and time for contemplation; to retrieve for the personal memory banks Adam Sweeting, that elegant essayist and social philosopher who poses as a pop and rock journalist, or Derek Malcolm, the God of cinema, rightly grinding one's favourite film extremely small; to slow time down, hold back, give the daily fix of news and comment its proper value. These journalists and critics we take for granted are *so good at what they do.*

The Bedside Guardian! How reassuring the suggestion is that we all not only have beds to go to, but bedside tables, bedside lights, and like to read a little before we go to sleep, the tradition of a culture behind us, the prospect of more to come. How civilized!

But then, of course, the *Guardian* is civilized. It assumes (and no doubt its researchers confirm it) a readership that is generally cultured, well read, properly informed, self-aware and community conscious. As the psychiatric institutions close and the patients drift out into community care, that care (I'm willing to bet) is more likely to be delivered by *Guardian* readers than by those who read the *Telegraph*, *The Times* or the *Sun* – newspapers that assume, to a greater or lesser degree, that their readers are primarily self-interested, and, by this assumption, make them more so. Newspapers themselves, of course, are self-interested and self-aware, let us not assume otherwise. I can feel the Editor flinch and murmur even as I write: 'But we do not want to be known as the newspaper of the muesli belt, the social worker, the self-righteous. We want to be seen as young, vigorous, thrusting, forward-looking ... Good God, what is she talking about, what about our new *type-face*?' OK, OK, but there's nothing wrong with the muesli belt – who doesn't want to live for ever, and in a decent society too? So don't lose your nerve. And there's nothing much wrong with the new lay-out – the final victory of the typographer over the sub – or the handy division into sections either, though the notion that more than one reader can now read the *Guardian* at any one time is too hopeful. Other people at breakfast simply want *both* sections first. But then no doubt if you're civilized, like the *Guardian*, you expect your readers to be the same, and good for you. Let the *Independent* take over as the nation's Thunderer; what we, the readers, expect and hope from you is daily guidance through the moral fog of contemporary Britain.

And that, of course, is what we have here in *The Bedside Guardian*. Hugo Young on Mrs Thatcher's political long-evity, Terry Coleman on Royalty Down-Under, Matthew Engel on Burnley, young Andrew Rawnsley (or is that just the policemen-getting-younger factor?), the Aggravator of Parliament, Ian Aitken on the self-destruction, self-absorp-tion (was there ever such a story of a snake swallowing its own tail and vanishing?) of the SDP – all stern moralists, though they may not want it said, and do what they can with wit and style to disguise it – Nancy Banks-Smith, scourge of the TV makers – wonderful to read, all agree, just so long as it's not your programme – and the elegant swansong of Waldemar Januszczak as art critic, who always knew what he didn't like, and seldom liked what he knew, but will perhaps have a little more mercy as the new literary editor. Or perhaps not – ah, the courage of it!

But that's the pleasure of *The Bedside Guardian* – you look for your favourites, and they're there, forget the day of the week. So may I wish you all good reading – and the slowing of the year . . .

Fay Weldon
June 1988

Made to measure, Honkers style

Among the many problems currently sent to try the venerable colonials of Hong Kong – the Taipans up on the Peak and the old members down at the Club – is the most pressing dilemma of What To Do About Mr Blackman's Suit. From the great mansions of Shek O to the floating palaces in Aberdeen harbour, everyone of note in the territory is discussing the matter – except, that is, Mr Blackman. He, it is believed, remains serenely unaware that the suit even exists.

Mr Archibald Blackman is a quiet and genteel old fellow, perhaps going on 70. It is said he once occupied his days running a great textile factory somewhere up near Boundary Street in Kowloon. Underwear, it is always said – something about a contract for Drawers, Cotton, Open Fly, for the Indian Police Service.

And then he retired, and his wife passed on, and the few investments he had made performed rather less well than he had hoped. He moved down from the Peak – 'so damn steamy at this time of year, you know' – to a very little flat. No one is quite sure where it is, exactly, but with rent so steep in Hong Kong (a single bedroom in the Mid Levels can cost £600 a month) everyone reckons it must be a rather shabby sort of place.

I say 'everyone', because everyone in Hong Kong knows Mr Blackman. He is as familiar a part of the colonial scenery as the Star Ferry clock or the circular windows on the Connaught Centre. Each morning, on the stroke of nine, he disembarks from the Hennessy Road tram and limps over – he carries an ancient umbrella, green with mould, to disguise his growing lameness – to the hotel on Connaught Road. He sits on a black leather armchair under one of the potted ferns, and for the next two hours precisely, reads what passes for news and gossip in the *South China Morning Post.*

Then, as the bells of the lobby clock sound 11, he rises and totters slowly upstairs to the Zoffany Bar – an oak-panelled clubroom of a place where a small number of old contemptibles gather each morning for pink gins.

The bar has dozens of prints, all by Zoffany – 'Sir Charles and Lady Parrish Arrive in Canton', 'Patna: A General View of the Godowns', that sort of thing. But according to Mr Blackman, only one of them is genuine. This, in fact, is Mr Blackman's only known recent public utterance. He usually sits in total and morose silence on his regular bar stool (no one else may sit there; a small brass plate fixed to the back says 'Archibald Blackman', and has space for two dates). He stares into his whisky and water, which the bartender keeps well filled. 'This damned bar,' he once declaimed. 'All the pictures bloody fakes – except one. Know which one? Find out for yourselves, I'm not telling you.' And other than that, he has kept near total silence.

He lunches, alone, in the Zoffany, after which he moves unsteadily across to the lift and transfers, for some unknown reason, to the Waterview Bar on the roof. Here he sits, on another brass-plaqued stool, for the rest of the day, gazing aimlessly at the bustle of the harbour below, and watching as the outbound jets glide upwards from the long concrete finger of Kai Tak airport, the fares costing more than he will ever be able to afford. Sometimes he takes a little more whisky than he should, and slides in a rumpled heap from his stool, umbrella and newspaper too. But the waiters keep a keen eye on him, and claim to be able to get to him before he hits the floor, and they prop him back up, and call down for a taxi. He is usually away by eleven.

Mr Blackman always signs his bills, with a flourish. The signature may once have commanded millions. Today, though he preserves the public illusion of riches, he is stony broke. His bills are all settled by his old chums – a few old textile merchants, a couple of brokers, a silver dealer – who have a whip-round at the club each month once the hotel has told them how much. Not that Mr Blackman is mean: from time to time, perhaps if the quinella's come up at the Jockey Club, he'll make an offer to settle. 'Don't worry, sir,' the waiter will murmur. 'All taken care of.' 'Really?' he'll say. 'Paid – did I? Dear me. Bless me. Must be getting dotty. Can't remember it at all.'

It was six months ago that the general manager of the hotel – an exceptionally proud man who runs an even prouder hotel – happened to mention the state of Mr Blackman's suit.

Yes, Mr Blackman's friends all had to agree – it was a rather sorry sight. An old grey thing, one button missing, the cuffs frayed, the seat shiny, the knees baggy. It had been a good suit, once. But now it was wanting, in many ways. The tennis shoes didn't look too good either.

And now, this being Hong Kong, something has been done. The friends had another whip-round – they needed about £200 to get a really decent suit. It took half an hour to raise. A fitting was arranged, cunningly, for the next time Mr Blackman fell out of his chair in the Zoffany Bar. They didn't have to wait long. It was just after lunch, about six weeks ago, and the great Shanghai tailor, Mr Wong Tin Sang, was on hand in the bar, and he slipped a couple of tape measures around the recumbent form of the old man. Mr Wong had made his original suit, so he used the tape measure just to check.

A week later, the cloth and the cut having been chosen, the suit was ready – a fine, plain grey worsted wool suit, fashioned in 12-ounce cloth that will look well in both the typhoon season and the colonial winter. And now it hangs in a wardrobe in the hotel, waiting.

And hence the problem. No one can be quite certain of the best way to give Mr Blackman his suit. His very considerable pride would be terribly hurt, everyone thinks, if he were to be told outright of the gift.

So, could it be contrived that somehow he wins the suit in a raffle? Could a waiter slip it to him when he next collapses into a sea of whisky fumes?

Out at the Country Club, deep in the vaults of the Honkers and Shanker, in the Captain's Bar and the Noon Gun Bar and the Dickens Bar, men sit and talk these days of old Mr Blackman's suit. There are more pressing problems that confront Hong Kong maybe. The Chinese are coming in a little more than ten years' time, and that should perhaps be of greater moment.

But not to the general manager of the hotel, nor to Mr Blackman's friends. They want him to enjoy his closing years dressed impeccably, the very essence of the English gentleman, the kind of figure whom the Chinese, when they arrive, will naturally expect to see. Suggestions, as they say, invited. Pink gins in the Chinnery for the best solution.

Simon Winchester
23 July 1987

Party timers

Like the ghouls who gather around particularly unpleasant road accidents, the Public Gallery looked on agog at the scene of devastation.

Order papers twisted into origami ducks, maps, books, bits of envelopes, and bits of MPs littered the chamber.

The better-informed spectators, proud to share the intelligence they had gathered from the radio with other members of the gallery, explained that the Commons was having one of its all-night parties.

They would do it quite regularly, on the feeblest of excuses, giving it a pompous name, All Night Sitting.

This was not the longest. On 31 January 1881, they had sat for 41½ hours discussing the Protection of Person and Property (Ireland) Bill, commonly called the Coercion Bill, before standing orders were introduced. In July 1935, they had managed 34½ hours on the Unemployment Assistance Regulations.

But what sort of party the Commons was holding was not entirely clear. The official title on the invites, the Felixstowe Dock and Railway Bill, suggesting a shindig for dockers and navvies, seemed to bear no relation to the conversation. It appeared to have been entirely taken over by the sort of bores who are normally left in the kitchen discussing the latest developments in compact disc technology or their wife's hernia operation.

A tall, grey man called Duncan Campbell-Savours was entertaining the rest of the partygoers by talking about birds – but of the feathered variety. As usual, Mr Campbell-Savours had only half understood the purpose of parties.

Labour partygoers insisted on dominating the conversation by talking about another party, organized by a shipping company.

Tony Banks said the invites had promised champagne flowing like water and dirty films. It had been cancelled. No wonder he was complaining.

This party was so boring that several of the partygoers had gone to sleep, sprawled along the green benches like wilting wallflowers. Perhaps it was a pyjama party? But nobody, with the possible exception of Nicholas Fairbairn, seemed to be wearing pyjamas.

As 2.30 p.m. passed, and the party crossed the parliamentary dateline, abolishing Wednesday, Mr Banks had complained about the engagements he was sacrificing to be there. 'Apart from Scottish questions, my own 10-minute rule bill on war toys has been lost.'

It did not impress Tory partygoers. There was a growing consensus that it was, perhaps, supposed to have been one of those fancy dress parties which fall embarrassingly flat when most of the guests still turn up in their lounge suits.

Only Bill Walker, the Tory MP for Tayside North, seemed to have made the effort, appearing at the beginning of the afternoon in a fetching mauve and brown kilt, with matching face. But it turned out that this, as with most things concerning Mr Walker, was a mistake.

Nobody had told him that the scheduled afternoon of Scottish Reels had been cancelled.

As parties are wont to do when they go on overlong, the guests got tired and emotional towards the end.

The Speaker, normally the politest of hosts, finally wearied of the attentions of the ugly overweight men who had been pressing their attentions on him and his stand-ins all night.

'I am not taking any more points of order,' he shouted, refusing further invitations to dance.

The ugliest and fattest of the bothersome Lotharios, Eric Heffer, rhino-charged to the mace to plead with him for one last waltz.

'I know we're all very tired and emotional,' wheedled Mr Heffer with the subtlety of an inflamed prostrate.

'Sit down for God's sake,' replied the Speaker.

Then Mr Weatherill called in the parents to bring the party to an end. They blamed, as parents will, each other's children for the mess left behind.

Andrew Rawnsley
12 November 1987

The wonder of Wallis

I can reveal, pretty jolly exclusively, that the bond between the Prince of Wales and Mrs Simpson was not passion but poetry. Like the theory that Queen Victoria was Jack the Ripper, this is one in the eye for serious historians who have never suspected anything of the sort.

In *The Woman He Loved* (HTV), she first attracts his attention by capping a quotation about lambs and linnets ('Mrs Simpson, you have such sensitivity!') and thereafter he woos her with verse and, worse, solos on the bagpipes:

> If I were king, my love, if I were king
> What tributary nations I would bring
> To stoop before your sceptre and to swear
> Allegiance to your eyes, your lips, your hair.

Seeing she was weakening, and who wouldn't, he follows this up fast with an encore:

> My friend with thee to live alone
> Methinks were better than to own
> The crown, the sceptre and the throne.

The slightly squashy nature of these poems and the fact that I have never stepped in them before, lead me to suppose that this may be an *undiscovered cache of the Prince of Wales's own work*! In which case flatten yourself against the wall because you are in the way of the biggest publishing gold rush since *The Old Man of Lochnagar*.

Sensitive Mrs Simpson realizes that poetry is the high road to his heart and, when he says 'God help me, I love you!', is ready with her answer:

> Among our ancient mountains
> And from our lovely vales
> Oh, let the prayer re-echo
> God bless the Prince of Wales!

It is hard to say if this means 'Yes, sir', 'No, sir', or 'Have you mentioned this to Mr Baldwin?' but it evidently goes down well, though not, of course, with Mr Baldwin. Considering that he was Rudyard Kipling's cousin, I find it odd that Baldwin did not contribute something, if only a limerick, to this poetic flow. Churchill does. Approached by the prince while he is painting in a sort of feathered sombrero, he offers abstractedly: 'Joy is the shadow of sorrow. Sorrow the shadow of joy.' By now even Edward is getting a touch tetchy about these curly answers to straight questions and says shortly, 'I *know* Winston, but how does that apply to Mrs Simpson?' God, who saves the Queen and blesses the Prince of Wales, only knows.

All this and Jane Seymour's performance leads me to believe that what we have here is not a play at all but a good old-fashioned, thigh-slapping panto. A prince who can deliver a solo on the bagpipes while scenery is being noisily shifted, a well-dressed Cinderella, a plumply affable fairy godmother and simple rhymes to cover your exit. There is a theatrical story that once, when a demon king's fire failed, he improvised: 'Dearie me, oh what a shame. Someone's pissed on the magic flame' . . . and exited to appreciative applause.

The prince is played by Anthony Andrews with his teeth welded together and several well-known faces appear, rather quietly and no wonder, under wigs. Actors must eat, I suppose, and this sort of thing ensures that a large number of them can sit down at a banquet for Baldwin and feast on what appears to be, quite suitably, Windsor soup.

This is the occasion when Mrs Baldwin, wearing the loose cover from a couch, says, 'Oh dear, sex is really so disagreeable.' I feel a sudden desire to defend Mrs Baldwin. Mr Baldwin first admired her when he saw her score half a century at cricket and, I seem to remember reading, she cheered him up by greeting him, on his return home, dressed as a Turkish soldier. We have no reason to suppose she was not the woman he loved.

Speaking in a whispering growl, like a bear in a cave who has a long, chilling winter's tale to tell his enthralled cubs, Wally Herbert teased out the story of Cook and Peary, two men who laid claim to the North Pole and, as neither would give way, died of the bitter exhaustion of it. Wally Herbert's conclusion in *Noose of Laurels* (Central) – delivered sighing, for never was a man sorrier to say it – was that they both lied.

Now this *is* a story that would make a good film: friends at each other's throats, a faithful black friend, a lovely and, surprisingly, naked Eskimo mistress and the beauty of that brutal place.

Cook and Peary had been friends – Cook set Peary's leg on their first journey – but there came a time when they wished each other dead. Herbert, who went to the Pole himself, seems to accept without surprise the icy hatreds that go with the job and make those of us who feel warmer whistle: 'It was in this hut that Peary first learned that Cook had survived and it must have really hurt.'

Cook's claim to the Pole could never be proved because Peary buried his records. Peary's claim stood until now, when Herbert's investigation led him, most reluctantly, to believe that Peary travelled the right distance but in the wrong direction. And knew it. The stricken face of Peary, lined and fur-framed, dissolved into a landscape of cracked ice.

The running huskies turned and, their tongues hanging out, laughed at the camera. There is no North Pole. It is salt water ice, ever shifting.

Nancy Banks-Smith
13 April 1988

Signs on the dotted line

In a sense, of course, it was all over long before Mr Gorbachev took his plane from Moscow airport. The INF deal existed from the moment it, with attendant summit, was agreed; not from when a clutch of signatures was appended to thick files of protocols. In another sense, the importance of this Washington summit rests on what else emerges at the white-knuckled end of a hard-talking Thursday. Is there a momentum which will carry an old President, in his dog days, through to greater things in Moscow next year? But, for the moment, because it resounded a little, concentrate on the thin meat of ceremony interposed for the cameras, and for history, between the slices of substance.

Ronald Reagan made one of his familiar, folksy speeches, with an impenetrable Russian tale about a pike, a crawfish and a snail. Mikhail Gorbachev quoted Ralph Waldo Emerson. Ronald Reagan went on somewhat about verification. Mr Gorbachev looked to the future. There was a high quotient of banter; proving, if proof were needed, that the President can still trade nightclub one-liners like a pro. There were many smiles; there was much hand-shaking; plus perceptible tendencies to clap at the breaks for translation. It all looked pretty warm and pretty jolly.

That was infinitely predictable. Both Mr Reagan and Mr Gorbachev are hardened politicians. They had a clear and vested interest in bonhomie. They were determined to make the outward and visible show a moment of history to remember. But, in doing so, they also said something else; something which, in particular, needs saying over and over again to an American audience. The United States does not, in any simplistic way, need to trust the Soviet Union; any more than a Red Army general needs to trust the director of the CIA. That is why wary, exhaustive negotiation and – yes – verification will be just as much a part of what happens next as they have been of the INF negotiations. But there is a step beyond that. There, yesterday, was Mr Reagan, the most conservative President for over half a century, the coiner of the Evil Empire, doing jovial and portentous business with the smiling emperor of darkness. A vignette to linger over, because it will need to be remembered when the flummery of summitry subsides and it is back to the business of bitter rhetoric, as usual.

Leader
9 December 1987

When the shooting stops

In a grove of trees headed by an ancient standing stone, near the cricket pitch used by the school in Hungerford where gunman Michael Ryan holed up, a body last night lay covered by a blanket and guarded by a single policeman in the gathering dusk.

Near by, on the corner of Priory Avenue and Hillside Road on the 1930s residential estate where mayhem had broken loose, a red Datsun, its lights still on and its windscreen smashed, stood parked. Inside was another body, its stained shroud failing to conceal the human form within.

That victim, according to one of the local residents

standing in bewildered groups along the street, was the father of the estate's beat policeman. he had come down to visit his son.

Further back along Priory Avenue, the neat privet hedge by Alan Lepetit's coal yard presented a gaping, earthy gash where a Ford Transit van had ploughed into it after its driver had been shot through the neck.

Next door, Mr Roy Fox stood by his mini-market, where Mr Lepetit had run across the road, bleeding copiously from a shoulder wound, after seeing the gunman casually approach his children, waving his weapons as if they were toys. The doorway of the shop was still splattered with blood, and inside Mr Fox showed the dark stain where his friend had lain in a pool of blood for half an hour until an ambulance arrived.

'I thought he was going to go, he's lost so much blood,' Mr Fox said. 'And when they did come they had the problem that stopping the bleeding risked cutting off his circulation.'

Earlier, at about 4 p.m., Chief Inspector Laurie Fray told reporters: 'Every time officers from the police or the ambulance have approached the area where the incidents have taken place they've been shot at. There are people lying there and we just can't get to them.'

For the same reason, it was not until 7 p.m. that fire engines were at last able to move into Southview. By that time Ryan's house and three adjoining dwellings were gutted. All afternoon, smoke from the blaze had hung over the estate – eerily silent, with the only traffic armoured police vehicles – in a thick pall. Watching the firemen at work from the flat above Mr Fox's shop, it was clear by nightfall that there was little left to burn. Only the structural walls remained. 'Thank God, I think the people in the next door houses are on holiday,' Mr Fox said.

Late in the day, the panic of lunchtime still sometimes broke through. 'I've been at work since 6 a.m. and I'm bloody well not going to let you stop me getting home,' a teenage girl shouted at a policeman who blocked her way.

But elsewhere on the estate there was a stunned calm. Residents leaned anxiously from their windows, asking whether it was safe to go out now. Others worried about elderly neighbours left alone. Telephone lines had been cut off by police, but the news about the dead and wounded spread across the estate. People compared notes across hedges and garden gates, conferring in shocked tones about those from their community – the taxi driver they had all known, and Mr Khan, the elderly Pakistani whom everyone knew – who had died in the shootings.

Many residents had been unable to get back home from work, and there were relieved and tearful scenes as the cordon relaxed a little after 7 p.m. and those who were simply delayed returned to their families.

David Rose
20 August 1987

Tatty mother of a town

The greed of developers has torn at Dublin's heart. Petty crime has soiled its style, congestion robbed it of an easy-going quality that was its own. Yet there is no city I know that is still as pleasant to walk through in the early morning before the traffic has arrived. The air is acrid with the smell of brewing. The light is startlingly clear. Seagulls scream, or perch on the Liffey's parapets. Only a few eccentrics are about.

I am, myself, a provincial visitor in this city. My earliest memory of Dublin is of my father driving the wrong way down Grafton Street, some time in the 1930s. 'Well, sure, you got here,' said the guard on point-duty at the other end, 'and isn't that the main thing?'

I didn't know then that the black pool of Dublin was a Viking foundation, later to become the centre of the sophisticated English Pale. 'The seat of this city is on all sides pleasant, comfortable, and wholesome,' remarked a sixteenth-century observer. 'If you would traverse the hills, they are not far off . . . If you will take a view of the sea, it is at hand.' Add to this the Georgian splendour of squares and thoroughfares, and there is Dublin in its later heyday: the 'grey brick upon brick' that Louis MacNeice wrote of, destined to become 'the bare bones of a fanlight/Over a hungry door.'

Long after my first visit I returned, sent up from the country to a school in what was then the modest suburb of Ranelagh. For the first time I met Dubliners: sharp-witted, sharp-tongued, sharp in appearance even, or so I've always thought. We dozen or so boarders from the small towns of Ireland, from villages and farms, were no match for the wily locals. This was their place and still their Pale. 'Dublin jackeens' was a term that passed our lips at home. It didn't here.

But I came to know the once-guarded territory well: the North side and the South side, Dolphin's Barn, Drum-condra, Rathmines and Rathgar. Harcourt Street was staid, Henry Street jolly. The blaze of the Bovril sign coloured the night sky above College Green. Ireland's pride was on pedestals: Grattan, Parnell, O'Connell, Davis, the Countess Markiewicz, the poet Mangan. Palatial cinemas decorated the streets of Europe's most film-conscious capital, and once in a while on a Sunday there were flags and favours as well, on their way to Croke Park for another all-Ireland final. The last tram took off from Nelson's Pillar, and not all that long afterwards Nelson's Pillar itself took off, blown tidily to smithereens.

You have to walk to get to know a city. When I was a Trinity student I walked at night, when the pubs and the ice-cream parlours had emptied. Weary dance-bands played the last waltz in the Crystal Ballroom and the Four Provinces; still-thirsty drinkers bargained with hackney-car drivers about the bona fide run to Goatstown and a few more jars. Within an hour the streets were given up to a handful of shabbily dressed women, and girls in head-scarves and liquid stockings. Only the famed Green Rooster remained open until the small hours, a piece of enterprise that earned this innocent grill-room an undeserved notor-iety. 'Good Food – that's all!' it protested, aggrieved, in its bus-side advertisements.

Guards loitered in O'Connell Street and Stephen's Green, the top button of their tunics undone, a cigarette discreetly cupped. But you could walk without meeting anyone at all in Cuckoo Lane, or Mary Street, where Michael Collins had his closest shave. Or in Islandbridge, where Oliver St John Gogarty presented the Liffey with a gift of swans in gratitude for the cover it had offered him as he fled pursuing gunmen. Or by Swift's cathedral, among the cruelly malodorous slums that Sean O'Casey brought to the stage of the Abbey Theatre.

Dear, dirty Dublin, you might even reflect as you wandered through its dark silence. Streets broad and narrow, the sluggish crawl of their river. Molly Malone, Biddy Mulligan, Anna Livia. Gammer and gaffer, as Joyce had it, and we their gangsters. The mother and father of a town.

It's different now. There are night-spots, discos, launderettes, and Bar-B-Q takeaways. Joy-riders rampage, drug peddlers peddle. A gliding police car accelerates in Capel Street, walkie-talkies disturb the peace of Bachelor's Walk. The fashion in insurance companies and multi-storey car parks has brought the melancholy blankness that is the twentieth century's ugliest trade mark. Yet fondness for the place remains.

Is such affection inspired entirely by the whisper of the past: by Gandon's Customs House, the enormous presence of the Bank of Ireland, the Halfpenny Bridge at twilight? Or by the velvet cubicles of Bewley's cafés, the timeless shout of the evening paperboys?

Whole lifetimes of familiarity or nostalgia would not give much of an answer. The mundane is more in keeping with Dublin's mood: hard facts are what matter here. No city has better barmen. No city is as quick on the uptake, or as swift with a loaded riposte. Pretension is forgiven only when accompanied by wit. Self-admiration has a short life. There's a swiftness to condemn, especially when condemnation seems like a talking point. Emotions are volatile, yet opinions are rarely less than measured.

It's a city notable for chance encounters, and beggars. In Merrion Row or Nassau Street, or anywhere at all, a face in a crowd is suddenly familiar. Polite exchanges as to health, and the weather remarked upon, preface the repairing to Toner's or O'Neill's or the bar of Buswell's Hotel. And when you're back on the streets again the tinker children are waiting, waggling their damp cardboard boxes at you. Shawled women press in to offer prayers for your spiritual well-being. 'Excuse me, sir'. In hushed tones, men outside turf accountants declare themselves temporarily embarrassed. The price of a cup of tea, the bus fare to Dalkey; a loan until Friday, here on the dot.

It's a disputatious city. Its gossip is merciless, its snobberies peculiar to itself. It's given to the grand gesture – like devoting an entire day's air-time to the reading of *Ulysses*, and frequently changing the colour of its buses. Assumptions are not encouraged; expected outcomes do not always materialize.

When first I lived in Dublin I had lodgings in a house where terriers were bred. I was occasionally bitten, and assumed that a mild complaint to my landlady would result in the offending animal being confined to its quarters. 'Ah, sure, he's only playing,' she assured me instead, and added after a moment: 'He's taken prizes, that dog.'

When in the early 1950s I took it for granted that I would be able to find work for which I was even faintly qualified, my presumption was similarly challenged. Without success, I offered myself to a variety of offices, shops, travel agencies, a cycle park, and a firm that manufactured telephone boxes. I ended up accepting a job for which I had no qualifications whatsoever. 'Suit an old or ex-nun,' the advertisement had said.

Dublin has changed; Dubliners haven't. The new excesses have long been deplored; the fight to regain a lost elegance continues determinedly. Yet something about the flavour of Dublin suggests that old stone and brick do not entirely reflect the essence of the place, let alone distil it. The new tattiness mocks the dignity there has been; but architectural charm, forever brushed down, can equally lead a city to the grave. Dublin's terraces and avenues, its courts and squares, at least do not sleep the sleep of a museum. The girls are still pretty. A pint of plain is still your only man. Dublin is its people.

William Trevor
20 February 1988

Meanwhile, inside No. 10 . . .

So Mrs Thatcher becomes the longest-serving prime minister since Asquith. Not, strictly speaking the longest of the twentieth century. There is Salisbury still to beat. When he retired in 1902 he'd held the job, off and on, for thirteen and a half years. Mrs T will need to win another election and carry on until Christmas 1992 to pass Salisbury.

Considering that even by the year 2000 she will still be younger than the Golda Meir who led Israel, one should remember that only the final milestone is definitive.

The surpassing of Asquith, however, is a moment worth noting. The leader certainly notes it herself. She delayed her journey to Africa so as to drink the toast under a British roof. Although highly selective in her attitude to history, she has never been less than fully attuned to her own part in making it.

Such longevity in office is a very large fact. Eight years and eight months. It's an achievement on its own, separate from its consequences. The consequences matter greatly. But the sheer length of it, in the friendless world of political leadership, deserves serious remark. A generation of opponents routed; a generation of rivals eclipsed; half a generation of voters upon whose consciousness no other prime minister has impinged. To my children, a male leader, royal or political, will come as an offence against nature.

So this has been an extraordinary story. But we should disentangle the remarkable from the banal. In the Thatcher mythology, the fawning astonishment usually starts too early.

It was not extraordinary that she became a politician. On the contrary, this is what she was born to be. Her lineage and formation allowed of few other possibilities. Politics infused the atmosphere in which she was reared by her father, alderman and leading citizen of Grantham. The political life, with its parallel attractions of service and of power, was the only life set before her as a model superior to that of shopkeeping.

Thus far, she was in no sense an aberrant case. Her origins accorded closely with those of the majority of Conservative leaders. A political family handed down the tradition of political action from one generation to the next. Unlike some of her contemporaries, she may never have exactly imagined she was born to rule, or at least to be prime minister. But her father laid out the path of duty just as clearly as any grandee who placed his sons on the road to Parliament. Through Oxford and beyond, released by the alderman, his child never for a second deviated from this ambition.

Nor was it extraordinary that, once at Westminster, she should do well. Women had before. Ambition, diligence and her husband's wealth were duly rewarded. She was an opportunist who took her opportunities, and ascended the greasy pole unencumbered by obstacles of her own making, such as blind faith or awkward conviction. In Macmillan's government she did what she was told, in Heath's she acquiesced in every twist that circumstance made necessary.

Although the mythology allots her the part of affronted critic, silently fuming at Heath's corporatist and inflationary errors, the truth is more congruent with the normal pattern of ambition. She swallowed it all. A prudent careerist could do no other. Her mentor, Keith Joseph, has said that he 'only became a Conservative in April 1974'. He meant, of course, a nineteenth-century liberal. The timing of the Thatcher conversion, the prelude to leadership, was identical.

This is where the story at last became extraordinary. She was elected leader, in circumstances well known. It happened at a time when the Conservative Party needed careerist pragmatism to be supplanted by something else. She had no difficulty in adapting. So began 13 years at the head of the party, and the eight years, eight months, which have ensured her, as nobody anywhere will dispute, a dominant place in any history of twentieth-century Britain.

That history will not be written for many years. The effect of the Thatcher era, for good and bad, will be a matter of argument never resolved to general satisfaction. And in explaining why it lasted so long, much must be attributed to highly adventitious factors such as the state of other people's politics and the state of the world, not to mention large doses of plain good fortune. But the personal contribution remains, massively visible in the three relevant organisms: the country, the party, and herself.

It is in part a tautology to say that an eight-year leader personifies the country's mood. And after so long, one cannot perfectly distinguish the contributions of leader and of country to a common ambience. Did she bask in a receptive climate, or did she set the temperature herself? Equally far beyond the reach of a firm answer is how long the mood, whoever created it, will last. Only when the leader has gone can we see whether attitudes changed, or merely behaviour.

All the same, no leader can last this long unless she speaks for some deep national sentiments. Three seem particularly conspicuous in her case. British masochism saw her through the unemployment crisis. British bloody-mindedness took on and won the Falklands war. A shared Little Englandism has been the reliable guide to most foreign crises.

These are enduring British traits which this leader has tapped more simply and openly than any predecessor in any party. She has done the same thing in more particular ways. It is hard to think of a single important issue on which, whatever her government may actually have done, her personal attitudes are not populist and universally known to be so. On Europe, on the Bomb, on South Africa, on hanging, on culture, on intellectual life, on welfare scroungers, on union bosses, Maggie could rarely be accused of failing to speak, alas, for Britain.

In the same vein, she has changed some conventional assumptions: again, one may hazard, in conformity with deep national prejudices. In the old order, fairness, equality, the benign State and the dispersal of power were common shibboleths. Fairness has been displaced by success, social justice by the business imperative. This has not been without benefits. But the key quote, a shocking but truthful epitome, was delivered to *Woman's Own* a couple of months ago: 'There is no such thing as society,' our leader said. It followed hard on a snort against those who 'drool and drivel about caring,' a phrase hastily withdrawn on the eve of the election, but immediately validated nonetheless.

So that is a first contribution to this long survival. To produce a stronger economy, she has appealed to some of the worst instincts of the British: instincts, however, which already existed. She articulated something new, but also stayed close to something already there. If Baldwin personified a national mood of quietism and complacency in the 1930s, Mrs Thatcher spoke with utmost eloquence for the materialism and self-interest of the 1980s.

Next there was the party. In eight years, age has not withered it nor custom staled its capacity to unite. Quite the opposite. Conservatives are more united after eight years than they were before the first Thatcher term began. This distinguishes the Thatcher party from most of its predecessors, especially the Liberal Party of H. H. Asquith, whose departure confirmed its disintegration.

There is no longer a single significant division in the Tory Party. A whole series of radical initiatives, highly offensive to old-fashioned Conservatives of both town and country, elicits only the spluttering of a few extinct volcanoes. The first victory was achieved with a totally split cabinet, most of whom thought Thatcherism was only a temporary phenomenon: the third by men with hardly an inch of difference between them, and none of whom view their leader with anything but the most respectful apprehension.

This is the product of formidable leadership. By dint of willpower and consistency, seasoned with well-judged deviations, the party's priorities have been remade and only a single Tory MP deserted to the Social Democrats.

And then there was herself. She was a big problem. Many people, looking at her eight years ago, doubted whether she could survive half the distance, not least because she was a woman, her one undoubted claim to historic uniqueness. Instead, one can see more clearly that her sex has been a key to much that she has got away with, a positive aid to durability.

It has made policies easier to sell. A woman found it easier than many men might have done to persuade the country to take its medicine, to talk her way through social outrage, to present her economic policy as a simple exercise in household management, running a balanced budget, not spending what you haven't earned, etc. etc.

It has made people easier to sack. No leader has sacked more ministers with less cause. Such ruthlessness was necessary, as she saw it, for the accomplishment of her mission. It has been visited upon scores of inconvenient presences, and somehow made more palatable by the lady's simpering complaints about how much she detests wielding the hatchet.

Finally, her sex has greatly helped the artifice of presentation. She does not mind being made up, and will do anything for the camera. Her reputation for honesty and directness, which is not false, masks an apparently artless guile. It complements the more admirable personal qualities: the forensic skill, the mastery of detail, above all else the inexhaustible enthusiasm for work which few men wanted to do for eight years (see Wilson and Macmillan), even when they had the chance.

Groping beyond Asquith for her place in Conservative history, you can soon make some connections. But the resemblances seem much thinner than the differences.

Like Peel she was a provincial, but unlike him she despised consensus politics. Like Joe Chamberlain she hated her party aristos, and she still sustains the illusion of herself as some kind of belligerent outsider. But he would surely have scorned the narrowness of her nationalism.

She is interested in science, like Balfour, but hardly a ruminant philosopher. She would like to be Churchillian, but the embarrassing frequency with which she stakes this claim disqualifies her from the league. Besides, the nation has never loved her, nor ever will.

With Macmillan it is hard to see any similarities of either character or outlook. Heath, of course, ought to supply the umbilical connection. But apart from all their other ruptures, the very thing which seems to bind them, their humble origins, in fact most signally divides them. Where Heath spent his adult life escaping from his past, hers has been presented as the source of all political wisdom.

In his history of the party, Robert Blake writes of Disraeli: 'At least there must be agreement that he remains the most extraordinary, incongruous, fascinating, fresh and timeless figure ever to have led the Conservative Party.' One day it may seem right to withdraw at least some of those adjectives and apply them to Margaret Thatcher. But meanwhile another effect of her record tenure is more obvious.

Such endurance, while a matter of just pride, carries its penalty. After eight years and eight months, any other government seems to belong to some remote museum. The old alibis slip over the horizon. What Labour did or did not do, long, long ago, makes an ever more empty argument with which to teach the senators wisdom. The state of the country is hers to explain and justify: hers and nobody else's.

Hugo Young
2 January 1988

Rock of ages

Mick Jagger couldn't remember if it was he or another of the Rolling Stones who'd been apprehended while peeing against a wall sometime in the sixties. His interviewer, from one of the Sunday supplements, had to correct him, better acquainted with the Stones mythology than the man at its centre.

Perhaps the incident never happened anyway, just as Marianne Faithfull now maintains she wasn't doing anything provocative with a Mars Bar the day the Drug Squad climbed through Keith Richard's living room windows. Rock doesn't really have that much history to recycle – not compared with the Royal Navy or English Literature, for instance – but it's been pumped up and embroidered so often that it feels as though it does.

'Why should I live in the past just for *their* petty satisfaction?' Mick Jagger wants to know, generous as ever to his once drooling public. His attitude would be all very well if he didn't expect the same fans to invest in his drab new long player, *Primitive Cool*. What an interesting thing for a semi-retired rock star aged 44 to do – make an album of mildly nostalgic AOR, performed with passionless competence by deluxe musicians carrying Filofaxes packed with session dates.

While letters appear in the *Guardian* arguing over the identity of the finest LP of the sixties, the rock-inspired dream of changing the system from the inside has come to a bitter fruition. The war babies are now taking charge, and are even more reluctant to relinquish their formative memories than their own parents were. While Mrs Thatcher is busily running the entire media establishment out of town, they're still listening to *Graceland* in their BMWs, or funding pedestrian documentaries about Elvis Presley. Johnnie Walker now fills Radio 1's Saturday afternoons with records most of his audience already own.

The recent *Omnibus* programme about Bob Dylan was so obsequious and inept that licence-holders should be queuing for a refund, or for complimentary CD copies of the artist's oeuvre as some kind of compensation. 'You know things go better with Coke because Aretha Franklin told you so,' Dylan observed recently, exasperated with the medium he once helped to pioneer. 'Everybody's singing about ketchup or headache medicine or something.'

Tellingly, *Omnibus* showed that while a generation

revered Dylan, they really weren't listening to a word
he said. They did follow leaders! They didn't watch their
parking meters! Rock never really grew up, it just lost all
its hair and developed a thyroid problem.

This may be ludicrous, but it isn't funny. If the value of
rock or pop is as a yardstock of social attitudes, an index of
the possibilities which might be available in the wider
world, then obviously we're living through a period of
lapsed ambition and failed nerve. Nowhere is this clearer
than in the plight of the *New Musical Express.*

Its circulation has declined drastically since its invigorating mid-seventies heyday, and attempts to revive the droop-
ing organ by endorsing Positive Punk, hip-hop or hitching
up with Red Wedge have only tightened the spiral of decline. Currently, in a faint echo of the war going on between
broadcasters and government, the *NME* is being ground
under the heel of its publishers, IPC, for daring to use the
f-word and for reproducing (among other things) the Dead
Kennedys' notorious penis graphics. There was a time,
probably around the turn of the decade, when the paper's
journalists would have gone on strike and whipped up a
fighting fund with the aid of a few friendly left-wing bands.
Fat chance of that in 1987. You can still read the word
'fuck' in *Smash Hits.*

Innovation or having an opinion have become liabilities,
unless you're Prince. Daily, the heavy tread of the past
thunders nearer, and it belongs to the postman. Poor man,
his sack stuffed with made-to-measure memories, his ears
ringing with the tinkle of quick cash-ins by artists who'd
long since given up any thoughts of yet another gobble at
the cherry. Who will it be today? Perhaps the re-formed
Jethro Tull with their new LP, a heraldically garnished
work entitled *Crest of a Knave.* You can tell at a glance
that age, experience and ownership of half the Scottish
highlands still haven't endowed Ian Anderson with dry,
sophisticated wit.

Yes have released a new single, the Bee Gees have re-
formed, Pink Floyd are on tour, the Grateful Dead are at
the top of the American charts, and Chris De Burgh and

Chris Rea are back (or perhaps 'they've never been away'). Fleetwood Mac and the Starship must be good for another decade at least, while Herb Alpert is helping himself to another hit with a little thing called 'Making Love in the Rain'.

David Bowie has just celebrated his fortieth birthday with one of his worst-ever records, and a hopeless live show. Eric Clapton has been repackaged yet again in the shape of *The Cream of Eric Clapton*, and rarely can a man have been less in need of a quick cash pick-me-up. His generation got the lot – sex, drugs, and a lifetime's guaranteed supply of platinum discs.

Nostalgia isn't just useful, it's virtually a prerequisite of success. It would take a deranged pundit indeed to put forward any sort of case for rock's continuing value as irritant or stimulant, and the naked statistics and fluent marketese of the trade magazine *Billboard* now embody not only the music industry's dominant logic but its sole *raison d'être*, too. It really doesn't matter what the product sounds like any more as long as it's malleable and contoured for comfort.

Adam Sweeting
2 October 1987

Go tie-less in Goolwa

Melbourne:
How splendidly 200 years of Australian history has unfolded during the royal tour. When the Prince and Princess of Wales danced in the hideous hexagonal ballroom at the Melbourne Hyatt it was the subscription ball at Ballarat all over again, circa 1854.

Ballarat, which was only a day's drive through the rainforest from Melbourne, is where gold was found in the 1850s, more than ever was found in California, and Australia was suddenly rich. Cigars were lit with £5 notes. And the newly rich held a ball. Those who couldn't get a ticket scrambled in through the windows.

Well, Melbourne this time was not so gentle a brawl as that. *Le tout* Melbourne, and Melbourne is rich, had tickets to be there, but the world's press were to be kept out for all but a few minutes. There's trouble for you.

'Play the game, mates,' implored the brave Australian appointed as their chief minder.

'There'll be a bloody game, mate, if we don't get in in good time,' came the gentle retort from *le tout* Fleet Street.

The approach to the ballroom was not up a grand staircase but up two narrow escalators, one after another. The pack rushed the first floor, and took 10,000 snaps of the princess floating weirdly upwards on that escalator, wearing a dress, 'with a train from a bow on the left hip'. Then she disappeared with the prince and their minders up the second escalator, leaving the photographers baying and desperately swinging their aluminium stepladders. There are always ladders – one, two, three, and four-storey ladders, so that the best equipped can be one up on their competitors.

'No ladders,' yelled the minders. 'Nobody, but nobody, goes up into the ballroom with a ladder.'

We swarmed up. Upstairs that archaic thing called a dinner dance was going on, something last seen in England in Nottingham, circa 1951. *Le tout* Melbourne looked up from its tables and scowled as the mob was let in. There was a band-leader on a rostrum, who announced that His Royal Highness had requested 'In the Mood' and struck up in Glenn Miller style, last heard in England circa 1944. Prince and princess took the floor alone, and danced at first sedately and then with many twirls. The cameras of the free world flashed. In the general uproar, the princess mouthed something to her husband, which was later reported to be 'Steady.' The unfortunate couple had to dance alone for a whole minute, which is an age, before they were joined, to their great and obvious relief, by *le tout* Melbourne scrambling up from its tables on to the dance floor.

It was Ballarat all over again. The dancers were the ones

with tickets. The hangers-in at windows were the hacks. Then, in a brilliant act of crowd clearance, the hacks were all ejected. The other side of the door, in what is known as the pre-function area, an equerry told us that the earrings and bracelets were a wedding gift from King Fahad of Saudi Arabia.

Spell it! The equerry spelled Fahad.

How much are they worth? 'We do not,' said the young equerry, 'guess the value of gifts.'

'How,' urgently inquired the *Daily Mirror*, 'do we get a jeweller to make an estimate?'

There being no jeweller in the house, not at any rate in the pre-function area, a value of £5 million was then informally agreed by the press, but immediately raised by general consent to £10 million.

We were chucked out long before the Prince of Wales made his speech. He said: 'Our lot, my wife and I, has been to start the dancing. I assure you it makes the heart sink, to have to make an exhibition of ourselves. Now how many of you would like to try it?' He then made a joke about both Sydney, the day before, and for that matter, the United Kingdom, being knee deep in cans of Foster's.

The hand-out of this speech did not reach the press till the next morning, by which time it was useless. The bane of hacks in Australia is that Melbourne or Sydney time is 11 hours ahead of London. Television satellite transmissions are instantaneous, but morning papers come out only in the morning. So something could be shown on TV-am in London a full day before it could get in a London morning paper. Seasoned hacks comfort each other with the thought that editors never watch the bloody television.

And these days there is no royal tour without the attendant hacks. Divinity may no longer hedge a Prince of Wales, but the rat-pack does. There used to be a famous gang of muggers called the Sydney Push. They have been superseded. And it's a hard life. Flying from Sydney to Melbourne to Adelaide to Darwin, everyone had to go through X-ray screenings, and there was an instant cry of 'What about our film?'

'Lost a lot of film that way on the Pope's visit,' said the minder laconically. 'It'll wipe the stories off your personal computers too, gentlemen.'

Then the security man added his words of encouragement. 'Don't want to have to drag you back with ropes like we did last year. Even if shots are fired, which God forbid, remember you'll still be under control.'

I wouldn't have betted on that. The tour is all timed to the minute, with everything detailed in four booklets, 127 printed pages of protocol with 30 diagrams and maps. Prince mounts polo ponies here; lunch in flight (at 10.30 a.m.); and, yes, 'mobile rope barrier will be used for local media'.

But of course half of it goes wrong. At Government House, Melbourne, a white palace like Queen Victoria's Osborne on the Isle of Wight, only with blue skies, we hung around for ages listening to the chairman of the Bicentennial Authority briefing local businessmen on how to conduct themselves when presented. 'Give him time to say hello. And the prince'll mingle around or whatever it is. It's a special baby of his.' The mingling had barely begun before we were all whipped off to get in place beforehand for the next royal engagement, miles away.

Mild exhaustion sets in, which nibbles at the character of a man. For the first four days, no matter what the temperature, I always wore a coat and tie. It was unthinkable not to. Only two others, out of a pack of 88, were equally formal. But then things fell apart. On the fifth day, at Goolwa on the Murray River, after two hours in 101 degrees waiting for the royals to return from a river cruise in a paddle-boat, with the band meantime playing Barry Manilow and 'Come Back to Sorrento', there I was lounging on the river bank with a can of cold Foster's in my hand and a slouch hat on my head, and no tie, and there I stayed lounging as the Prince of Wales passed within two feet. Thus climate corrupts good manners. That is my explanation and I know it won't do.

It was on that bank that Harry Arnold of the *Sun*, being asked along with the rest of us not to stand in the way of the public who had been waiting for a glimpse of the royals since dawn, told the police they were an ignorant and stupid lot. Anglo-Australian relations would have been noticeably improved, police morale would have soared, and there would have been a mighty cheer, if Mr Arnold had somehow, quite inadvertently of course, found himself up to his neck in the Murray.

But then, no one who goes along on one of these trips is in any position to cast the first stone. 'Ho,' said the amiable and vastly experienced *Daily Mirror* man to me one day at breakfast, he who once found the prince in his bachelor days in the bushes with a Miss Wallace. 'Ho, the *Guardian* still here, with your integrity? Ho, ho.'

Fair enough. The day of the bicentenary itself was a great state occasion, and Prince Charles, going back to the beginning, admitted to George III's transportation of inconvenient people, but put in a good word for the British Empire and for the courage and resolve and quest for knowledge of the likes of Captain Cook, which made pleasant hearing. But for the rest of the tour what were we all doing, all of us, but observing a marriage? You don't start off intending to do that, but you're blind if you don't see it's what you're doing. After a week, you've seen a lot of little things. You can't help it.

Prince Charles is always at ease, or if he isn't he's a marvellous actor. He does owe something to his tailor and shirtmaker, since he's always the best-dressed man there, and I wonder if he's setting some kind of fashion by wearing his coat sleeves pressed with sharp creases, as Edward VII did. But the princess, though her dresses are always Ooh'd and Ah'd at, is neither at ease nor an actress, and it shows.

He makes his off-the-cuff speeches and she stands looking down at the floor. At a conservatoire of music he plays a few notes on a cello, and then she, rather defiantly I thought, knocks out a bit of bad Rachmaninov on a piano, which wasn't in the programme. They plant a small tree together, she shovelling in three spadefuls of earth and then her husband doing the same, and there's immediately a buzz-buzz of talk; doesn't that show things are fine between them?

But then at the awful three-hour fashion show on the last evening in Sydney – an evening of which all wool-growers were proud, where Michael Parkinson was MC, and where models paraded interminably and couturiers talked rot about their creations catching the scent of so vast a country – it was Prince Charles who for a moment nodded off, as any sane man would, while the princess, for the first time that I saw on the tour, was animated and went up to the models at the end and chatted away. If you watch all this, and I watched it, you are playing voyeur.

But back to those photographers for a moment. They are men of natural resource, and God help anyone who gets in their way. I saw them got the better of just once, and that was by the no-nonsense stewardesses of Ansett, the domestic airline that flew us around Australia.

'No ladders on the plane as hand baggage,' said the stewardesses, and there were no ladders. The magnitude of this achievement cannot be overemphasised.

Then on the plane there was a scrum, with each photographer trying to stow his three cameras, zoom lenses, monopods, tripods, and other aids. 'This', said the Ansett girl, 'is flight 4005 to Melbourne, so would you please all hurry up and sit down? And smoking [practically seizing an offending cigarette] is prohibited. By law.' So there.

One of the stewardesses was wearing a maternity smock. I asked an airline official if this could be so. He told me they could fly till they were nine months pregnant. He said this was a land of no discrimination. Except, I am happy to say, against French photographers who behave like oafs. I think it was that stewardess who, moaned at by a Frenchman who wanted yet more beer, told him he'd drunk the plane dry, and that he could make do with champagne like the rest.

The coldest, hardest remark of the whole tour was made not by one of the heavies, not even by a French photographer, but by an English girl journalist, who wasn't working for one of the tabloids either. 'It's a deathwatch, isn't it?'

she said. It takes a young woman, unaware of mortality, to say that. But no shots were fired and, on the evidence of this tour, Australia will not become a republic just yet, not for a generation or two.

Terry Coleman
6 February 1988

3 and 4 February 1988

Invisible people

From that great and justifiably self-congratulatory public banquet which is the Australian bicentennial anniversary, 200,000 people have been virtually excluded.

They are the Aboriginals who occupied the country before Captain Cook set his flag down near Sydney for the British, and who now scrape a living on the mostly arid land allowed to them by the white settlers, with only primitive tools for their professional self-respect and only alcohol as a substitute for hope.

Over the years, after the initial uneasy respect between colonizers and colonized, they have been taken out of the bush by the white man, shot in the back of the head and piled up like logs or chained together like dogs. If it were not for a minority of people like Pat Dodson, they would not have been able to muster the 40 of their number to stand outside their Tent Embassy facing Sydney harbour: a gesture intended to tell a genuinely compassionate Prince of Wales about one of the most pathetic sagas in the copious chronicle of man's inhumanity to man.

Now 38, Dodson is used to being self-sufficient and resourceful. Descended from Aboriginals in Broome, Western Australia, he was orphaned at 12, and sent to a Catholic boarding school. He became a priest, but gave it up eight years ago because, as one colleague put it, 'he could not accept that the European way of worship was the only right way.' He went on to marry, start a family and become a stalwart of the Aboriginal land rights movement.

A magnetic bearded figure, he has been both speaker and organizer. He is now director of the Central Land Council, one of the three government-backed land councils of Australia which aim to give freeholds back to Aboriginals.

He is also an elected member of the 76-strong Council of Aboriginals, which meets four times a year, not in the offices at Alice Springs but always in the bush – because decisions about Aboriginal land must in dignity always be taken on the land itself. He is national coordinator of the Federation of Land Councils.

The Australian High Commission in London said yesterday: 'We have a number of biographies and photographs of people here, but nothing on Pat Dodson.' That simple fact may say more than a manifesto about white attitudes to the Australian Aboriginals as people.

Dennis Barker
26 January 1988

Wellies will be worn . . .

Whatever did the county set deck themselves out in before Mr Barbour invented his solemnly shiny, mud-brown mini-mackintosh? The waterproof jacket at least makes for, at first glance, a sudden new classlessness among the centuries' old class-ridden clans of country folk.

The famous dun donkey-jacket was donned by the thousand at the weekend when the new point-to-point season thunderingly got under way and a jolly good time was had by all – with winners and losers, plebs and debs all hoorayingly hip-flask happy and bitter-beer chasers still at only 80p a pint.

The only way a modern Mayhew can spot the class difference on these winter's end Saturdays is that the posh tent serves up the liquor in glasses while the common man sups from plastic.

Cars are parked in the very same field, but the prices are graded at £7 and £10, and you get more bangers in the former patch. I suppose Volvos, BMWs and Range Rovers simply think it's worth three quid extra not to be parked alongside a clapped-out Vauxhall van. There are also a lot of horses about the place at a point-to-point: but nags are not snobs, some of them only look it. They don't mind mucking in together and at a point-to-point they blooming well have to. And how. It is a whole new fall game.

On Saturday – which was a sensational, snow-threatening, wintery, windblown watercolourist's day – you could drive through a longish lunch-hour across half the width of southern England and every county seemed to have at least a noonday traffic jam up the most unlikely of lanes that led to a telltale couple of hillsides and hillocks speckled already with the serried ranks of cherry reds and primrose yellows and ol' banger blues of the western world's motor industry. Many were pulling horseboxes in the same dingy, half-glossy brown of the owners' statutory Barbour overcoat.

The Army show was at Tweseldown, in the very heart of officer country. Horsey sons and daughters of Betjeman's thirties. Surrey & Hants and terribly terribly. Very up-market. Doughnut sellers spelt it 'Donuts'. The picnic hampers were of genuine wicker, and the girl on your arm was pronounced 'gel', and they had complexions of porcelain and voices of tin and looked nearly as haughty as the horses.

Wellies were not half as green across country on the English borders at north Hereford; old black working jobs there, with genuine working mud on them, and Doughnut Tent spelt properly and wives answering to Joyce and Jennifer, and aunties to Edna.

There was a strictly ordered announcement at Tweseldown for 'William Henry please report to Mummy, who's waiting by the car' – at Hereford a similarly echoing PA announced the forthcoming attraction: 'On 24 March at the Village Hall a talk on "The Horse and its Respiratory Problems"'. The same voice also boomed urgently at one stage – 'would the veterinary surgeon please get pronto to the jockeys' tent!' To hell with the human, how's the horse?

Devotees of *The Archers* would twig Saturday's culture gap. The military will resent the analogy, but Tweseldown had about it a touch of the Snells of Sunningdale. The North Hereford, on its blissful, rolling course at Whitwick Manor on the Ledbury road, was much more genuine Ambridge.

'How's Mark bearin' up?' asked a tweedy TA type at Tweseldown, meaning (I presumed) Capt. Princess Royal, who is still on crutches after fallin' back'ards orf a lorry at Luhmuhlen in West Germany in the autumn. Everyone's favourite, Foggy Phillips, would be back in the saddle by July at the latest, said the chap in the know.

At Hereford, it was less glittery gossip, and if not quite Grundy or Gabriel and over the top, very much Jack Woolley, Phil and Jill and Shula. More sausage rolls and bananas in a plastic bag in the boot and, in a way, more succulent eavesdroppers' droppings – 'So I said to Sandra, get up and ring the ruddy vet yourself, woman. It's you who's made the damn mare so frisky in the first place.'

Still a thumping good day out. The season continues till May. The sport has changed enormously. Traditionally, meetings were simply an end-of-season 'Thank-ee' from the local hunt to farmers who had tolerated them jorrocksing all over their land through winter. It was a sort of four-legged village fete to greet the spring. Now it is far bigger business than that.

Any point-to-point worth its salt nowadays is sponsored by such national combines as Christie's, Land Rover, Audi or Times Newspapers. They all have their sponsors' tents and free booze and soft sells. Every whip and crop, mare and marquee seems to have a sponsor now.

Last winter, 12,430 steaming, snorting hunters ran, jumped and/or stood still at a total of 176 meetings at 113 different courses. This year the figures will be far higher.

On Saturday, some 3000 enjoyed the fun near Ledbury, with an astonishing entry of over 300 horses.

'Not so long ago,' said Richard Lee, the celebrated point-to-point trainer now exclusively under Rules, 'this meeting might have drawn just 25 runners for the whole day. It was just a day out for the horses and riders from the local hunt. Now it attracts owners who are butchers, bakers, and, literally, candlestick makers, who like the idea of owning a "racehorse" and having a rattling good day out into the bargain. Well, prize money of 70 or 80 quid isn't going to make anyone a fortune when it costs at least £60 to keep a horse for a week, is it?'

Lee says it is 'just a different sport now, a different entity: you have to enjoy it for what it is' – and he certainly was on Saturday, as he revelled in his last day off before the up-coming Cheltenham meeting.

On the card before every race across England on Saturday it announced: 'Entries must have been hunted during the current season with any recognized Hunt in Great Britain.' That is mere waffle now and, as Lee says, the sport actually is very different to the ancient one it still pays lip service to.

The idea that a top point-to-point is just a frolicky fiesta for the amateurs who hunt through the bracing, bleak, coffin-like days of winter is now, frankly, baloney.

Any hunt is happy to get new subscriptions. All a point-to-pointer has to do is pay his sub each year – and no questions asked when he enters the paying spring carnival. Masters of Foxhounds are snooty at the best of times: they are not going around checking up on who's hunted and who hasn't like an office-boy sneak, are they?

The freemasonry of it all does not jump to take the *Guardian* into its confidence, I can tell you. Everyone knows what's going on, but what the heck, no one cares either. At least it's been evolution not revolution, ol' boy, what?

Had every entry at every point-to-point been hunting that season, as the rules stipulate? I put the question to the engaging trainer, Jackie Skelton, of Eardisley, a few miles west of the lovely, red-soiled pastures that were galloped over on Saturday.

'I'm jolly well sure they haven't,' she said. 'Mind you, they don't know what they're missing. But it's now become a bit of a businessman's sport. The emphasis has altered. Professional yards can pay as much as £12,000 for a horse, so they aren't going to risk him with their local hunt, are they? No, just get him ready for Feb and the point-to-point.'

Would the veterinary surgeon please go to the jockey's tent, pronto – and is Mummy still waiting by the car?

Actually, there can still be very good days out in Mrs T's olde Englande.

Frank Keating
3 January 1988

Half a league onward

The roll call of urban decrepitude is read out on Radio 2 every Saturday at about three minutes past five ... Rochdale 0, Halifax 0; Stockport 0, Scunthorpe 0 ... the usual dismal news for the sad-sounding towns of uttermost England.

The Fourth Division of the Football League has come to seem like a repository of the Britain left behind in the 1980s: uneconomic, dated, provincial, and kept going out of unfashionable sentiment. But Thatcherism has reached even this forsaken corner of English life. It used to be extremely difficult to be kicked out of the Football League. Now the old featherbedding has finished: the bottom club is automatically demoted. Over the next few years many of the old names are likely to vanish from the pools coupons to be replaced by teams from thriving Thatcherite places like Barnet, Weymouth, and Maidstone.

If their football clubs go, some of the towns may vanish from the national consciousness completely. So it seemed a good idea to investigate the condition of part of Fourth Division England before that turns Tory too: Burnley, for instance, who last May were one desperate last-day win away from being the first club booted out.

Burnley, for heaven's sake! In 1921 Burnley F.C. were champions of the Football League and went 30 games without defeat. The town, meanwhile, wove more cotton than anywhere else in Lancashire or the world; there were 100,000 people and 100,000 looms. It was said that the Burnley weavers clothed Britain before breakfast and spent the rest of the day clothing the world. Fancy stuff came from Blackburn; checks from Nelson; the peasants of India and China did not wear fancy stuff or checks. They wore Burnley greycloth; the town thrived and the names of the half-back line – Halley, Boyle and Watson – echoed round the country.

In 1960 the football team were League Champions again. By now Asia had its own textile industry but the town still knew what its strengths were: cotton, coal, Burnley F.C., then run by the fat and famously autocratic pork butcher Bob Lord, and the Burnley Building Society.

In 1988 all the old certainties have vanished. Bob Lord is long dead. The 18 Burnley pits nationalized in 1946 have all closed. Even the building society has gone. The football club clings on – just. Likewise cotton. But no peasant is likely to be wearing Burnley cloth unless the fashion is for bandages or household dusters.

With failure has come cleanliness. If you stood on the hills above the town in 1960 all you could see were the tallest mill chimneys poking above the pall of smoke. The privet hedges were black and the moorland bracken stunted; even the sheep were smoky grey. One day at Turf Moor when Spurs were in town Danny Blanchflower, their captain, watched the crowd trudging through the drizzle and said to Jimmy McIlroy, Burnley's star inside right: 'How the hell do you live in a place like this?'

McIlroy still lives there, along with a decreasing number of other people: the population of the old county borough area is down to around 63,000.

Yet it is actually a very likeable town, one that makes you realize that on the most important indices, the levels of sheer human friendliness and decency, the southeast is bottom by a very long way. But what is Burnley now for?

Cotton is one answer, sort of. Just outside town there are hundreds of looms at Brierfield owned by Smith and Nephew turning out medical gauze and swabs in a gaunt stone mill, just the sort there might have been trouble at a century ago. Now there is hardly anyone there to cause it. This is textile hi-tech. There are 500 looms in weaving sheds Nos 1 and 2, rooms the size of a football ground with the unmistakable weaving-shed racket: ker-ponk, ker-ponk, ker-ponk. I looked round for the people. In the distance there were a couple of mill girls in denims. In the thirties there was much unrest in Burnley when the mill-owners tried to enforce a system of six looms per weaver instead of the traditional four. At Brierfield, the figure is 90.

A mile away the real, old thing still exists at the Queen Street mill, which has been turned into a working, steam-powered museum, rather a good one actually, which ought to be playing its full part in our new but precarious growth industry, taking in each other's folklore. It remains chronically, and maybe terminally, short of cash. The council are ambivalent about Queen Street. It is one of the glories of Fourth Division England that its towns still have Labour councils of the sort that in more sophisticated spots would themselves have qualified for a heritage museum.

I attended a meeting of the Burnley Policy and Resources Committee and in the hour before I nodded off not a soul mentioned the implications for lesbians of the new shopping centre and it was 50 minutes before the token trendy mentioned South Africa. Burnley's ratepayers have been saved a good deal of money and crassness by the councillors' conservatism but it has left the town short of good ideas as well. 'They're decent, honest working men,' says the local journalist and conservationist Richard Catlow, 'but they are a bit short of imagination. They'd still knock anything down to build a superstore. You try and convince them to preserve a cotton mill and they say "I worked in a cotton mill, lad. Who'd want to preserve that?"'

Even now the cotton remains sewn into Burnley's heart. There are still plenty of women deafened horribly by the constant ker-ponk ker-ponk but perfectly capable of lip-reading a passer-by from the top deck of a bus. Sam Hanna, now 84, went to work aged 12 in a gaslit weaving shed in Trafalgar Street: 6 a.m. start, 53 hours per week, wage – two and sixpence. Mr Hanna is a sort of filming Lowry who has spent 50 years recording dying crafts and the living town. On the weaving sheds he remains firmly unnostalgic. 'They treated us like animals.'

Burnley's cotton industry was probably past its peak when Sam Hanna started work. As early as 1890 mill-owners anxious for a fast buck were selling off their old, unwanted looms to India, not stopping to think what the Indians would do with them: undercut Lancashire with infinitely cheaper labour. Meanwhile the coal seams were getting too difficult to be worth mining.

'Burnley has declined faster than any other large town in Lancashire because, uniquely, it has lost all its large industries,' says the borough historian Roger Frost. When the mills closed so did the firms who made the looms; there were five in town with solid Lancashire names like Pembertons, making solid Lancashire looms. Only one is left, eking out life ingloriously as a jobbing foundry.

You can get over-depressed about Burnley. It has a tra-dition of self-reliance, and it is reviving slowly, pulling in new industries (the town's biggest employer is Lucas) and even the football team is now respectably and safely in mid-table.

But there is a pessimistic view of everything here. 'If a firm comes to Burnley, they come because they're exploiting low wages,' says Roger Frost. 'Very few of these jobs are in locally-owned firms. Come the next depression Burnley will be vulnerable again, I'm convinced of it.'

Would Burnley have more confidence if it still had a winning team? Daft as it might sound, many people feel much the same about both the football and the Burnley Building Society. That too was one of the top 12 nationally but still homely and rooted. If the dahlia society or the karate club wanted a little sponsorship on its big day, the answer was always yes. The people were loyal in return.

In the eighties that was no longer enough. The Burnley began slipping down the league table, as inexorably if not as spectacularly as the soccer team. Eventually it was eaten up. Now it is part of something based in Bradford called the National and Provincial, which sounds like a bank. It is still making a PR effort in Burnley and even paid to reopen the railway to Todmorden. But you wonder whether it will last, PR effort and railway both.

In the end, though, no one gets passionate about a building society. People do talk in the most graphic terms about the game against Leyton Orient which Burnley had to win to keep in the League: 'As near to a religious experience as you can imagine,' and 'The most emotional experience of my life except the death of my parents.'

Jimmy McIlroy, now the deputy sports editor of the *Burnley Express* ('I know more about local lady darts players than about modern footballers') watched the occasion more cold-eyed than most. He is convinced that Burnley – like the other Lancashire cotton teams, Bolton and Preston and Blackburn – were finished as great clubs when the £20 maximum wage was abolished in the sixties.

Burnley's decline was the most dramatic, partly because the chairman was immortalized in the over-grandiose concrete of the Bob Lord stand, partly because the club lost its old knack of finding good players cheap and partly because of management which at one stage in the post-Lord era behaved as though it had someone else's Visa card. But you cannot divorce the club's fate completely from the story of its surroundings. Turf Moor is probably the best-appointed workplace for miles around. But it needs a strong town to do it justice as well as a strong team. Maybe a fat dictator would help if he were the right strong man.

Robert Maxwell is only a plastic imitation of Bob Lord; it would take Charles Laughton to re-create the rôle. It will certainly not be played by a director of Lucas or the National and Provincial, hunting for the Burnley branch on the balance sheet, and possibly the map. And even a chain of butchers' shops is unlikely to have its head office in Burnley these days.

I left Turf Moor rather sadly and went for a pint at the General Scarlett on the Accrington Road. General Scarlett was a Burnley man who led the Charge of the Heavy Brigade at the Battle of Balaclava several hours earlier and much more successfully than the other, more celebrated charge.

By temperament, the British prefer to wallow in heroic defeat rather than in victory; Burnley likes past glories, which is just as well, the present being so disappointing. They ought to name a pub after Halley, Boyle, and Watson.

Matthew Engel
24 February 1988

Marilyn according to Miller

Only the most veteran and watchful of brokers would have spotted the portent on Wall Street a full year and a half ago. It was a relatively small transaction which should have chilled those with long memories: Arthur Miller sold out his blue chip shares.

He could have waited a year and made more. But the theatre's child and great artist of the American Depression and its postwar aftermath preferred to take no chances. 'This is going to sound absolutely nuts,' advises a financier in *The American Clock*, his play about the 1929 crash, 'but when you get your cash, don't keep it. Buy gold.'

In 1986 it didn't look quite so bad, so Miller bought bonds. But in principle, he says, 'I took my character's advice. I chose not to participate in the next collapse, which I was absolutely certain was on its way. I knew a certain number of companies were valued far above their actual value – many per cents above – and yet they were still going up. I don't know who finally decided time was up but they moved a lot of money awful fast.

'And I don't think we're necessarily finished yet because nothing fundamentally has changed. Instead of doing what we always did in the past – inventing, researching, planning ahead – we simply decided to turn a fast buck by selling Japanese. Same thing here, I think.'

Miller, now 72, is here to celebrate his 260,000-word

autobiography, as well as a continuing British renaissance of his plays, with this week's West End transfer of the National's staging of *A View from the Bridge*. He has already talked himself hoarse because the book, a work as dense and lyrical as Chaplin's memoirs, came out in the States two months ago.

He has talked about his craft and about the Depression but even more so – in response to demand – about his second wife, Marilyn Monroe. He talked about her to me openly, patiently, and with an almost despairing sadness.

But afterwards he was invited to nominate the question he himself would most like asked or answered in 1987.

Leaning closer, he said: 'There is one question I care about very much. I don't know the answer but I know the question. Why is it so difficult now to deal in written art with the forms that life has taken?

'Why is it that so much of our work is lacking in human empathy? Why do we care so little about the characters that are put before us? Is this a real picture of the way we think now and feel about ourselves as a race; that basically we are an exercise in black humour, particles of consciousness that don't deserve very much empathic interest?

'That is what I keep wondering about. In my plays – where they do succeed – I think you care a helluva lot about whoever you've been looking at. And I would like to see more in my own work and that of others of that kind of relationship.

'That is what's of interest to me and it's a mystery. Why there are so few great works of modern writing? I don't know whether they are not being written or not being made public. In other words, whether the fashion of the time is such that they are not encouraged?

'I don't know that, but it does concern me a lot. The reason is not aesthetic, it is that if we are so cool towards ourselves, it does not bode well for the species. There is an ingredient in any hope for a democratic and just society that we all tend to take for granted. That is, that it has got to give a damn.

'The theatre is the most obvious example of this coolness

but it has got into films too. There is a terror of being caught
with your feelings hanging out. The really popular art
seems to be mechanical. In films there's a vast calling
for space epics with no trace of human dimension. In my
boyhood, we had Pearl White and Flash Gordon but we
knew they were a side road of society. Now they're a highway.'

We don't often raise – or get asked – questions as large
in Britain. But the question was in character, as was his
unwillingness to throw out easy answers and his expectation that the mystery might still be settled by social
discourse. It was asked in the voice of the author of probably
the twentieth century's most tearing line of dramatic
empathy – 'Attention, attention must be paid to this man,'
in perhaps the century's most humanly unified play, *Death
of a Salesman*.

This is a public voice, and a mode of questioning, which
it has been our fortune to have with us for nearly 50 years
now. It first began to take on form when he was told the
story of Peter, a member of his first wife's family who
became unstable and committed suicide in the middle of an
apparently cheerful and hopeful youth.

'I was almost nakedly ignorant of formal psychiatry, and
it never occurred to me to write Peter off as a case,' Miller
says in the book. 'Instead, I sensed the mysterious motion
of spirit in his illogical behaviour.'

That sense – on which all his stage writing has depended
– led both to his first published play *The Man Who Had All
the Luck* and to *The Golden Years*, a radio study of the
conquered Aztec emperor Montezuma. Both are studies
in what he calls 'the illusion of powerlessness' to which
individuals are prone.

The Depression was a forcing-house for that insight. He
was 14 when it broke, the college-bound son of Izzie Miller,
founder of the Miltex Coat and Suit Company, New York,
one of the country's two or three largest. In prosperity
his father was celebrated for fastidiousness – 'a man who
will not eat in restaurants where there are thick water
glasses'.

Among Miller's earliest recollections is lying at his mother's feet in Harlem while she listened to the Columbia student she paid $2 an afternoon to come in and talk about novels. Within a year or so the family was struggling to find $50 a month to pay the mortgage after moving to the smallest chicken-coop of a house they could find. Izzie took to dozing whenever money, and especially the topic of college fees, was raised.

Miller's friends spent the week playing touch-football in the street. 'I once walked into a basement room to find our whole football team masturbating each other,' he says in one of many passages which relish the wild anarchy and comedy of even that phase of American life.

Instead of joining that lifestyle, he spent two years working in an auto parts warehouse and elsewhere to save the $500 fees deposit he needed to get into college. What he saw then gave him not only a guilty sense of luck and a rage that has hardly yet subsided but a richness of 'democratic education' experienced by virtually no British playwright of his century.

He and his first wife Mary were radicals so instinctual that, in the middle of labour pains with their first child, she cried out 'Oh, those poor Yugoslavs!' whom Hitler was that night invading. For a period after his first hit *All My Sons* (1947), which was earning $2000 a week, he carried on doing a factory job for 40 cents an hour until the inauthenticity of it overwhelmed him.

His only formal links with Communism were desultory discussion groups, he says. These were to return to pain him in the McCarthy years of the 1950s. But first there was *Death of a Salesman*. Its director Elia Kazan became the earliest of a multitude to say it was about his father. Lee J. Cobb, cast to play Willy Loman, the little salesman at the end of his tether, said before rehearsals, 'You know – or do you? – that this play is a watershed. The American theatre will never be the same again.'

The afternoon of opening day, Miller, Kazan and Cobb went to a performance of Beethoven's Seventh to get Cobb in the right mood. 'We thought of ourselves, still, as a kind of continuation of a long and undying past,' Miller says. The word 'still', relegating such faith to his own and other people's past, is indicative of his present sadness.

Instead of clapping, the audience at curtain-fall turned and talked to each other. Then came the apparently endless applause. The head of Gimbel's stores chain, who was in the audience, ordered at once that none of his over-age employees be sacked. And, reputedly, a salesman stormed out, shouting, 'I always knew that New England territory was no good.'

Six years later during the run of *A View from the Bridge*, a story pulled out of the air by Miller from his Brooklyn stevedore friendships and his personal sense of his father's feelings towards his sister, a docker kept coming quietly to performances. He was obviously much moved. 'I knew that family,' he told an actor who eventually spoke to him. 'The whole story is true, except that the ending has been changed. The girl came in while Eddie (the father in the play) was having his nap and stabbed him in the heart.'

But by then Miller's personal life had clouded. The day he had been due earlier in the 1950s to go to Salem to research *The Crucible*, his most widely performed play, his great friend Kazan confessed he had decided to cooperate with the Congressional Un-American Activities Committee. Salem now has a tourist Witches' Trail in honour of the play. But when Miller got there that day, all he could think about was that the will and capacity of the State to 'break charity' between individuals seemed timeless and inescapable.

And Marilyn was on the scene. In the autobiography he tells how, while he was waiting for his divorce in Nevada, she phoned to talk about her problems on the *Bus Stop* film set. He felt a sense of lifelong love for her so strongly that he fainted in the phone kiosk. He saw ahead '. . . a creative life with undivided soul . . . to be one thing, sexuality and mind, appetite and justice, one.

'All our theatre – my own of course included but that of the masters too – seemed so paltry now beside the immensity of human possibilities.' In youth Chekhov, Sophocles and Ibsen had seemed mighty creatures, 'natural eruptions of man's will to survive.' But now all he could think of was that they had been unhappy men.

'With all her concealed pain, she (Marilyn) was becoming enviable, the astonishing sign of liberation and its joys. And soon, an amazing life.'

As we know, it was not to work out like that. Sitting in a London hotel over 30 years later, Miller recognizes, as if it were yesterday, the malicious 1950s and 1960s press scuttlebutt: that they'd have nothing to say to each other, that they'd be sexually incompatible; and the stories after her suicide that, unlike her first husband, the baseball player Joe Dimaggio, he had neither attended her funeral nor laid flowers on her grave in the years after.

He said, 'We had discovered something far deeper than they ever knew. We found plenty to talk about. She was a very politically interested person, interested in the society, interested in living. She wanted to survive into her middle and old age. She wanted children.

'I don't think there was any question of us being sexually incompatible. It was an attempt on my part and on hers to transcend the barriers between two kinds of living – the one which was more sexual, the other more intellectual.

'There used to be, way back in ancient Greece, the ideal of the whole person. We have now come so far from that that it's not capable of being discussed.

'I am sorry to say I don't particularly know how to deal with funerals. I have a tendency in general to separate matter from spirit in a way that makes it difficult to conceive of a relationship with a dead person. I feel that they are not there any more.'

Arthur Miller has been married for the last 25 years – his best, he says – to the photographer Inge Morath, a survivor of Nazi Germany who matches his own sense of 'the tragedy of humanity' but brought him an optimism and internationalism he had not known before. They have a grown-up daughter, Rebecca.

Yet he is open enough to reply, when asked in another context whether his feeling for Marilyn was an obsessional infatuation or a mutual and authentic romantic love: 'The latter. That's the difficulty.'

John Ezard
5 November 1987

Timebends: a Life by Arthur Miller (Methuen).

Verses for adversity

In the circumstances, I suppose it was inevitable that some-one was going to quote Browning's 'The Lost Leader'. From the opposite angle, someone was also bound to offer us Yeats on the birth of a terrible beauty. Perhaps more unexpected, though equally apt, was Shelley in defence of polygamous relationships.

For this was the Social Democrats, the party which has managed to show in its seven short years of life that it can combine an unrivalled capacity for political illusion with an even more impressive capacity for literary allusion. What else would you expect from the organized middle classes?

The poet who came most readily to my mind yesterday, however, as speaker after speaker coupled their attacks on each other's leaders with appeals for a friendly parting of the ways, was Robert Burns. Just as the Labour Party likes to conclude its conferences with the 'Red Flag', it might have been appropriate if the SDP had wound up for the last time with 'Ae Fond Kiss'.

How nice it would have been to see Shirley and Bob, Roy and Bill joining hands on the platform to sing those touchingly immortal words:

> ae fond kiss and then we sever,
> ae fareweel alas forever
> deep in heartfelt tears I'll pledge thee,
> Warring sighs and groans I'll wage thee.

But it was not to be. If there was much reality in the sense of anguish at yesterday's parting, it was much more like the anguish which accompanies a really nasty family divorce than the sentimental pain of true lovers torn prematurely apart. What we saw on the platform, as Shirley Williams announced the result of the vote on the proposed SDP merger with the Liberals, was certainly not sentimentality, it was raw triumphalism.

And by and large, Mrs Williams and her pro-merger colleagues were fully entitled to their sense of triumph. We had been led to expect something more dramatic than the steamroller figures she finally announced: Yes, 273; no, 28; abstentions, 49.

Mind you, Mrs Williams (by the way, must we go on calling her that? just like her party, she has re-married) was perhaps pushing it a bit when she claimed that this represented an 80 per cent majority instead of the two-thirds required.

As Dr Owen pointed out later, the anti-merger faction had deliberately stood aside from the vote, so that the total poll was 200 short of the number entitled to take part.

But there it is: no one can any longer dispute that the merger has the backing of a substantial proportion of the grass roots of both the SDP and the Liberal Party. With only the formality of a simple majority in a membership ballot to be surmounted, it is fairly safe to assume that the Social and Liberal Democratic Party will be a going concern by the autumn.

Yet one cannot help feeling some degree of sympathy with the opponents of merger. As many of their speakers argued, it is an over-simplification to claim that they represent nothing but a David Owen fan club. If they still declare their belief in the *raison d'être* of the Social Democratic Party, that was a conviction they acquired from the eloquence of Shirley and Roy as well as from the doctor.

That was why there was something mildly distasteful about Mrs Williams' presidential address at the start of the whole marathon debate. It was clear from the first few sentences that nice, rational, reasonable Mrs Williams had deliberately decided to abandon her familiar image as a conciliator and go for the jugular.

By the end of her speech (from the advance text of which, to be fair, she excised some of the more brutal passages as she spoke) any hope that the weekend was going to be conducted in the warm spirit of Robert Burns instead of the cold fury of Robert Browning had effectively vanished. It was going to be war.

Indeed, that was apparent as soon as one arrived in the headquarters hotel. Pushing through the swing doors into the lobby was like stepping into a time capsule, carrying one back to the hairy days of the Labour Party conferences at their very worst.

At first glance, one could grasp that a nasty row was in full swing. Rival factions caballed in corners and whispered in doorways. Predatory reporters, notebooks in hand, slithered from one group to another before hurrying to the hotel phones to immortalize the scene.

As Mr Ian Wrigglesworth, a former Labour MP, ruefully remarked from long experience: 'It's quite like old times, isn't it?' And so it was, save for one minor difference. The row was about nothing more cosmic than the booking of a meeting hall; in the Labour Party, even at its worst, it would have been about the Bomb, the survival of the human race, or some such.

But then, that is what really nasty family divorce rows are frequently about. How often one has watched in horror as old friends drag each other through the courts over who owns the piano and who gets the portraits.

One was surely entitled, however, to expect better of a party which had founded itself substantially on the proposition that politics could be conducted in a rational and civilized fashion. As one despairing speaker remarked, it was dismaying to find that the Liberal Party could wind itself up in dignity and good fellowship after 200 years existence, while the young SDP displayed all the characteristics which sniffy Social Democrats had denounced in Liberals.

But all that is history now, even if the history has proved to be nasty, brutish and short. The real questions now are about the future. They concern not only the prospects for some kind of political success for the merged party but also the role of the unmerged SDP in deciding the fate of the new party.

The new party, whatever its honourable intentions, is much more likely to perpetuate Conservative rule than to assist in ending it. Though there are sophisticated psephological arguments which should suggest it might prove otherwise in certain circumstances, the broad-brush reality is that the more successful it is the more likely Mrs Thatcher will be to benefit.

But the entry of a fourth party on to the stage could easily modify all that. Though many Owenite speakers insisted yesterday that they are not planning to put up candidates against the merged party, Dr Owen himself made clear on Saturday night that they stand ready to field candidates in every constituency in the land.

To be sure, he made it plain that he would only take this aggressive step if the new party refused to co-operate with his party – a proposition which I took to mean if it refused to give him and his two parliamentary colleagues a clear run. But there has not been much encouragement for that sort of expectation from either Mr Steel or Mr Maclennan.

So the odds are – indeed, the logic is – that the merged party and the unmerged party will almost inevitably end up fighting each other in some, if not all of the 650 parliamentary seats. And that won't just split the third party vote, it will also strike a devastating blow at the credibility of third party politics in general.

If so all those millions of voters 'out there' whom Liberals and Social Democrats like to think are yearning for some alternative to the traditional parties will simply be turned off altogether. And that can only be good news for Mr Kinnock in his struggle to recreate a credible Labour Party capable of winning votes again.

It would be ironical if this key service to Mr Kinnock turned out to be the ultimate destiny of the SDP's Man of

Destiny himself. Getting the Labour carthorse back on the road is hardly the role Dr Owen chose when he left the Labour Party seven years ago.

But that's life, I suppose, even for Men of Destiny. Yet it is surely proper to reflect at this historic moment on the curious circumstances which now seem likely to see one of the most charismatic political figures of the postwar years marching voluntarily on into impotence and isolation. In the words of another (though anonymous) poet: 'Ain't it all a bleeding shame?'

Ian Aitken
1 February 1988

Champagne in the dark

Beirut:
Some people have a nose for news. I have an ear. Whenever the burden of work becomes overwhelming, my right ear starts producing the pain that only ears and teeth can.

Thus it was that, in the first days of Terry Waite's disappearance, I found myself pounding on the doors of the emergency department at the American Hospital. The department was closed, a scruffy notice informed us, because of the kidnapping of yet another intern.

Over the street and up to the ear, nose and throat floor of the main hospital building I went, squeezed in the lift among militiamen redolent with BO and Eau Sauvage. Then followed an hour's waiting for the duty doctor to complete his rounds of other sufferers – most of them with their ears blown off or out.

'Still here?' he inquired, committing murder with a blunt-ended instrument and clearly more concerned with the complete person than the suffering part. 'What on earth for?'

Later that week, my driver took the cross-eyed kitten, the last in a long line of camps-war cats, to the vet for an ailment which was not, as I feared, fatal but rather, we were assured, the kitten equivalent of teenage acne. 'She's still here?' said the vet. 'She must be mad. She doesn't even need a visa to get out.'

Several days on, only the kitten feels up to indoor sports. The vet had medicines aplenty – most of his patients are long since gone, with their masters – but the chemists have half-empty shelves. No ear drops. It is only half the explanation that today's prices are tomorrow's cut-prices; shops are simply not ordering as they did before.

With the collapse of the Lebanese pound money is short and those who seem to have an endless supply of it, the militias, have other ways of doing their shopping.

West Beirut is still a long way ahead of other Arab capitals as regards daily consumer necessities, but it doesn't compare with its former self: the champagnes are still there, but the port and oak-smoked kippers are gone. There are no catnip mice.

There are also, at least on the face of it, no Westerners. It is quite possible these days to go to Smith's supermarket, or the Commodore Hotel, where foreign journalists were tumbling off their barstools like falling rain not so long ago, without seeing a single Western face. The same is true – or would be, if one actually did it – of a walk along the seafront.

'You can feel the xenophobia,' an Eastern European journalist commented the other day, leaning over the balcony of a Western embassy with a glass of French champagne, Grande Cuvée, in hand. 'I sympathize with a lot of what lies behind it, but I really don't feel obliged to explain that to them.' More pertinently, there is no explaining. A former Shi'ite fighter of my acquaintance was berating me the other day for having been spotted on the Palestinian side of the contested village of Maghdousheh.

It was useless to point out that the Palestinian return to Lebanon cannot be described from the Shi'ite side of the line.

It is enough to be seen with the enemy to be the enemy. And the enemy, in these days of atomization, is very difficult to avoid. It very often changes from block to block. A Druze friend involved in the search for Terry Waite this week offered to combine talking with feeding me. What was my pleasure? My first three choices were, apparently, no-go areas for the Druze, although in the very heart of the city.

We were reduced to hamburgers in a joint where the other clients had to put their pistols in their pockets before shaking hands. And then there are the logistical problems, which at times like this become overwhelming.

In the past three months, I have succeeded in making two international telephone calls. In the last few days, strange gentlemen have been constantly interrupting my conversations, against a background of even stranger noises. Telexes died for 36 hours. There are no foreign newspapers and Beirut Airport is again closed.

There are constant electricity cuts and permanent water shortages – not to mention the sniping, with heavy machine-guns, that has been cutting down the street in front of the house ever since President Gemayel and President Assad kissed and made up in Kuwait.

What makes it bearable, desirable even, is the Lebanese themselves – the knee-high boy who runs the newspapers up to the house every day to save valuable time; the fruit seller who throws away, for you, the ones with soggy bits; the friendly militiamen who have been standing in the shadows all night long, shouting 'don't be frightened,' ever since a gentleman not of my acquaintance telephoned around midnight one night to say, 'we're coming now.'

Then, last but not least, there is the long-suffering driver who is not only willing to drive anywhere, anytime and through anything, but who fixes generators, humps butane bottles, shops, banks, stakes out and, in these kidnapping days, changes cars several times a day – always with one of myriad relatives suitably equipped in the back seat.

As the last Western diplomat in West Beirut points out,

'the chances that something might happen to us are much bigger than they were a week ago. We're it, darling.'

Julie Flint

First published 4 February 1987, and reprinted 6 February 1988, when Julie Flint was named International Reporter of the Year by Granada TV's What the Papers Say.

God's club tie

After the traumas of the past year, MCC perhaps deserved the rub of the green for their bicentenary match. But not even the biggest optimist could have wished for a better day than that which streamed down on London. Lord's looked glorious – an outfield chequered with the nap of green velvet, a summery, picnicking, packed house which chattered animatedly through the day, and the new Mound Stand, resplendent.

The Coldstream Guards were there too, with their incidental music. But, above all, there was a century from Graham Gooch. God, quite obviously, wears an egg and tomato tie.

The cricket was in keeping – mildly competitive while lacking the jingoism of a true Test match. By the end of the day, 96 overs, MCC had made 291 for 4, with Mike Gatting unbeaten on 68 and looking odds-on for a hundred today if he survives the new ball first thing.

For most, it was supposed to be a day of celebration. For Gooch, it was more than that. It has not been an easy season for him. Last winter he opted not to tour, and although he never pretended that a Test place this summer was his by divine right, not even he could have anticipated the way in which he was forced to retreat into the shell of county cricket.

He hadn't so much lost form as changed persona: for

whatever reason – lack of confidence, too much responsibility for carrying the Essex batting, or even changing his tried and tested bat manufacturer – his runs, still prolific by ordinary standards, were those of the journeyman accumulator, not the destroyer.

Indeed, he is only playing in this match because Martin Crowe is injured. So the moment, after just over four hours, when he nicked Kapil Dev off the inside edge to square leg for the single that took him to his first hundred for two months could be the most significant, from an English viewpoint, of the match.

Until then, there had been some who doubted his value in the World Cup and Pakistan tour for which he is available. Now the idea of omitting him would be unthinkable. As the crowd rose to him, he gave that sheepish wave of the bat that some mistakenly take for indifference, But, inside, you can bet he was mighty pleased to be back.

Conditions for a rehabilitation could not have been better. Mick Hunt, the groundsman, had prepared the sort of featherbed pitch that emasculates fast bowlers: the kind we never seem to play the West Indies on. Gooch meandered out, dragging his bat in careworn fashion, in the fifth over, after Chris Broad had been lbw, deceived by Imran into offering no stroke. Gooch is fond of batting at Lord's: three of his seven Test centuries have come here. But yesterday he was under the sort of pressure not to fail that the likes of Athey, say, or Moxon, or the young Gatting even, felt every time they went out to try and establish themselves. And it showed at the start as he left things very much in the capable hands of Greenidge, who obliged with 52 of the 96 pre-lunch runs. All were scored with that exaggerated limp, a cliché now, which generally precedes a double hundred.

Not this time, though. Greenidge launched at Qadir's second ball after the interval and was caught overhead by Harper at mid-on. Gower, never in touch, scratched eight wistful runs in 20 overs before touching Harper's second ball to Dujon. Gatting, before tea, was similarly circumspect.

Gooch, however, was starting to look like his old self and some bounce came back into his step as he began to clip the ball clinically through mid-wicket.

He rid himself of his batting helmet and donned his battered old sun-hat. It was like a casting-off of shackles. In the afternoon session only 14 of the 81 runs scored came from the bat at the other end. A straight drive sent Qadir to the X-ray machine, to the disappointment of the crowd.

It's not easy to keep Gatting out of things, though, and with a cuppa inside him he started to attack Harper, the best bowler of the day, from hitherto uncharted territory yards down the pitch, hitting him straight and over mid-wicket, and driving Imran.

It took a very special piece of cricket to get rid of Gooch. The stand was worth 103, and looked set for many more, when Gooch – emulating Gatting – skipped down the pitch to Harper, over the wicket, and drove firmly just to the onside of straight. Harper, 6ft 5in tall and telescopic – armed, pounced and in the same movement threw out Gooch's middle stump, leaving the batsmen two yards down the track, grovelling incredulously on all fours. It would have been worth the entrance money for that moment alone.

Mike Selvey
21 August 1987

In the green heart

Umbria is supposedly an unknown quantity in Italian tourism, there being no sea. But it would be a rash traveller who claimed to 'discover' it. Most Christians, not to mention Mrs Thatcher, will immediately connect it with St Francis of Assisi.

For art lovers it conjures up Giotto, Piero della Francesca, Perugino. Historians of an older, pagan world will recall the classic victory devised by Hannibal, though he was down to one elephant and one eye, when he ambushed Flaminius between the mountains and the shore of Lake Trasimeno. Wine bibbers will sigh for the authentic *abboccato*, or semi-sweet flavour of Orvieto. Now holiday-makers are asked to join the list, and think of Umbria as 'the green heart'.

Like any other heart it is served by a main aorta, in fact the highway that runs, via Rome, from one end of Italy to the other. And in Umbria there is little of the competitive strain of the heroic Italian driving met with elsewhere. The roads are generally good, though they may forget to post a sign which tells you that the excellent road you are breezing along will come to an end after 20 kilometres. Most often, however, the end is a spectacular destination.

The many hilltop towns of Umbria, rising with austere definition above the valleys, have the effect of an archipel-ago, with rural exchanged for marine life, swimming in a haze of sunflower, cypress and corn.

Our villa was on a slope of sunflowers and faced another such slope: not so much fields as forests of sunflowers, acres of gross discs like giant gas rings, sizzling with bees. A rather loutish plant seen close up, the sunflower's jolly crowd behaviour is exemplary. Two irrigation ponds in the fold at the bottom had been extensively colonized by a species of equally cheerful and vulgar frog, whose bright green and yellow livery seemed to have been modelled exactly on those in souvenir shops.

The house whose ground floor we occupied, with a ver-anda for al fresco meals and a tree for garage, was one of those plain brick rectangles which the natives are thrilled to find suit the tourists, so they themselves can move in to nice new modern buildings. Naturally, it's not just a dim old barn any more, but a proper Tuscan conversion job, as per investment portfolio limelight, with three bedrooms and two bathrooms, more furniture than I can remember in a villa before, and even sharp knives.

We had a slight dilemma over the electricity, since we couldn't have the light and the oven on at the same time.

Hot water turned suddenly icy in the shower, too. The engineer on frequent visits pronounced the system *benissimo*, but it took the removal of a wildlife corpse from the flue to solve the problem. The two cats were great hunters, and accompanied us on expeditions as outriders, but made no distinction between prey in the fields and what they could hunt down on the kitchen table.

I thought we would have a scorpion problem too, when one showed up black and fearsome against the white wall above a bedhead. My early tropical conditioning prompts me to violence, and sleeping with my shoes safe under lock and key, but now the conservationist faction in the family, doubtless urged on by the mana of St Francis, prevailed to save its life. It was collected in a picnic bag – I hope it was not too cold for it – and released among the sunflowers: a strange habitat for it, but rich in insects. And, incidentally, the black variety is harmless; it is the wimpish-looking albino that gives you a nasty sting.

Though there were common birds around us, and the crow is indestructible and pigeons roam mob-handed in Assisi, in high summer it seemed that the forces of St Francis were losing their battle against the pollutants. On a trip to Polvesi, one of three islands in the 376 square kilometres of Lake Trasimeno, a distressing number of fish floated by belly up. But in the high spots of the woods the insect carnival continues.

We had this relaxing place a dog-leg 15 kilometres from the principal town on the lake, Castiglione del Lago, which is a mix of pretty resort (fastidious swimmers prefer the police pool to the lake), suburban sprawl served by some frabjous supermarkets, notably the cooperatives, and a kernel of old town.

The latter is, inevitably, up a hill, but a modest one by comparison with the hulking bluffs of Orvieto, Montepulciano, Cortona, Assisi, Perugia. It has a piazzetta to loll about in, a tranquil restaurant terrace overlooking the lake and a frenzied one up an alley, called La Cantina.

But neither beats the Jolly at the foot of the hill, with TV competing against music, and family rows competing with both, a lugubrious waiter behaving as foil to the exuberant boss, and a bubbling pizza called 'dustbin' because anything and everything the cook lays hands on is heaped into it.

Of course the town has a castle. Umbria has castles the way the moon has craters, from broad-shouldered fortresses that loomed implacable until the advent of the cannon, to country manors that prop up the esteem of some poor hamlet, or decay like biscuit in the sun.

The 50-odd-kilometre perimeter of the lake is festooned with them. And every one has its extraordinary story of rivalry and conspiracy, of cankers in the bud, hoky-poky behind the arras, trials of strength, and nasty pieces of work opening the postern gate to the enemy at midnight. The romances of Rafael Sabatini are by comparison sober documentaries.

The jaunty little hotspurs that owned them set up more armies than there are teams in the football league, and with a more congested fixture list. A mercenary might march out one day against an army whose strip he would wear on the next.

And as one stands on one broad platform after another, scanning fertile valleys below, as the robber barons did, perched above the wonderful labyrinth of gloom of a Montepulciano, or breaking clear of 100,000 pairs of shoes in a Perugian street market for that gigantic prospect of the great plain with the mountains beyond, one must recognize that there is no making a sensible pattern in the medieval mosaic.

Better perhaps just give up and wallow in the confusion, and enjoy reading Luigi Barzini on the Italian psyche. But I should just acknowledge that Castiglione's main event in history is rather a dismal one, when it betrayed Umbria into Tuscan domination. Today the courageous can get a clear view right across the lake from the tall tower of the castle, and there's probably nothing sinister in sight.

Come to think of it, though, that was quite a fright we had on the island of Polvesi taking a picnic by a ruin, when a couple of fighter bombers banged out of nowhere, monastery hopping, low enough to read the serial numbers.

It's the sort of thing that could give cardiac arrest to the green heart.

Alex Hamilton
26 March 1988

The groans of grunts

'God has a hard-on for Marines because we kill everything we see. He plays his games, we play ours.' Thus says Lee Ermey's raucous drill instructor to his shaven-headed recruits at their boot camp preparation for Vietnam in Stanley Kubrick's *Full Metal Jacket*. And it would be dangerous for these grunts to think he was only play acting. It's 'an eight-week college for the phoney tough and the phoney brave,' and it's meant to hurt.

So is Kubrick's loose adaptation of Gustav Hasford's *The Short Timers*, a Vietnam movie, made substantially in Britain, that's about as far from *Paths of Glory* as could be. That film railed against the horror, wastage and cynicism of war as if the young director had just discovered it. *Full Metal Jacket* shakes its bloody locks at us with a wearier, harder anger. Kubrick as drill instructor perhaps, pushing us, like he did in *Clockwork Orange* and *The Shining*, towards the surreal, and making a bitter, almost theatrical farce of all our best hopes.

Not surprisingly, given the man's obsessive insistence on technical perfection and his determination to prove that naturalism is never enough, this is a Vietnam movie like no other. Which is different from saying it is either the last word, or the best. In fact, it lacks warmth, except where the fires of hell are concerned, and its humanity and breadth of vision are at least questionable.

It pursues the ice-cold logic of its opening 45 minutes at training camp as if it's too late for any of us to call for help.

Gentle Jesus has no part in this film. If He had, He would have been crucified earlier. Marx, one feels, would have fared as badly. The world's not capable of the saving.

From boot camp, where Vincent D'Onofrio's porcine country boy is driven into violent madness as maggots are made into Marines, virtually shaped into M-14s loaded with bullets (the full metal jacket of the title), we progress to Vietnam a moment before the 1968 Tet offensive. Rafterman (Kevyn Major Howard) and Joker (Matthew Modine) are now engaged in reporting the facts as optimistic fiction – 'Welcome to Vietnam, the Movie.' They know differently in their hearts, but haven't the intellect to draw more than simplistic conclusions. There's party rock on the soundtrack, and it points up the acid futility.

Finally, we go on a sniper shoot. The enemy killer is good but armed only with a rifle, and it's a she rather than a he, terrified and shaking, pleading for mercy after leaving her own trail of bloody destruction. Should they shoot or leave her to wriggle herself towards death? Here's where, at long last, the film stops momentarily to think, through the attenuated brains of its participants. That, too, is a bit too late.

There is no question that this is a brilliantly made film, and the fact that it was fashioned about as far as Kubrick could get from Vietnam (those East End palm trees look very sorry for themselves in our greyness, but then war might have had the same effect) does not matter. It's like *The Vietnam Revue*, the props are incidental. What does matter is Kubrick's icy stare, which renders much of the wit sour and the horror like only a ghastly pantomime.

The film, unlike *Paths of Glory*, seems to say that there is nowhere for human decency to go, that the absurdity of things is all too much. That makes it shocking but seldom moving in the real sense of the word. Its power ought to have been tremendous but it is dissipated by an odd lack of pity. Pious hopes would not have been enough. But one does need a horizon to look for, with or without a rainbow. It's not there.

At one point a pretty teenage prostitute, riding pillion

on a Vietnam boy's scooter, bargains with the Marines for her favours. She'll give them a good time, whatever they want and take a long time about it too. But not the Negro. His penis will hurt her. So he ups and shows her that it's not too big. What is the purpose of this scene? One knows Kubrick's work well enough to be certain that it is not to titillate. But with *Full Metal Jacket* he is standing so far above us, like a kind of God, that sometimes you can't tell what he is feeling, or how you are supposed to react.

Unless, that is, we can really encapsulate everything in those final words, appropriate to a lot of other things apart from Vietnam and perhaps what he hopes us to take from *Full Metal Jacket*: 'I'm in a world of shit. But I'm alive. And I am not afraid.'

Derek Malcolm
10 September 1987

Neil and the Big Idea

By an inspired stroke of conference management long ago, the Leader's speech at a Labour conference is always prefaced by another ritual occasion: the Lovely Old Lady's speech, and the speech of a Lovely Old Man.

They are there to receive from the Leader's hand the merit awards which conference bestows each year on two ancient and faithful servants. And somehow, for all their age and uncertain frailty, the recipients seem to succeed, year after year, in leaving the hall glowing with nostalgia, pride and affection of a kind which on some other occasions Labour looks almost to have lost.

This year Will Thomas was too ill to travel from Torfaen in South Wales to collect his award. But at 102 – the oldest person whom most in the hall yesterday had ever seen – Catherine Griffiths, who grew up in South Wales and worked (like Neil Kinnock's mother) as a district nurse, was there on the platform, ancient and bowed but still full of spirit, to recall her days as socialist and suffragette in a sweet little speech of thanks.

The Leader, as ever, gained more than he gave in this transaction. By the time Mrs Griffiths had gone the hall was again in the mellow, receptive mood which was just what he needed for the bagful of hard home truths he was going to offer them.

Nor did the parade of Old South Wales heroes end with Mrs Griffiths' departure. It was there again in Neil Kinnock's speech as he enlisted even more of them in support of his major theme: that Labour must change with the times or perish.

Nye Bevan first, since what he said and wrote (one famous Brighton speech apart) remains for so many Labour people largely indisputable. 'Guard against the old words,' Bevan had taught 'for the words persist when the reality that lay behind them has changed . . . Long before we realize it, we become the prisoners of the description.'

Then the Tredegar neighbour to whom, in the wake of the 1959 election defeat, the 17-year-old Kinnock had turned for confirmation that the new wave of affluence which had helped to cause Labour's defeat must be welcomed, not disparaged. And finally his own father, with a wry and bitter warning about just what the Tories meant when they preached about Opportunity . . .

All part of the continuity, part of Labour's family history; and offered on this occasion as a kind of guarantee that these phases of solemn and hurtful re-examination were not the modern invention of opportunists chasing yuppies.

It was, by Neil Kinnock's standards, an austere kind of speech, eschewing at least in the early stages those well-documented oratorical tricks which milk an audience for applause, going light on alliterations, even excluding jokes until, some 20 minutes in, a bit of expert mimicry of Ron Todd's east London wisdom brought the first release of laughter topped by applause.

There was little open protest against what must have seemed to many a dangerously revisionist message. Some plainly didn't like it: Dennis Skinner on the platform, Eric Heffer and Brian Sedgemore in the MPs' pen gave little or no applause. (Those who looked for Tony Benn on the platform, radiating dissent, didn't find him; he listened from the hall.) Here and there, there were strangled shouts which sounded like 'stop the witch-hunt,' one eerily emerging just as Mr Kinnock began to warn that Labour had nothing to gain from gesture politics.

But if Labour is so ready to change, and to talk, as he did, of a new commitment to industrial efficiency and economic competitiveness, how shall we tell the new changed party from the Tory alternative?

That was the second theme, developed through a scathing dismissal of those who classed Thatcherism as the sort of Big Idea that Labour was no longer thinking.

Mr Kinnock found that ludicrous. Mrs Thatcher's so-called Big Idea was no more than a ragbag of small-minded prejudice. When John Moore talked of eliminating dependence, what he meant was not ending need, but ending provision. 'Teaching people to fly,' Mr Kinnock added contemptuously, 'by pushing them off the roof.'

Why, Mrs Thatcher could not even recognize a real Big Idea when it reared up in front of her, as she had shown by her mean response to the new US–USSR peace process.

And then the appeal to unity. Unity not, he said, on his terms, but 'on the terms of those who support us and would like to support us' (though as Monday showed, there is still much anguished dispute between those who measure such preferences from the polls, and those who prefer to rely on the twitchings of their thumbs).

If the applause at the end seemed to lack the whole-hearted passion which greeted Mrs Griffiths, that was scarcely surprising. There are clearly many, quite apart from those who condemn it outright, who deeply fear Mr Kinnock's re-examination, who suspect that it could very well end in the pouring away of socialism. But they have read the runes well enough to suspect that substantial change is inevitable.

People had to decide, he said at the end, whether they

wanted victory, or whether they were content to settle for belonging to a party that could offer the British people nothing but sympathy, that did little more than attend the funerals of hopes, of communities, of industries – 'a party of permanent condolence senders.'

Those might not be words that they wanted to hear but, to judge by the way they responded, they were hardly disposed to challenge the truth of the analysis.

David McKie
30 September 1987

5 October 1987

Joker in the Kremlin pack

Exactly a year ago, the *Guardian* devoted four whole pages to publishing a remarkable document, the manifesto of a Soviet group calling themselves the Movement for Socialist Renewal.

Its basic theme was that 'the crisis of the Soviet economic system is closely connected to the political crisis which concerns such fundamental constitutional principles as the freedom of speech, press and assembly, freedom of personal immunity, private correspondence and telephone communications and the freedom to join organizations.'

It called for the democratization of the Soviet system, for a choice between candidates at elections, and eventually for a kind of political pluralism, for 'different political organizations, all with the ultimate aim of building a socialist society, and competing between themselves for the best programme of action in the interests of our ruling class, the workers, peasants and intelligentsia.'

Its deeply pessimistic analysis of the Soviet economy concluded that 'our country has reached a limit beyond which lies an insurmountable lag in economic and scientific technical development behind the advanced industrial nations.'

The only remedy, it went on, was the decentralization of the economic system, the introduction of free market mechanisms, curtailing the role of the state planning board, changing the price system, and the legislation and encouragement of private enterprise.

The importance of the document, and the reason why the *Guardian* printed it in full, was that it was leaked to the NBC television correspondent and to the *Guardian* in Moscow not by dissidents, but through senior Soviet official sources who feared that the cause of reform was faltering in the Kremlin.

My commentary on the document said that it had been collated from a series of papers prepared within several Soviet think tanks and submitted to the central committee as outline plans for reform. I suggested that much of it had been read by Gorbachev himself. This was a remarkable opportunity to observe the Soviet elite debating with itself about the future course and parameters and possibilities of reforming such a system from within.

The document had a curious reception among the professional Sovietologists and Kremlin watchers of the West. They accepted that it was a genuine Russian document, rather than a CIA concoction, and that it had been put together by a group of academic intellectuals. But they doubted that it had official provenance. They judged that it was inconceivable that senior Soviet officials, party members and central committee staffers could have had anything to do with a document so subversive, so bold, and so challenging to the political primacy of the party.

Who could blame them? Everything that we know of Soviet and party history since at least the 1920s justified, indeed dictated, their caution. But it now seems clear that the document printed in the *Guardian* a year ago contained the blueprint for the Gorbachev reforms we have seen enacted over the past 12 months. That document fore-shadowed to an uncanny degree the increasingly radical lines of the Gorbachev perestroika, or reconstruction.

All of the economic reforms that the Movement for Social-ist Renewal put forward have now been presented formally by Gorbachev to the central committee. And almost all of the political reforms, for secret ballots, for a genuine choice among candidates, for the legal right to take errant officials to court, have now been enacted.

There are limits, clearly. Witness the way in which the trial of the Chernobyl managers and technicians was opened to the press only on the first day, and the full charges have still not been made public.

The astonishing strides made by glasnost have not yet asserted the rights of a free press. But the bold spirits of Soviet journalism are coming wonderfully close. It is now commonplace for us Western journalists to write uncen-sored in the Soviet press and to broadcast live on Soviet radio and television, talking freely of Stalin, his crimes, human rights, and the good sense spoken by Trotsky in the early 1920s.

But glasnost is about far more than just the media. I suspect that in 50 or 100 years' time, historians will write of Moscow in the perestroika in much the same terms that we now think of Weimar Berlin, or Vienna just before 1914, or Victorian London; as a discrete and magical time when the mood and the culture and the possibilities of life all suddenly exploded together.

It has all happened so fast in Moscow, that all at once it seems there are long-banned books available, there are newspapers that we have to read each day, novels that have to be devoured, television programmes that everybody rushes back to watch, art exhibitions that deliberately push forward and tease the public consciousness.

The moment is all the richer because it is living on the secreted cultural fat of three generations. We are now relishing the art that has been banned since the 1930s, all suddenly flooding over us in a great and exciting way. We can watch Nikolai Erdman's play, *Suicides*, banned since 1930. We can watch the Taganka Theatre's brilliant performance of Bulgakov's *Master and Margarita*, and we can watch his long-forbidden and savage satire of proletarian-worship, *Heart of a Dog*

We can watch at least some of the movies and read most of the books that the censors have kept on the shelf for years. We can watch Panfilov's *Thema*, but not yet *The Commissar*; we can read Pasternak, but not yet Solzhenitsyn.

We must not fool ourselves. As Dr Andrei Sakharov keeps saying, hundreds of prisoners of conscience remain in Soviet camps. Thousands of Jews still wait for their exit visas, and not a few of them take full and proper advantage of their new right to demonstrate their protests openly outside the visa administration office.

Above all, there is now, and there remains for the foreseeable future, no prospect of any challenge to the Communist Party's monopoly of political power. Capitalism is not breaking out across the Soviet Union. The Gorbachev reform programme is aimed at saving socialism, not dismantling it.

But there is a challenge to the nature of the Communist Party, if not to its role, and that challenge is coming from Gorbachev himself. The extraordinary party conference that is to be held next June will be made up of some 5000 delegates elected in secret ballot by the 19 million party members. This secret ballot is a deliberate attempt to sidestep the traditional grip of the regional party bosses on the composition of such delegations.

Gorbachev has hinted strongly that he wants the conference to rewrite the party rulebook, apparently to impose limited terms of office for party bureaucrats and to require regular re-injections of new blood into the party's ruling bodies. *Pozhivyom, uvidim*, as the Russians say. We shall live, and then we shall see.

But there is one thing that still makes me think twice about that document we published last year. In the news story announcing it, I wrote the following cautionary sentence: 'It remains possible that the leak of this document is a deliberate provocation, concocted by anti-reform groups who are seeking to discredit the Gorbachev reform strategy by linking it to an openly political programme which threatens the Communist Party and its monopoly of power.'

Even though I know the identity and the senior posts held by the leakers, that thought still nags me. And that nagging doubt reminds me that for all the cultural ferment, for all the bold excitements of glasnost, and for all the emerging into life of those heretical proposals the *Guardian* printed a year ago, this remains a mysterious and peculiar society.

Whenever something out of the ordinary happens, we journalists are well advised to think of six simple questions. In the case of the manifesto, I can answer five of them. I know the who, the how, the what, the where and the when. I still do not know why.

Maybe this time next year things will have moved on yet further with the remarkable dizzy progress of the official dissident who rules in the Kremlin. Perhaps then I might be sure of the answer to that simple question which still haunts me one year on from that manifesto.

Martin Walker
22 July 1987

Love in a cold climate

Many labels have been attached to Lucian Freud in the course of his deceptively long career but the two that seem to have stuck are Herbert Read's postwar description of him as the 'Ingres of Existentialism', and, more recently, Robert Hughes's big-league claim that Freud is 'the greatest living realist painter'.

The large and impressive Freud retrospective that has finally arrived on the South Bank having wowed them in America and by all accounts made them feel queasy in France ('*les cadavres abominables*') challenges the accuracy of both these oft-quoted summations.

The artist who painted the roomful of slouched female nudes that lies like a peep-show at the heart of this exhibition's architecture was no Ingres in technique or disposition. Ingres, remember, was the artist who gave his smooth Odalisques extra vertebrae in order to perfect the elegant curve of their backs.

Freud's women are often as lumpy as the old settees they are slumped across. There are places where their flesh has clearly had to be sanded down, so boulder-strewn is it with re-workings. And where the women of Ingres recline in queenly repose, the women of Freud are out cold as if the painter has shot them with a tranquillizer gun. They lie there, legs open, comatose, offering up beaver-shots and close-ups of their knees, while the painter examines their inert bodies with unwavering interest. The Renoir of Realism?

Freud's nudes are justly famous. They rank alongside Stanley Spencer's as the most distinctive and disquieting British contribution to the genre in this or any other century. But it is easy to see why French observers found them misogynistic and ugly. Bonnard he is not.

Viewed one at a time, as they should be and indeed are in the exclusive private collections from which most of them have come, they succeed in capturing a brazen and rather shocking corporeality, as if art, after centuries of obfuscation and wishful thinking, has finally found the honesty to show us what a naked body really looks like.

But by displaying so many together, crowding them along the same stretch of unmade bed like baby seals, the Freud retrospective heightens the unfortunate impression that you are watching some form of painterly cruelty at work. Like Spencer, he appears to dwell too keenly on imperfections, stretch-marks, blotches, moles. His nudes contort themselves into poses of Mannerist discomfort, arms, legs, breasts akimbo. They wear expressions of animal dumbness.

'I used to leave the face until last,' Freud explains unpleasantly in the catalogue. 'The head must be just another limb.' You do not have to be Lucian's grandfather, Sigmund, to see in this imposition of animal nakedness a possible desire to control or humiliate. Certainly the psychological forces guiding the artist's hand are infinitely more complex than a mere appetite for realism.

Lucian Freud is 66, so I suppose we must try to think of him as an artist in old age, which is difficult. He is for instance already three years older than his idol, Rembrandt, was when he died. But where Rembrandt arrived at a splendid artistic old age, a way of looking and painting that was unmistakably wise, Freud's art shows no sign of turning all warm and humanitarian on us. The heating in that seedy studio, in which so much of his art is set, remains comprehensively switched off.

Instead, Freud's vision seems to be stuck in a perpetual middle-age, a painterly attitude described and defined by its obsession with the ageing process itself. What is true of his nudes is true of his yuccas and his brilliantly grubby sinks. They are being observed at moments of mounting decrepitude. The brown leaves of the yucca, like the brown stains in the sink, reverberate to the drip, drip, drip of time.

The show begins with a fresh-faced Lucian painting his fresh-faced wife as if she had feline blood in her. She was called Kitty. So perhaps the stylisation of her face into perfect wide-eyed ovals was intended as a deliberate play on her name. These early portraits are like Elizabethan miniatures, full of secretive allusions and floral correspondences, love tokens at heart. The catalogue writer, Robert Hughes, claims great things for them. But in situ, the rest of the show rather puts their thinly charming stylisation to shame.

The story of the exhibition from here on – and it is a completely involving one – might therefore be expected to tell of a gradual loss of innocence, a pictorial Rite of Passage, as the wide-eyed stylisations of youth progress relentlessly towards the hard-core realism of old age.

In fact the exhibition reveals a powerful sentimentality at work in Freud's art, continuously disrupting the painter's expected progress. Most commonly it is a strong, almost Picasso-like sense of masculine protectiveness towards his female sitters, as evident in the early love-pictures as it is in the sleeping babies of his middle years and the marvellous late portraits of his mother. The comatose final nudes are probably as interesting as they are because the division between protectiveness and voyeurism seems disquietingly blurred.

Freud was born in Berlin in 1922 and only moved to Britain at the age of 11. One of the points made recurringly here is that in calling him a British artist we are overlooking the importance of his Central European origins. The art itself seems never to overlook them.

Just as the late nudes are somehow Germanic in their unglamorous, jarring corporeality (the Dürer of Deconstruction?) so the early likenesses have the rather affected and stiff charm of early Northern renaissance portraiture.

Looking into the moist eyes of Freud's portrait of John Minton, where you can see the window lights reflected in the water-film, Van Eyck-style, or at the irresistible sequence of likenesses of his second wife cast as a kind of eternal 12-year-old, it seems nonsensical to speak of him as a realist, the world's greatest, living or otherwise. The projection of sadnesses and vulnerabilities is obviously from artist to sitter, and not the other way around.

Even at the other, realist, end of the show the impression persists of a nudity that is as much symbolic as observed. Freud never for instance paints body hair on legs or arms, only in the neat triangles of pubic hair. His female skin is a painter's confection, at first perfect, unblemished, then gradually becoming blotchy, like Caravaggio's ripening fruit used to symbolize the passing of time.

The sense of symbolism is strongest in the middle of the show in some of the curious subject pictures interspersed among the portraits, figure-studies and views from the kitchen window. The strangest of them shows the artist himself standing behind a huge foreground plant with his hand raised to his ear as if listening to it talking. Mother-in-law's Tongue?

In the same room, the creepiness of late Freud emerges fully formed in a perfectly horrible set-piece of a naked young man sharing a dirty settee with a rat. Clearly such paintings have iconographic secrets to yield up. When Freud is being so melodramatically macabre you feel it is probably best not to know.

But all that cold air in the studio is clearly keeping the old painter's mind edgy and alert. The show contains thousands of awkwardnesses to keep viewers off balance and interested, and numerous passages of amazing *trompe l'oeil* where he does indeed become a brilliant realist, painting the water dripping from the tap of his studio, capturing every varied texture of close-up vegetation.

But what I admire most about this retrospective is its unswerving ambition to investigate life experiences, however impolite, directly as they come. The anti-bourgeois nature of Freud's art is complete and thrilling.

And Freud – thank God – shows no sign of regressing into one of those awful Great British second childhoods. His work grows more rather than less ambitious as the show progresses.

You never catch him ignoring the guidelines of adult and authentic life-experience. Which is why he strikes me as a much more important painter than Francis Bacon who devoted the tail-end of his retrospective at the Tate to silly tributes to Ian Botham.

This is my last column as the art critic of the *Guardian*. I have been doing the job for the best part of a decade and feel as if I have had my say. Indeed I am tired of saying it.

There are far too many pleasant memories to begin enumerating them here. But to my successor I bequeath an old Lithuanian proverb: While the farmer fattens up his prize bull, the clever pig steals his turnips. Find that pig!

Waldemar Januszczak
5 February 1988

Queen of Hanover Square

Once, in the land of the fashion people a great Queen ruled. To a few select intimates she was known as Beatrix. To the rest, whether high or low, she was Miss Miller, august, powerful and rarely glimpsed editor of *Vogue*.

She dwelt in a tower in Hanover Square and went about in the world only on matters of great importance. But she did send forth her four beautiful princesses to do her work in the world. They were called Grace Coddington, Anna Harvey, Mandy Clapperton and Liz Tilberis. And they were a bit august, too, and powerful and sometimes folk quaked a bit around them, but not much. Because they were as charming and nice as they were beautiful. Well, most of the time.

And they were surrounded by handmaidens of a very superior class and, among the people, they were called the Voguettes – which was partly affectionate. With the help of the handmaidens who scurried hither and thither collecting the raw materials from which the princesses made their beautiful pictures, the great Queen ordered the affairs of fashion land. And some were raised up by her and some were cast down and some praised her name and some bitched. And all was as it should be.

And then the time came for the great Queen to retire and the folk wondered which of the princesses would succeed her to the throne in the tower in Hanover Square. And, lo, great consternation. The mighty Emperor from the West, the awesome lord of Condé Nast, spoke and told the people that he had a new princess for them and her name was Anna Wintour and she was to be Queen. And Anna, beautiful and clever, came and changed things a lot. And some praised her name and some bitched.

But the new Queen had left her prince behind when she crossed the ocean to sit on the throne in the tower in Hanover Square. And she missed him. So just 16 months after ascending the throne, she quit. And this time one of the princesses was chosen to ascend the throne and, as is the way with princesses who are beautiful, wise and good, she's damned if she's not going to live happily ever after . . .

'You see before you,' says Liz Tilberis from behind Anna Wintour's dramatic black desk in *Vogue* House, 'a totally incoherent person. I only seem to be able to speak in dreadful clichés. It's a dream come true, the best thing ever, totally breathtaking.'

Doubtless the circumstances surrounding her elevation have done as much to rob her of breath as the actual promotion. For, when the announcement was made, Liz was only days away from leaving her job as fashion director at *Vogue* to cross the Atlantic to take up a splendid new appointment at Ralph Lauren, the New York company whose fortune is based on a canny, glossy recreation of classic English (and New English) upper-class style.

Her goods and chattels were packed, her house was let, her husband, Andrew, an artist, and their two small sons were all psyched up to New York, hamburgers and Disneyland. Liz had put behind her regret at leaving *Vogue* after 17 years and had focused ahead on the new job, a new life style and the pleasure of spending more time with Grace Coddington, who is already in New York working for another American designer, Calvin Klein.

Then, three weeks ago, when she was in Paris to cover the couture fashion collections, Condé Nast's Daniel Salen took her aside for a little word on the subject of the editorship of *Vogue*. 'I discussed it at length with Andrew, of course,' she says, 'but, ultimately, it is what I have spent my entire career working towards, wanting desperately yet being terrified of. Impossible to turn it down. And Ralph Lauren was so nice about it. He understood completely.'

Condé Nast has seized the opportunity afforded by Anna

Wintour's departure to change the editorial structure at Hanover Square. Mark Boxer, editor of *Tatler*, becomes editor in chief of both titles with Liz editing *Vogue* and Emma Soames editing *Tatler* under his overall command.

'My primary task,' says Liz Tilberis, 'is to get the fashion absolutely right. You have to have a balance in a magazine like *Vogue* between fashion as dream, as fantasy, as frozen image that expresses something very powerful about the mood, the feeling of its time, and fashion as the garments we put on in the morning and which are going to give us confidence and give us fun.'

It is arguable that under Bea Miller the dream dominated, particularly through the stunningly lyrical imagery created by Grace Coddington. Her work was often not so much about the nature of frocks as the nature of women. It was terribly rich, with references culled from art and literature, and illuminating in a way which qualified them more satisfactorily as art than as fashion illustration.

'Anna shifted British *Vogue* over in the other direction,' says Liz. 'Her arrival here coincided with one of those rare dramatic moments when fashion really does change completely. It is a myth that fashion changes drastically from season to season. It doesn't. It mostly evolves gradually, the emphasis changing subtly, a new palette of colours superseding the old. But once in a decade or so, the complete volte-face occurs. And this time it was the hemline going up, up, up. And the hemline changes everything. Every proportion is affected. Designers cannot tinker at a moment like that. They start from scratch again.

'Anna was marginally ahead of most of the designers in judging that this moment had come. She pressed the button at exactly the right time and was absolutely firm and uncompromising in her commitment to the new look. She was right. *Vogue* has to take fashion forward. It has to break the limits – not in a ridiculous, deliberately outrageous, desperate for novelty way, of course, but it must set the pace. And with the new, short skirt, it did.'

In fact, when Anna Wintour first pressed that button, ruthlessly shortening skirts on photographic sittings, many a fat-kneed 'expert' was convinced that it was a purely wilful and arrogant exercise which stemmed from nothing more compelling than her own slender figure and excellent legs. Theirs, however, was the egocentric view, not hers. Alas.

Liz Tilberis trained as a fashion designer at Leicester College of Art and Design and was a finalist in the 1969 *Vogue* Talent Contest. She was called Elizabeth Kelly then and remembers the lunch to which the finalists were summoned as one of the great ordeals of her life. 'We had to *eat* in the presence of Lord Snowdon, Lady Antonia Fraser and Quentin Crewe, and it was as if someone had maliciously concocted a menu of the things one looks least attractive eating – spaghetti, spinach . . . It was quite dreadful.

'Anyway, they must have overlooked the spinach between the teeth because they took me on for the summer holidays to make the tea and then hired me when I left college in 1970. From making the tea I was promoted to ironing, then to pinning, then, but only when I proved worthy of the promotion, to gathering the information for the captions.'

Hers has been a single-minded career. She started buying *Vogue* at a tender age in 1965 and has every issue. She has never really wanted to work anywhere else. 'I started off being enchanted by, fascinated by clothes – not to buy hundreds for myself – but by the whole magic world of fashion. It is a kind of addiction.

'Nevertheless, I am far from unaware of the contradictions inherent in the business, the kind of things which do upset some people. When children are starving in Africa or being neglected or maltreated in Britain, it is hard to justify devoting your life to something as ephemeral and sometimes as elitist as fashion. Of course a frock that costs £10,000 is an insult to the poor sections of society. Yet no one gets as upset about pictures, motor cars or polo ponies that cost even more and are an even greater self-indulgence on the part of the buyer. There's a strange sort of puritanism mixed into the motivation which has a distasteful killjoy aspect to it.

'The fashion industry employs an enormous number of people. A love of fashion makes the economy go round. The £10,000 dress is part of the glamour that fuels the love of fashion that keeps the high street buzzing. It's not brain-surgery but it's not totally parasitic or pointless either.'

Entertainment is an acceptable concept. The puritans don't knock entertainment. So they might be able to cope with fashion as entertainment. Liz Tilberis quite likes that thought. 'I always try to find the fun side of fashion – the biggest gloves with the spikiest feathers. That's what it's really about, fashion. It's about fun.'

Brenda Polan
26 August 1987

Unshaped genius

Simon Callow is a phenomenon among actors. He is not only a brilliant and exuberant performer: he is a writer – and a very good one too. Few people can match him in catching with words the physical excitement of a great performance. His first book *Being an Actor* is the best description of a modern actor's life that I know.

Now he has written a biography of Charles Laughton. It is an excellent and entertaining read. Callow's enthusiasm for his subject is very engaging, even when his claims for Laughton's talent lead him into rhapsodies which overstate his case. His self-identification with his hero is complete – so complete you wonder occasionally whether Callow's Laughton is not often wish-fulfilment rather than reality. In the end, you finish the book knowing rather more about Callow than Laughton.

All the facts are there – but their interpretation is sometimes what Callow needs them to be. But if I quarrel with him, I still enjoy him. There is, after all, an honourable tradition in subjective biography. It is why we all love Boswell.

Callow charts all the agonies of this great and complex actor: his dislike of his own ugliness; his desire to *show* his characters, warts and all, rather than to explain them; his hatred of his own homosexuality; his political timidity; his obsessional love of America – a country where the man who always felt an outsider in England believed he could belong; and his fanatical love of Shakespeare: 'Shakespeare was his breviary, his rosary, his private devotion. Shakespeare was also his crossword puzzle, his unsolved equation, his everlasting riddle. But most of all, Shakespeare was his great white whale, haunting and mocking him, appearing tantalizingly on the horizon of whatever waters he might be amiably paddling.'

Callow's main thesis is that Laughton's film performances of the 1930s – Henry VIII, Quasimodo, Rembrandt, Captain Bligh – were so revealing of the remoter parts of his own dark psyche, that he decided consciously or unconsciously, as he moved into middle age, to endure less as an actor. In consequence he worked within more comfortable limits.

I do not believe in this division in Laughton's work. That there is a change is unarguable. But I think the explanation of his life's progress is much simpler and sadder than Callow believes. In the performing arts, it is not enough to have great talent. You also have to have great talent for handling your talent.

Like many star actors of our century, Laughton lacked this talent. He was a worried man who felt increasingly a failure. He allowed himself to get out of condition physically, and he stayed away from the stage too much. Great film acting requires genius, and Laughton had it. But the theatre, whilst also requiring genius from its giants, is a gymnasium which challenges the actor not only mentally but physically.

Two obsessions haunted him, one personal and one professional. They drove him to a life of increasing evasions. The first was his homosexuality. It is difficult for us in our more open society to recall the guilt-ridden world of homosexuality when it was still a criminal offence.

In the thirties, Laughton's career was on the point of ruin. England was no place for him. America provided a freer and more liberal atmosphere. Yet it was in England I believe where his heritage lay – the heritage of the English classics.

Laughton's second obsession was Shakespeare. In the thirties he did a season at the Old Vic with Tyrone Guthrie, and, like many great actors setting out on the classics along an original path, he was derided by the critics as unclassical and unShakespearean. This happened among others to Olivier, to Gerard Philippe, and to Richard Burton. But they tried to fight it out.

Laughton left for Hollywood and world stardom. He then began a life of justification.

He told me repeatedly that the English classical tradition was unimportant if you compared it with the extraordinary ability of the new medium, film, to reach the whole world. Yet every day of his life, in his house in Hollywood, he read and pondered and spoke Shakespeare. He was a king who had banished himself from his kingdom but who was always waiting the call to return. By the time the call came, to Stratford in the late 1950s, it was too late.

Laughton's spellbinding personality was plain to see. But as a Shakespearean, he was like an Olympic athlete who had neglected his training for 25 years. He was full of intellectual theories – some of them crazy and the result of those long years of meditation in his Hollywood study.

He believed that a capital letter in Shakespeare's Folio and Quarto texts indicates an emphasis. No amount of pointing out the vagaries of Elizabethan typesetters could shift his conviction. So as King Lear, he was left accenting in all the wrong places and fighting for breath.

It was our great loss that he could not, like Olivier, combine film stardom with the theatre. His repertory would have been immense – Falstaff, Leontes, Shylock, Malvolio, Prospero, and all the parts that Molière wrote for himself. He needed to belong, and went on trying to persuade himself that he belonged in Hollywood.

He needed a mentor, and one of the more touching things

in Callow's book is Laughton's near-adulatory working relationship with Brecht in his Hollywood years. Yet this also ended suddenly and inexplicably. Was he frightened ultimately, as a good American, by his left-wing friend?

Simon Callow makes big claims for Laughton's perform-ances. And certainly those that exist on film are landmarks of dangerous, unsentimental acting. Yet I feel his greatness was never fully achieved, even in film. Put him by Spencer Tracy and you begin to see the difference between truth and display, however brilliant.

He made one great film, directing *The Night of the Hunter*. Like Welles and like Olivier he became in one leap a major film director. But to Hollywood's shame, because it did not make money, he was never asked to direct another picture.

Laughton's life is a tragedy which England and Holly-wood partly brought about, but which he mostly brought on himself. Callow tells the tale movingly, and leads us into the heart of an actor. It is, for anybody, a very exposed position.

Peter Hall
11 September 1987

Charles Laughton: A Difficult Actor by Simon Callow (Methuen).

A for Hang-Me-Down

You may not be aware that the apple that fell on Newton's head was a Flower of Kent. I doubt very much if a Golden Delicious would have had the same effect. There is, or was, an apple called Improved Hang-Me-Down, and pears called Golden Balls and Bloody Bastard. Life was altogether more colourful and confident in the kitchen garden 100 years ago.

For some time I have kept *The Victorian Kitchen Garden* (BBC2), the most serene and dreamlike programme on television, to myself like the blackcurrant pastille in a tube of fruit pastilles and given you the lemon. But today I will not write about brain damage in Glasgow (*Coma*, BBC1) or Aids in Africa (*Antenna*, BBC2). I will comfort you with apples: Prince Albert, 'a good cooker and good looker'; Gladstone, 'which some gentlemen would not have in their gardens'; Beauty of Bath, 'a good scrumping apple'; and Ashmead's Colonel, 'which is still winning tasting competitions'.

That's Harry Dodson talking. He was the head gardener at Chilton, near Hungerford, in its heyday. On the husk remaining, a derelict acre surrounded by a tall, rosy wall, he and the BBC have created this splendid tribute to the Victorian stomach, a great kitchen garden.

Great Victorian houses grew their own supermarkets, and expected plums, nectarines, pineapples, melons, and grapes to be available on demand. When this garden was a going concern Harry grew 40 kinds of pears so, whenever pears were required, pears were available and at the point of perfect ripeness.

Thomas Rivers, the nurseryman whom even Charles Darwin approached humbly ('My name may possibly be known to you. I am working on a book on the variation of animals and plants'), sold 1000 different pears. His son, by the way, bred Conference, almost the sole survivor of the frightful modern massacre of fruit.

Harry, who ran the garden with 14 men under him, has revived it in his old age with one young girl, Alison, to help. His green and gold melons hang plumply again in nets like udders, his pink and gold peaches are unmistakably buttocks. Grapes are the only thing he has not been able to recreate in a year; they used to overwinter in their own house, each bunch drawing rainwater from its own patented grape bottle.

The invigorating bounce of the Victorian mind was never more apparent than in the patent cucumber tube. 'An enthusiastic cucumber grower', explained Harry, 'was very disappointed because he couldn't grow them straight.' After a lengthy tussle with recalcitrant cucumbers, he invented a sort of milk bottle open at both ends. Harry tried this out in the garden and the frustrated cucumbers grew straight; they had very little option. There was a slight flaw in the idea or the enthusiastic cucumber grower's name would now be on a par with Newton and Darwin. Unless you stood there, wound up and ready to pounce, the growing cucumber filled the tube and stuck like a ship in a bottle.

Glorious Victorian assurance booms in the names of the plants Harry has grown again. Magnum Bonum, a potato; Ne Plus Ultra, a pea; Best Of All, a tomato. It is remarkably restful. There seems all the time in the world to watch the pears taking on the rosy glow of the wall, the cardoon, like a green peacock, growing vaster than empires and more slow. Time to keep your seed in your waistcoat pocket from one year to the next. A time to sing, 'Oh, thank the Lord,' without being altogether certain which lord you were singing about.

'Enjoy the summer innocently while it lasts,' said the Shilling Kitchen Garden in 1859. 'Treat your master well if you happen to be a servant. Treat your servant well if providence has made you a master. Be thankful to Heaven.' The summer didn't last, of course. The big house went or the big money went. The kitchen garden with its 40 sorts of pears went, and the nurseryman with his 1000. The chauffeurs and the grooms and the gatekeepers went. Only the shell of the kitchen garden, the wall, remained.

And Harry of course. And a packet of peas which the presenter Peter Thoday's father had given him and he had thrown in a drawer for years. They were Ne Plus Ultra and they germinated. I find that cheerful.

Nancy Banks-Smith
26 November 1987

Litter lady

Attendants in St James's Park, London, were hard at work just after dawn yesterday spreading rubbish across a patch of grass close to Horse Guards Parade.

They had been instructed to make the area look sufficiently disgusting for the Prime Minister to use it for a televised lecture to her subjects on the need to mend their mucky ways.

The backdrop – or more accurately the litter drop – for the Tidy Britain publicity stunt included banana skins, rail tickets, plastic bags and drinks cans, which had been collected from other parts of the park on the day before.

'We were out here at 7 a.m. putting it all down,' said Mr Paul Hallsworth, a park sweeper who normally spends his time picking it up.

'We have seen this morning a beautiful park disfigured by litter. This is not the fault of the government. It is the fault of the people who knowingly and thoughtlessly throw it down,' said Mrs Thatcher.

She had arrived bringing in tow a rather despondent Environment Secretary, Mr Nicholas Ridley, a man whose walk through a park could normally be tracked without too much difficulty by following the chain of his cigarette ends.

The Prime Minister, dressed in a smart three-quarter length check coat, with pearls and imitation crocodile handbag, set to work on the rubbish which had been arranged for her convenience with pieces about a yard apart.

Some sedate practice with a contrivance called a rubbish claw was followed by increasingly frenetic clearance activity, using the hand without the handbag.

After about 15 minutes she repaired to Admiralty House where she warned: 'We want to do as much as possible to restore civic and national pride but if that isn't enough we may have to consider changing the law.'

She said she was 'very ashamed' at having to drive other heads of state through Britain's untidy streets.

Workmen have since returned the park to its normal state.

John Carvel
23 March 1988

Ironing in the soul

Jill Tweedie came with me to see Germaine Greer, because we happened to meet that morning and, it being May, 1988, I thought the three of us might ruminate on the last years. The sun was shining for the first time in weeks and Germaine's lunch and her country garden, as well her conversation, were enticing. 'We cannot miss this historic meeting,' she said with a dry irony when I phoned her to ask if Jill could come too, and I thought, too late, that perhaps it might be a dreadful mistake. I don't think it was.

Germaine was in the kitchen making chapattis. In the stone-flagged dining room an exquisite summer lunch lay on the table, with a cold bottle of white wine on a sunflower yellow cloth. There were curried potatoes, chick peas, broad-bean salad, guacamole, and some other grain or pulse I couldn't put a name to. During lunch, we talk about the non-emergence of this elusive New Woman – the awfulness of little timid girls and young women, as feminine as ever, mincing, speaking in baby voices, and acting helpless. There are as many about as ever there were, because it's still what men want.

We talk about how almost nothing has changed for women in 20 years. Everything keeps coming back to that. Style, image, chic, not substance. 'All that power dressing crap,' says Germaine, and stabs meaningfully at my shoulder pads. She wears a T-shirt with three parrots on it (and a bra underneath).

Inevitably we run straight into dangerous waters. The

Alton Bill is fresh in mind. We recall the potty madness of
some of the demos at the time of the 1967 Abortion Act,
marching down the street yelling: 'What do we want?
Abortion! When do we want it? Now!' As if abortions were
ice creams or Christmas bonuses. And then Germaine harks
back to some of her *Sex and Destiny* themes. She really
seems to think most women desire children most of the
time. Abortion wouldn't be necessary in a society that
supported and cherished its women and children, she as-
serts. Every pregnant woman wants her child, if only
society made it easy for her. Jill says that sounds just
like a Life or SPUC argument. Bearing and bringing
up a child is a great burden, and not all women want all
their pregnancies, not even in the most perfect society.

Here Germaine comes up with her rosy view of how life
could and should be for mothers and babies, loved and
supported by all around them, the babies shared, the burden
spread. I say, a little acidly, that the truth is that the
burden always falls upon one, and one alone, and it always
will. I try to explain the desperate uniqueness of that bond,
the awesome, and oppressive sense of a newborn child's
vulnerability, and the strength of the mother's feeling that
she and only she really cares. When the chips are down,
only she stands between her child and disaster. It is very
difficult for anyone else to step in and relieve her, or ease
that burden significantly.

Germaine is indignant. It's society's fault. She has, after
all, taken in mothers and children, tried to take her share
of that burden in her time. She has many god-children for
whom she has played this role. She continues in praise of
motherhood. 'Every moment of that child's life should be
precious, treasured. Not a moment wasted.' I am stricken
with guilt and anxiety. Have I enjoyed my children enough?
Am I letting those precious moments slip by? Jill looks
distressed. We argue back that life isn't like that. How can
you possibly treasure every moment? And children just
aren't utterly treasurable every minute of every day, not
in real life. Germaine thinks and talks in absolutes. It is
what makes her wonderful, and infuriating, both at once.

Motherhood is good – an absolute good, so it must be good everywhere, in all situations, and if it isn't, society (Western) is to blame. She burns with a loathing of Western materialism.

Here she strikes a chord with Jill's view of the world. I have never seen much wrong with materialism. Given a shred of a chance, peasants are pretty keen on transistors. Are they pure in their poverty, admirable in their need? Third World women are as badly treated, or worse. Worse mostly. But in her wilder moments Germaine even has an apology for female circumcision. She is a romantic and a Utopian. She started out in Sydney as a libertarian anarchist. Her opinions change – why shouldn't they? But they spring from the same fount. I think her sometimes wildly wrong – as in much of *Sex and Destiny* – but she is always wrong for the right sort of reasons, and always in an interesting way.

After lunch, sitting on the grass in her garden, we watch her ginger cat, Christopher, stalking in her beautiful flower beds (amongst other things, she is a gardening expert). She is besotted by her pets, talking to them, cajoling them, completely admiring. Christopher plods past, the sort of cat that looks as if it is wearing furry flares. As we talk, Christopher catches a small furry animal. Jill shouts out in horror, telling Germaine to stop him quickly. The cat continues to maul the animal, letting it creep away, then pouncing again. Jill is now almost in pain herself watching the suffering of the creature, while Germaine (the vegetarian) is laughing with pride and delight at the cleverness of her cat. I just watch, having not much instinctive liking for either cat or rodent. 'It's a poor vole' Jill says. 'No it's not, it's a rat,' says Germaine.

Then the thing, whatever it is, suddenly makes a wild rush at us where we sit on the lawn, and dives straight under my skirt, and I get up and scream loudly. The others roar with laughter and Jill is allowed to shoo the cat off until the vole/rat has escaped into a bush. As we continue the conversation, however, I notice the cat quietly catching the vole again and eating it all, except for its face.

About this time it occurs to Germaine that I have not interviewed her properly, or indeed at all, about her book, which was supposed to be the point of this meeting. Jill wanders off to chat with some of the waifs and strays currently residing with Germaine; generous host to various passers-through, she always has a collection of the wounded.

The book is daunting, and mysteriously titled *Kissing the Rod*, an anthology of seventeenth-century women's verse, a mighty academic tome (at an academic price). Finding seventeenth-century poetry anyway difficult – all that dum-de-dum rhyme jars in the modern ear – I need some persuading that this is a book I want to read. Especially when Germaine says she doesn't consider most of the poems of great value. And, on reading the introduction, and the notes on each poet, it becomes clear how difficult it is to know who wrote many of them anyway, because women often wrote anonymously. They were abominably abused, and rewritten by their publishers, who spiced up their poems, and presented them as titillation, signed by 'A Woman of Quality', 'A Lady of Honour' or some such coy come-on.

However, under Dr Greer's excellent tuition, I begin to see the point of this lengthy exercise. There were certain kinds of poems that only women wrote, the best of them written and circulated privately. They were often written as therapy, as moral lessons, as occasions for fortitude, often on the advice of pastors and doctors. Here are collected certain favourite themes, poems written in farewell to husbands by pregnant women who expected, and often received, the worst from childbed. Poems written to surviving children by their mothers on their deathbeds. Poems written about dead children by their grieving mothers, struggling to find religious consolation in unbearable suffering. Some are mad and morbid, others overwhelmingly moving. Like this of Mary Carey's written on the death of yet another child:

I only now desire of my sweet God
the reason why he tooke in hand his rodd?
What he doth spy; what is the thinge amisse
I faine would learne; whilst I ye rod do kisse:
Methinks I heare God's voyce, this is thy sinne;
And conscience justifies ye same within;
Thou often dost present me with dead frute;
Why should not my returns, thy presents sute:
Dead dutys; prayers; praises thou dost bring,
affections dead; dead hart in every thinge.

The book is not a pointless dredging up of unknown work, simply because it is by women. It shows a different strain in women's writing, and the strain they had in writing at all – most of them semi-educated, discouraged, and the respectable ones certainly not permitted to publish. The book is also another reminder of the many splendours of Germaine Greer, her extraordinary diverse skills and enthusiasms: writing, (academic or controversial), cooking, gardening, and above all talking. Her talking is a performance art of stories and ideas, turning the obvious inside out, taking nothing for granted, not even what she herself said five minutes ago. I went down to the Press Association to dig out all the old cuttings, every yellowing clip since she arrived. The scandals, the outrage: that photo in *Suck* magazine (if you are too young to know about it, I shall not describe it here, nor the story about the whole Manchester United football team). I tried to remember what it all meant back then. Sex was anarchy and revolution. It was the metaphor, it was the message. Screwing was screwing the system, a little obvious perhaps but all I can say is, it seemed to mean something then.

So in these post-Aids days she decries sexual liberation (sounds as dated as a bust bodice). She looks at what it has done to women. They can't say no; they are enslaved again, a pointless, meaningless and now dangerous coupling, she says. Her berating of sex is as fierce as was her celebration. Look at the abandoned wives. What did they get in exchange for their security? And Jill and I agree.

But what shocks me in those cuttings is the gallons of vitriol that have been poured upon her over the years. Such fear and loathing, such 'I told you so' whenever anything bad happens to her. Such outlandish praise: 'The profile of a Garbo, the rump of a show-jumper' is followed by such detestation. Now she can't have babies, this high priestess of sex, they gloat over her tragedy. 'The Loneliness of the Liberated Lady', when she admits (she always 'admits' everything) that maybe she misses having a family after all.

Small minds, small spirits affronted by the sheer size and magnetism of the woman. It doesn't help that she's never been a joiner (neither have Jill or I). Never part of The Movement – whatever or wherever it might be. She slammed into the Greenham women, laid about the more frightful manifestations of Women's Lib in its day, which made her few friends. Like Gloria Steinem, she is beautiful, and above all a star. That is contrary to the orthodoxy of the true faith, which says such self-promotion is patriarchal, hierarchical, and unsisterly. (Neither Jill nor Germaine could hide in a crowd of sisters if they tried.)

We end where we began. Twenty years have delivered little to women, we agree. *Plus ça change* – it's all on the surface, except for a handful of super-educated lucky women at the top. For the rest, life may actually be worse. None of us is optimistic about things getting better. None of us offers prescriptions or solutions. I do not know if it is because we are 20 years older and wiser and sadder or whether the cause is really nearly hopeless. But we had an exceedingly enjoyable afternoon talking about it.

Polly Toynbee
19 May 1988

Kissing the Rod, edited by Germaine Greer, Jeslyn Medoff, Melinda Sansone and Susan Hastings (Virago).

After the deluge

The great theologian Bishop Usher calculated that God created the heaven and the earth in the year 4004 BC. At nine o'clock in the morning. He set a good example, did God. I didn't start work till half past ten this morning, but from now on I'm going to try to do better. If I got down to work at nine o'clock perhaps I too would be capable of such mighty achievements. Who knows?

The flood that swept away everything except the Noah family and their pets occurred (according to Usher) in the year 2348 BC, after it had rained for forty days and forty nights, which is very much like the weather conditions we have endured of late.

You have to take your hat off to Noah because according to the Bible he was 600 years old at the time. Unfortunately neither the Bible nor Bishop Usher says what time of the year the flood took place. I thought of asking the Meteorological Office, but their recent performance does not inspire much confidence.

Perhaps it is something the Bishop of Durham could look into. We really ought to know, because it is obvious that the hurricane the other night was just an early warning. I don't know about you, but for the last few weeks all my spare time has been spent in building an ark. I'm making it out of gopher wood, and the length of it shall be 300 cubits, the breadth of it 50 cubits, and the height of it 30 cubits.

At the same time I've been rounding up two of each of every animal in the neighbourhood. It's amazing how much room two horses take up, especially when they are sharing the garage with a bull and a cow and a couple of goats. Elsewhere in the house it's sheer chaos since the cats chase the mice and the dogs chase the cats. And I still haven't found the essential dove for when the good news comes.

The Comtesse thinks I'm bonkers and is threatening to

leave me, in which case I will have to go on my own. This will mean the end of the human race. Then the rats will take over, as I have always predicted.

But to get back to Noah. When they had mopped up after the flood God blessed Noah and his sons (Genesis chapter 8) and said unto them 'Be fruitful and multiply.' They must have followed his instruction with extraordinary rapidity because by the very next year (2347 BC, according to Bishop Usher) there were enough of them to start building the tower of Babel, with the intention that it should reach to heaven.

This was the first high-rise building, and the consequences were appalling. Genesis tells us that 'the Lord came down to see the city and the tower.' He didn't like what he saw at all. Whether or not he called it a monstrous carbuncle is not known, but he made it clear that the children of men were getting above themselves. His actual words were, 'Now nothing will be restrained from them, which they have imagined to do.'

Throughout the Old Testament God displayed an extremely quick temper, and never more so than in the early books of the Bible. On this occasion his options were slightly limited. He couldn't do another flood because he had promised not to, signing the treaty to this effect by putting a rainbow in the sky. On the other hand he could still have turned our ancestors into pillars of salt, or given them plagues of toads, or boils, or carbuncles for that matter, or just smitten them in their hinder parts.

But he did none of these things. Perhaps for once he was in a good mood. What he came up with was a totally unexpected wheeze. Up to then everyone had spoken the same language. Now God said, 'Let us go down, and there confound their language, that they may not understand one another's speech.' The result was babble.

It all has a strangely familiar ring, doesn't it? First there's a period of freak weather conditions, with a constant downpour and a flood. Then comes a dramatic fall in the city, a hard time for upwardly mobile people, and a confusion of tongues.

It's a good book, the Bible, and bang up to date. I looked ahead a few chapters and it was all about conflicts in the Middle East, with the Israelites and Palestinians (Philistines) and everyone else in the region either smiting one another or else taking them into captivity.

But enough of all this reading. Back to work on the ark. Where am I going to put the giraffes? The man from the builders' merchant just dropped by for a chat. I told him I needed some more pitch and a hundred-weight of nails and some more gopher wood. Or three by two if he was short of gopher wood, for which apparently there is at the moment an exceptional demand.

He promised early delivery but there was a lot on at the moment, guv. Still, he'd make sure I had it all by Monday. Or Tuesday. Might be Wednesday. Could be Thursday. Without fail Friday. At the very latest early next week. Guarantee it by the end of the month. Thanks for the drink, squire. Blimey, you've got a lot of animals.

Damn it, the cat's just eaten one of the mice, so I'll have to get another one. So much to do. It's not surprising that Noah was 600 years old by time he had everything ready.

Richard Boston
5 November 1987

I spy . . .

Spycatcher is a very interesting book, first because of all the brouhaha regarding its publication and second because it is a very good read.

But it raises a large number of serious questions for those interested in the workings of intelligence services, whether they support the policy the government has been pursuing, or the policy of 'publish and be damned' of certain newspapers.

Let me say at the beginning that as a former professional intelligence officer, I am shocked at the detail revealed by Peter Wright's memoirs, but more of that later. The point the government has been trying to make in various courts is not what Wright reveals, but that he reveals it at all. The 'obligation of confidentiality' is the crux of the matter.

Sir Robert Armstrong claimed in court in Australia that some of Wright's revelations were dangerous to security. But he also claimed that Wright was in breach of his contract to keep his intelligence work confidential. I served in the Security Service (MI5) and the Secret Intelligence Service (MI6). When I left in 1953 I did not sign any form of declaration relating to confidentiality. I think this was for the simple reason that no such prepared document existed.

Such a document was produced, and all officers leaving the service were required to sign it, after the Philby debacle. This document headed 'confidential' was called 'Supplementary Declaration on Termination of Engagement'.

In it the leaving officer accepts that the head of the Service has carte blanche to cancel any entitlement the officer may have to superannuation or other benefits.

I believe Wright would have signed such a document because it was policy to do so when he left, and also since he was in receipt of a pension this would have been the basis of an ongoing and continuing contract. It is important to consider why Mr Wright should have written his book.

He complains his pension was small – and it was if the figure he gives of £2000 per annum is correct. He says he wanted to reveal the wrongdoing in MI5. To me this reads as the sprat to hook a publisher. The only important point is if part of the government's security agency actually worked against the prime minister of the day.

Wright himself is an odd character, whether as first seen in his TV documentary, or as the old man in the Australian hat during the hearings in Melbourne, or from what one gleans about him from his book. From the cover of the book one would tend to believe Wright was a very important officer in MI5: 'A key figure'; 'The central figure in Britain's relentless and sometimes humiliating efforts to detect and expose Soviet espionage'; 'Britain's principal liaison with American intelligence officials', are some of the descriptions his publishers give him.

The uninformed could assume from some of the descriptions bandied about that Wright might have been the number two in MI5. Far from it. Neither of the intelligence services, MI5 or MI6, have a cadre of ranks like the services. Indeed, a recent head of the MI6 office in Hong Kong was so anxious not to be overlooked that he put in his *Who's Who* entry that his position carried the equivalent rank of Major General.

The British intelligence services divide primarily into junior and senior officers, with heads of department above them becoming directors, and above them the head of the Service and his deputy. The breakdowns in the different levels of junior and senior officers relate primarily to salary, and not to the position or function the officer has.

It is said that when he joined MI5 Wright was told that he would be a senior officer, but also that he would never be eligible for a promotion. This seems an odd basis on which to start a career which after more than 20 years' service only merits a £2000-a-year pension. Either Wright has magnified his importance or there must be something in the nod and the wink he said he was given about extra ad hoc payments.

Victor Rothschild's involvement in the Wright allegations intrigues me. When Maurice Oldfield decided to confess to lying in his positive vetting, he told me he discussed it with only three people: Sir Robert Armstrong, Victor Rothschild and myself. For six years Maurice's secret lay fallow until Chapman Pincher revealed it earlier this year. Who was Pincher's source? Wright and Pincher were brought together by Rothschild. Was the revelation about Oldfield timed to take the heat off the Wright case?

It may be useful, however, to consider the present position of the secret service officer who wants to write a book. The convention before Wright was that manuscripts concerning activities in the intelligence services would be submitted to the service concerned. Sometimes they were acknowledged with a note, 'You would not expect us to comment.' On other occasions there was no acknowledgement and publication went ahead.

In 1965 I handed Oldfield a novel I had written about the collaboration of the KGB and MI6 to prevent the Chinese obtaining a nuclear device. Oldfield asked me to drop it ànd I did, but it would have been a very successful novel.

In 1985 a former SIS officer published a book about his experiences in Greece. When I brought this up in discussion with MI6, I was told, 'It slipped through.'

On 16 September 1985, I wrote to my former employers, MI6, advising I intended to write a book 'to protect Maurice', for I knew then there was a book in the works to smear Maurice Oldfield's reputation. I sent with this letter a synopsis of my book. On 4 December 1986, I submitted to MI6, with an accompanying letter, 'the chapters of my book relating to my service in MI6'. I asked for written comments by 15 December. To date I have heard nothing more than demands from the Treasury Solicitor that I undertake not to publish.

Having read Wright's book I am not surprised at the row that erupted. It describes matters which have always been the most sensitive areas of intelligence. I find the detail that appears in *Spycatcher* shocking. It seems to me that the government's case should have been to attack the revelation of confidential information and not to attack the contentious obligation of confidentiality. I realize that brings into question the recent flood of spy books, where retired officers have given information to authors.

Certainly new laws are required, for a secret service is nothing if not secret. Meanwhile, my publishers and legal advisers seek to persuade the Treasury Solicitor that the *Boy's Own Paper* accounts of the adventures I went through 30 years ago which have been mentioned in other books are harmless, and that the object of my book which is to try and mitigate some of the damage done to the reputation of that loyal public servant, Sir Maurice Oldfield, can be accepted and permitted.

Anthony Cavendish
24 July 1987

Anthony Cavendish worked for MI5 from 1946 to 1948 and MI6 from 1948 to 1953. References to specific material in Spycatcher *were removed to comply with the government injunction against the* Guardian.

24 July 1987

High drama, real soap

Scene 1: A high-rise, medium-vandalized, low-life housing estate. Surrounded by gawpers, the mayor is about to plant a ceremonial tree. Television cameras are there. Suddenly, a woman turns up with an ironing board. She unfolds it, and starts pressing clothes. Cut. Cut. Cut. The intrusion is not scripted in the episode of *The Bill* being filmed by Thames Television.

The intruder cheerfully continues ironing, seemingly unaware of the disruption she's causing. 'Do you know Douglas Fairbanks Jr?' she asks the mayor. 'He's an old friend of mine.' The mayor, apparently, does not. Extras grin in complicity. The producer decides to call off the location shoot.

Scene 2: A heated meeting of residents' reps of the South Acton Estate. All its meetings are heated. They're drafting a letter to the director general of the BBC, complaining about plans to film an episode of another cop series, *Rockliffe's Babies*, in front of their homes. 'No consultation with tenants was deemed necessary,' the letter states tartly, 'as it was probably presumed that they must enjoy the filming of so-called action scenes on their estate.'

'Well, they do not,' says Diane Potter, alias the ironing lady, alias a law graduate, alias a single parent and community activist who, along with other residents, is campaigning against their neighbourhood being used again and again for scenes in crime-cop films and series.

You can see what they mean. It's a bit like an ordinary family living in Albert Square or Coronation Street and not being in the cast, when everyone else is. Those two locations, of course, are imaginary. South Acton is for real. It's been featured in dramas as often as Tottenham's Broadwater Farm estate has in documentaries.

Being a favoured location – between the Television

Centre and the BBC film studios – is full of hazards. One lunchtime, Potter was talking on her way home to a friend when a complete stranger came up and said 'Shhhhhhhh.' *Only Fools and Horses* was being filmed. Potter, then a novice saboteur, went to her flat, phoned neighbours in other tower blocks, and got them to have loud conversations through open windows. Flight of cameras.

However, even she was flummoxed when, one evening, a film crew working on what was supposed to be a night scene got the hapless caretaker to knock on every door, asking residents to switch off their lights. The self-importance of producers is staggering: they throw cordons of silence round public areas where they work, turning them into little, temporary fiefdoms. But there are more lasting consequences.

'It's the stereotyping,' says Yvonne Say. 'It's always heavy cops and robbers things they film here. We wouldn't object so much if it was children's programmes.' Firmly fixed in the minds of location managers is the image which equates big estates with crime. It has to be said right away that South Acton is not an estate of alms houses, tenanted by the blameless elderly.

Potter and the campaign posse admit that the estate has been noted for its share of problems, though a group of 12 or so tenant associations are working to improve the environment and change its image. 'The moment you move to South Acton, you're labelled and you're likely to be criminalized as well,' says Potter.

The issue of filming has brought home to concerned tenants just how powerless they are. When Potter complained to the location manager about *The Bill*, she was told: 'It's nothing to do with you. Whether you like it or not, the housing department [of Ealing] has given us permission.'

And when Beatrice Questroy complained to the producer about using an empty shop to stage a siege in which a policeman is held hostage by a gunman in *Rockliffe's Babies*, she says she was told: 'The violence is inside the shop and anyway, the story is fictional.' She says: 'I told

him, the series might be fictional, but the estate isn't. He
then said a lot of money had already been spent on the
programme.'

Right now, both sides are considering their next moves.
The BBC has been warned that crews face strong protest
action from residents if they return to the estate, 'unless it
is with the intention to right the wrongs done to residents
by the company,' as that letter, now smouldering on the
DG's desk, makes clear.

There, surely, lie the seeds of a solution, and the salvation
of British television from its summer doldrums. How can
telly producers who have been on location at South Acton
have ignored the material which lies in front of their lenses.
There's a rich, raw vein of endless soap. Like an Arthur
Haley novel, it could be titled simply *Estate*; like the *News
of the World*, all human life is there.

There are heroic human stories of single women bringing
up children and managing to get degrees; of tenants' leaders
battling to revive community spirit among desolate tower
blocks. There are power battles, worthy of a city boardroom,
at committee meetings of the Oak Tree community centre.

There are mysteries and tensions awaiting a script-
writer's attention: why do so few old people from the estate
attend the fortnightly tea dance? Why was the mums and
toddlers group so antagonistic when the first black and
Asian mothers attended? Does the National Front still try
to recruit in the Osborne Road area, as it did a few years
ago?

'Racism isn't so bad here, because we've got so many
nationalities,' says Douglas Sampford, a retired bank
official, who is a leading light in the tenants' federation.
'We have eleven nationalities in our block alone,' says his
German wife. 'Twelve, Hildegard,' says the precise Mr
Sampford.

So many incidents have passed into the mythology of
South Acton, the producer of *Rockliffe's Babies*, or any other
programmes would have no need of invention. In several
blocks, former patients from mental hospitals are being
rehabilitated: 'There's one guy committing hara-kiri on the

landing, and I've got another in my block who pisses over the balcony on the nurse below,' says Diane Potter.

'People here regularly jump off blocks,' says another single mother. 'A woman once jumped off with her children. When I moved here, the residents said they painted the place red, so they wouldn't have to wash the blood off.' With material like that, who needs to set up a gun siege in a chemist's shop?

As it happens, Diane Potter would like to convert that same disused shop into a drop-in centre and café for women, and sell health food there. But at the moment, it seems that the immediate use of the premises is as part of a set for the BBC. So the campaigners are bracing themselves at least for a battle of words.

But when the cameras eventually turn on the real dramas of South Acton, rather than the fictional ones filmed there, there is a talented cast of naturals on hand. Doing her stunt with that ironing board, Diane Potter was the shrewdest actor on the set. And Douglas Sampford still plays a bank manager to the life. And there is surely a role for Hildegard, too.

John Cunningham
5 August 1987

First Person hijacked

Let's be clear: 'First Person' is not I. Not just now. If you're reading further, suspend judgment about the writer and editor, Christopher Driver. True, my own body has belonged to me for 55 years and it still works for me: skin, bone, muscle; appetites, taste, affections (especially affections).

If you know me, you can tick Identikit boxes. Colleagues won't spare a glance: minute hand, accurate typing, odd fellow – but the *Guardian* has employed plenty odder, some still in circulation.

However, on the first Saturday of the year my person was hijacked either on a Lake District hillside or done over even more thoroughly during my blackout on a helicopter ride. Most obviously, this person of mine was robbed of my syntax, including a valuable bundle of pronouns and tenses.

The terrorist's weapon has been identified as a 'cerebral infarct'. But you won't want to hear the jargon: just a slight 'stroke', plenty of incidents – about 50,000, the Registrar-General told me after kissing this particular statistic on the stretcher.

So please forget that First Person who's been forging my name. The editorial tactic is to reveal, that's publish, the psychology of the hijacker who's still in occupation of the left hemisphere of my cerebellum.

Here's the briefing. The anti-terrorist neurological unit in Newcastle General Hospital releases the information that my *right* hemisphere seems at freedom, operating on the visual-spatial-creative network. On day three, for instance, I was understanding Latin elegiacs, remembering my telephone numbers, and distinguishing Cotherstone cheese from mousetrap.

But *on the same day* I was taking two hours over scribbling a postcard, mishearing/misunderstanding every word spoken in a particularly clear voice, and communicating near-gibberish. Here is an example (wisely censored by my wife) from a letter I addressed to musical friends: '. . . she, and he but was 9.30 p.m., so I was not out in bedroom was I carrying nurse. So, folly, and the *Guardian* and orchestra the week, and down paper's and orchestra's see go. I think it is good half full because his to physical health, his the from speaking and the speaking brain health. Oliver Sacks find his Latin because his book because my Alistair Elliot was poet and Latin and Newcastle so other it Christopher other found in the hospital . . .'

At this period, I had to be handled rather tactfully. I've always prided myself on my spelling and I wrote out a word-list. I could spell my words splendidly, but the terrorist had interspersed vaguely probable quadri-syllables: 'cunctuation' and 'titulation' particularly pleased me. Even my classical and poetic friend in Newcastle and my wife with her old-fashioned English degree, barely overruled those words, and I still hanker for them.

On day four, I began to realize that syntax was fog. Just the naming of parts of speech clarified emerging shapes after the terrorist had exploded a smoke-bomb over my pronouns, prepositions, and tenses. But even at day 14 (when I started this article) I can be kept unaware of saying 'she' for 'he' or 'besides' for 'between', with hilarious results. My colleagues may allow me to describe the outrage on the hillside, but I don't think they will let me edit somebody else's copy until I shall have been taken back into the pilot-trainer.

Now that I can read the books I have borrowed, I learn that the left hemisphere 'is said to be better at associative thinking and analytic reasoning, while the right is more efficient not only for visuo-spatial processing and . . . the interpretation of music.' Just so, but I found a variant for myself when I got to a piano. As any composer could have told me, most Western music really does need 'syntax' and 'argument': it's hardly a metaphor.

At this time (while my useful language was confined to pictorial nouns and active verbs) my pleasure in music could also be called vertical – chords and instrumental colour – rather than linear. Memory recognized a familiar Bach theme, and fingers obeyed me (or not) in the fugue, while a sense of span and counterpoint meant nothing. The music went in no direction. Later, these two linear senses – the linguistic and the musical – grew back together.

At least the terrorist – unlike most of his kind – shows a sense of humour. During the second week, I was enjoying colleagues' vivid sketches and columns and even trying to write verse at a stage I could not have written prose. But in the same week two magazines published articles of mine that I'd written six months ago – I'll spare you the titles. I opened the pages eagerly. I found them totally unreadable . . .

I'm still uncomfortable without my syntax. Please remember that I'm not my First Person. The terrorist is still leaning on my pen. I'd sooner prefer myself – even if you'd prefer him.

A year later:

The terrorist went quietly – till the next time. Not that strokes often recur, short of obvious indications (smoking, blood pressure, obesity). But psychologically, the victim can be terrorized or tempted into the role mapped for him. For instance, a mild stroke is a wonderful excuse for doing (or not doing) everything one has always wanted (or shunned). Or so I am told.

Technically, for anyone professionally concerned with language, the 12 months that followed this article were instructive. There have been other minor neurological complications, but initially my linguistic faults fell in the sphere of speech defined by Broca: confusion with syntax, negative/positive mistakes and very short-term memory losses (the kind you need to transcribe a telephone number).

Thank heaven, all kinds of writing came back in weeks rather than months, some of them usefully spring-cleaned during their absence. Editing took much longer to return, and thanks to an adroit and sympathetic speech therapist I now have a better understanding of that familiar process. Everyone has his or her own vocabularies and syntax, however rudimentary. An editor is watching, as it were, a split screen in the brain, as in a VDU. On one half of the screen lies the other person's text. On the other half, the editor puts up on the screen his own preferred solution for conveying the same meaning. But mere substitution of one's own phrase for the other person's is normally unacceptable and the editing brain has to set up a third, compromise channel. I'm back to my old high-handedness I suppose – but that can't be blamed on the brain.

Stroke

Dun tone, fellside, January grass;
Swollen beck; a leap, a slump.
Prism fountained; hearing head
Centred, still, on busy clump.

Luck of orange chopper; sleep.
Catch me kind and scan me quick.
Who'll believe my gibberish.
Dr Lin and Dr Dick?

Book the hemisphere preferred;
Pitch my tent beside my brain.
Pronouns, tenses – clear the peaks;
Syntax-blind with cloud and rain.

Christopher Driver
January 1987 and January 1988

Cambridge fellows

Robert Hewison in his book *Monty Python: The Case Against* describes at one point the differences between the Pythons in terms of their universities. The personalities and comedic styles of the Oxonians, Terry Jones and Michael Palin, are presented as warm, absurdist and visually imaginative; those of the Cantabrigians, Graham Chapman, Eric Idle and John Cleese, as logical, ruthless and full of verbal sarcasm.

Oxford in its warm valley is worldly and social, throwing out politicians, modern novelists and other hideous affronts. Cambridge, thrusting up stone fingers from a howling fen, is puritanical and moral, offering a steady output of mathematicians, scientists, philosophers and treacherous sodomites.

In every field of human endeavour this difference seems to obtain. In religion, Oxford is known for its brightly coloured Anglo-Catholics, Cambridge for Erasmus, Oliver Cromwell and stubborn purists like Thomas More and the trio of Cranmer, Latimer and Ridley who were fried to a crisp, appropriately enough in the town of Oxford itself, rather than succumb to the icons and lace of Rome.

In literature and aesthetics the worldliness of Oxford's Wilde, Ruskin and Pater seems a universe away from Cambridge's George Herbert, Milton and Wordsworth. Yes, Byron was at Cambridge too – the rule is riddled with exceptions – but it seems clear to me that Oxford and the world are inseparable; scores of prime ministers up to and including Thatcher, against Cambridge's lonely Walpole and Pitt cannot be a coincidence.

Nor can Cambridge's strange catalogue of scientists, mathematicians and philosophers from Newton through Hardy, Russell, Moore, Wittgenstein and Turing be ignored. There the atom was split, DNA discovered and the meaning of meaning thought long and hard about.

There are even physical differences in the human product. We think of the Oxford drawl and the Cambridge gabble (exemplified by the great Jonathan Miller). Virginia Woolf (Cambridge, and herself, as Oxford's Alan Bennett has written, 'in a very real sense the tallest woman writer I have ever known') noted how long and lanky Cambridge men were, and another comparison of the Pythons shows Jones and Palin failing to match up to Chapman and Cleese's 6 ft 4½ in.

But so, you might well be asking, what? Well, what it all comes to is an admission that I went to Cambridge. Why I chose Cambridge over any other university I have no really clear idea. I had no family reasons, only a dim sense that somehow I would never have considered any other. Perhaps it was because I am tall; I gabble; I'm often accused of being reserved and sarcastic; and I don't like politicians much. Anyway, one thing led to another and there I went and now here I am about to do my bit in a play about six Cambridge graduates.

The Common Pursuit, by Simon Gray, takes its title from a book by F. R. Leavis, perhaps the most Cambridge man who ever lived. Born, bred and entirely educated in the town, there seems to be very little evidence that he ever strayed out of it, and if anyone personified that tradition of moral purity, ruthlessness and integrity it is surely he. Generations of English teachers and critics have been raised on his rigorous doctrines of concreteness, morality and purpose, but while a few Leavisites remain now to haunt the courts and libraries of Cambridge it is true to say that, in our cruel way, most of us who were up in the early eighties regarded the man and all his works as a joke.

In our last weekend of freedom, before the previews of *The Common Pursuit* began in Watford, I took the cast members on a trip to Cambridge to show off the town and university to them, and there it dawned on me that the place is irrelevant to my experience of it, for my experience of Cambridge is exclusively to do with people, not buildings.

If I had been in Moss Side or Milton Keynes with those same friends I should have enjoyed myself just as much. Well, all right, architecture has some point to it, I suppose; I would have enjoyed myself *nearly* as much, let's say.

While the cast all had an amusing jaunt (the full story of Rik Mayall, the private lavatory and the irate night-club manager is one for which the world is not yet prepared) sporting on the Backs and being buttonholed by charming undergraduates, it became clearer and clearer that just as the place was irrelevant to me, so it is to the play.

The Common Pursuit is not about Cambridge and it is certainly not about Leavis, literature and criticism. It is about friendship, I suppose; betrayal, disappointment, ambition and all that; but really it is about the six people of the play, just as *Hamlet* is about Hamlet.

Who wants to see a drama about six Cambridge types, after all? I certainly don't. Simon Gray suffers, I feel, from the unfortunate fact of still being alive. I suppose in Shakespeare's day some people moaned 'Oh, not another play about Verona' when *Romeo and Juliet* was first presented.

Chekhov, who set his plays in far more remote a milieu, isn't charged with being elitist. Jane Austen isn't castigated for wasting her time on parsonical gentry; she is praised, *inter alia*, for being so honest as to write only about what she knew. There is, for instance, no occurrence in her works of two men speaking alone together – it was, by definition, something she had never experienced.

Simon Gray is similarly honest. He writes about what he knows, and he writes extremely well. That's why I, and Rik Mayall and John Gordon Sinclair and John Sessions and Sarah Berger and Paul Mooney wanted to do this play.

Simon Gray had never heard of any of us, of course. It had been agreed that the play should be cast with actors who could play, with reasonable conviction, characters who moved from their early twenties to their early thirties. Gray had complained, with a characteristically despairing drop of the shoulders, that Alan Bates was the youngest actor he knew and so it came about that he had to sit through hours of cassettes of our 'work' – something I wouldn't wish on a dog.

We had another problem: Rik Mayall and I in particular have never really done this kind of thing before. Rik has blazed a trail across the showbiz firmament baring his soul and his botty to an adoring world and I, with my chum Hugh Laurie, have trembled on *Saturday Live* or *Friday Live* when we weren't Blackaddering or just trying to be nice. But acting in a proper grown-up play, being a lovie, doing the West End, 'shouting in the evenings', as the late Patrick Troughton had it: all a little bit scary.

In what I believe is called, by the kind of new reader the *Guardian* redesigned itself to attract, a 'worst case scenario', the traditional West End audience will look upon us as gimmicky TV casting and the younger audience who might usually trot along to see what Mr Mayall's up to will think we've sold our souls to the grown-ups.

One of the problems of the West End play is that it has been almost exclusively upper middle-class, upper middle-brow and upper middle-aged for years. In the end the spectacle of clever people articulately ironizing about their lives and adulteries in a room has limited appeal and, while at first sight *The Common Pursuit* may appear to fall into that category, it is important to all of us in the production to demonstrate that it is real theatre and as funny, moving and boundless as life itself.

The Common Pursuit is not a 'well-made' piece: it is life-shaped, not play-shaped. But in a world where every fashionable magazine devotes pages to music, film, TV and fashion but ignores theatre completely, where theatre journalists can solemnly ask you if you are doing this play because you want to be taken seriously, thus demonstrating the very attitude towards drama that has been killing the straight play for a decade (why do they think it's called a *play* for goodness sake?), in such a world it is hard to promote an evening on the basis that it is good theatre, for there are generations who have been trained to regard theatre as institutional culture rather than dynamic art. One thing's for certain: it's more fun being in a play than being in a work.

Stephen Fry
2 April 1988

Hick snix nix

First on this same sunny Taunton ground, 93 years ago, came Archie's Match. MacLaren's 424 for Lancashire was one of bludgeoning brilliance and is still talked about graphically by members born a generation or two later.

Then in 1985 came Viv Richards. He scored 322 with mighty and murderous intent against Warwickshire, whose weary bowlers congratulated him with generous spirit and said they were thinking of taking up another sport.

Yesterday, it was Graeme Hick's match, as future record books will testify. Worcestershire declared at tea on 628 for seven. The tall 21-year-old Zimbabwean, in the process of qualifying for England by residency (the selectors must wait until 1991), wondrously talented and still supposedly and ominously learning, was 405 not out.

He has scored 815 runs this season and we are still in the first week of May. Records, we suspect, are not of paramount importance to him. 'I must admit I didn't even know of the MacLaren achievement,' he said, minutes after coming in with a tired step and an exalted face to a members' ovation.

Phil Neale, the Worcestershire captain, also confided that he was unaware how close Hick was to the championship record, set by the irascible Lancashire skipper before the turn of the century. He would not tell whether he would have stalled sentimentally for another over or two if he had known, but he must, in retrospect, agonize over the timing of his declaration.

Worcestershire could not bat too much longer, four-day cricket or not. They still had to bowl out Somerset twice and there were optimistic murmurs out of the side of the mouth that the wicket might eventually be turning. For heaven's sake, they might be needing Hick for his bowling. And, as we soon found out in the pale evening sunshine, they did.

He had been at the crease for nine and a quarter hours. He had given a hard chance or two early on, might have been caught off somewhat tired shots to cover and backward point towards the end, and was perilously near being stumped as he lifted his heel playing and missing at Roebuck.

But it was a magnificent amalgam of timing, discrimination, unflurried temperament and dazzling maturity. 'Not as good as my double century at Old Trafford,' he said with unassuming candour.

His bolder shots were straight and true. He never resorted to a wanton slog. The emotions were mostly hidden in the nature of this young man, but he wore a third-former's grin and raised his bat high as he reached his 200, 300 and then 400.

Hick faced 469 balls. He hit 35 fours and 11 sixes. He dominated the innings, as lesser mortals stood at the other end to take minor roles and lead the applause. Ian Botham watched with admiration. 'It was one of the greatest innings I've seen.' The books tell us it was a Worcestershire record and the eighth highest in the first-class game.

There is something quietly engaging about this emerging genius. His style lacks ostentation, just like his persona.

He has an old head and relishes the unmitigated strain of concentration that a marathon performance like this demands. As he awaits the bowler's run, he holds the bat horizontally in the way MacLaren favoured.

The Somerset bowlers pounded away with aching limbs, willing hearts and wry looks. The fielding faltered badly as MacLaren did his despotic deeds, but there were only occasional lapses yesterday as the contest veered inexorably towards Worcestershire and the 1300 spectators – oh, if there had only been more – became obsessed by the sheer statistical grandeur of a feat of historical significance.

David Foot
7 May 1988

Heavenly bodies

As I stood within the Colgate zone of Michelangelo's Adam, so close that I felt the need to stoop in order not to rub my head on the Sistine ceiling, I had a flash of insight concerning Michelangelo's vision of Eve.

This high up, in this company, in this place, any dumb thought is apt to seem deeply significant. But squinting over the restorer's scaffolding away from Adam's creation towards the scene of his upcoming seduction and exile from paradise, I could see Eve very clearly – more clearly than all but a handful of humans had seen her since she was painted in 1510. And quite definitely she had the body of a man.

Eve's weight-lifter's thighs and pectorals, her python-esque biceps, the curious way her waist was a man's waist rebuilt four inches higher than usual, gave her body a masculine outline which the two awkward appendages attached like rubber balls to her front did nothing to feminize. Only her head, hands and feet were convincingly girlish. Michelangelo had probably never seen a naked woman in his life.

In the room the women come and go,
Talking of Michelangelo.

To reach the restored ceiling you must first negotiate a small obstacle course called Vatican bureaucracy. Among the forms you have to sign the most important is the one declaring that in the event of an accident up on the scaffolding you will not hold the Vatican responsible for the damages. In the event of an accident up in the scaffolding there will not be much left of you to seek damages with. It is an awfully long way from the realm of Michelangelo to the chapel floor below, packed solid, all morning, with a rich assortment of mortals.

In the corner of the Sistine Chapel, now somehow sundrenched since the cleaning, is a covered tower. Inside the tower is a tiny yellow cage-lift powered by what appear to be rubber bands and a lawn-mower motor that phut, phut, phuts you 60 feet up into the air. Going up in that rickety lift was one of the most exciting experiences of my life.

First you must witness from close up a bloody murder, the beheading of a screaming Egyptian who had maltreated a Jew, Botticelli's beginning to the story of Moses, painted on the walls of the chapel. Then a large bulging knee appears, and above it a huge bearded head, deep in thought, Michelangelo's Jeremiah. A few phuts more and you are up there in the gods.

The restorers work on a scaffolding designed in imitation of Michelangelo's, for even in scaffolding-design he was a genius. The same holes that he used are being used again in an arch-shaped arrangement that grows more secure the more weight presses down on it.

Up here the three wise Vatican restorers have created a little kingdom for themselves, a kind of caravan home in the sky with chairs, telephones, visitor's book, a marvellous roof, and a wizard's assortment of brushes and bottles. Most of the cleaning is being done simply and meticulously with small sponges moistened in distilled water.

I am surprised, and pleased, by the seeming irreverence displayed by the loudest of the three restorers who, in explaining to me the various complexities of both the cleaning process and the original painting, never misses the opportunity to give Michelangelo's fresco a good firm slap and rub, like a groom enjoying his special relationship with a favourite horse.

In the room impeccably turned-out Italian schoolkids
in unending herds come and go,
Talking (perhaps) of Michelangelo.

In *The Agony and the Ecstasy* Michelangelo was of course played by Charlton Heston with Rex Harrison as the domineering Pope Julius II who had comissioned the ceiling from him and who spends the film pacing up and down like an expectant father shouting: 'When will you make an end of it? . . . You dare to dicker with your pontiff?' In fact Michelangelo lived through the reigns of 13 popes and worked for seven of them. The first number seems to have determined his relationships with them.

He was, as we know, a small man. Charlton Heston is not. So Rex Harrison, who was a sturdy six-footer himself, wore built-up shoes in an attempt to look Heston in the eye during the interminable painter to pontiff confrontations out of which the bulk of *The Agony and the Ecstasy* was made.

'As the film went on,' Harrison remembered, 'it seemed to me that he was growing. Eyeball to eyeball he was once more a couple of inches taller than I. He must have grown through sheer tenacity.'

Groucho Marx, on hearing how much the film had cost, said to Charlton Heston: 'You could have saved a lot of money if you'd painted the Sistine Chapel floor instead of the ceiling.'

Those scenes in which Heston was seen flat on his back miraculously completing his fresco were shot using a very tricky special effect developed for the movie. What he was actually doing was uncovering a recreation of the painting which technicians had hidden beneath a thin layer of gunge.

The set, which won the art director an Oscar nomination, was at the time the biggest indoor movie set ever created, a full-scale reproduction of the Sistine Chapel built in Dino de Laurentis's Rome studio. In 1965 it cost nine million dollars. The present restoration of the most important and celebrated painting in Western art is costing the Japanese television company NTV just three million dollars. In return they have exclusive rights to all photographic and film material of the cleaning and will continue to do so for three years after the work has been completed.

In the room three giggling Malaysian nuns looking slightly out of place in their stern Catholic habits come and go,
Talking of Michelangelo.

Work on the ceiling began in 1980. It is due to finish this year when the restorers move on to the fiendishly difficult task of cleaning *The Last Judgment*, that huge, dark, apocalypse of a fresco that stretches up from the altar to the roof at the far end of the chapel. It is in *The Last Judgment*, painted 20 years after the ceiling, that Michelangelo included a grim self-portrait – sagging human skin lacking a body.

At present the restorers are over half way through cleaning the most famous panel of all, the *Creation of Adam*. I position myself beneath the celebrated gap between God's finger and Adam's and reaching up add a third digit to the configuration. I cannot tell you what a thrill this silly gesture gives me.

From close up Michelangelo's masterpiece looks surprisingly rough. The plaster is criss-crossed with wide cracks. Shine a light on it and you see that the surface of the vault undulates like the Umbrian hills. The restorers are able to chart his progress across the quarter acre of painted ceiling with complete precision. Each day's work has left its bumps.

Adam was painted in four days. God took three. Every day a fresh area of plaster was put down and Michelangelo had a maximum of eight hours to complete the work before it dried. The watercolour he used fused with the wet plaster to become one tough, bright, glowing surface. If he made mistakes there was no undoing them.

'Oil painting,' he is reported to have mutterd, 'is fit only for women and lazy people like Fra Sebastiano.' Fra Sebastiano was Sebastiano del Piombo, a friend for 30 years before they fell out and Michelangelo turned (characteristically) nasty on him.

In the room the tour guides holding up car antennae
with different coloured roses inserted into them to
distinguish each particular group come and go,
Talking (loudly) of Michelangelo.

What is the connection between the Sistine ceiling and the English monarchy? The answer is: the tombs of Henry VII and Elizabeth of York in Westminster Abbey sculpted by the Florentine, Pietro Torrigiano. Torrigiano was the man who broke Michelangelo's nose.

'I felt the bone and cartilage crush like a biscuit,' he recalled, unrepentant, for according to him the young Michelangelo was a jealous bully who could not tolerate any artistic competition. Torrigiano remains probably the most unpopular man in Florence (what a shame that his projected tomb of Henry VIII and Catherine of Aragon was never completed) but I suspect that the Michelangelo he punched bore more of a resemblance to the real thing than the man/God preserved in the annals of artistic folklore, Ariosto's 'Michael, more than human, Angel divine.'

Like most other indisputably great artists, like Picasso for instance, who was positively poisonous on the subject of rivals ('Alberto tries to make us regret the works he hasn't done,' he said of Giacometti), like Leonardo who wrote a childishly hostile treatise on the shortcomings of the Michelangelesque sculptor ('the marble dust flours him all over so he looks like a baker'), Michelangelo tolerated no competitors ('Why, my serving-maid would have written better,' he replied to Leonardo's taunts).

Certainly the Michelangelo-approved life-story that has

come down to us is largely the product of autobiographical myth-making. He boasted that he was descended from Italian counts which he was not. He told his first biographers the story of a miraculous DIY apprenticeship that determinedly suppressed the role of his first teacher, Ghirlandaio. Later on in life he liked to claim that he painted the Sistine ceiling entirely by himself, which he did not.

There is a professor William Wallace from Washington University in St Louis who is now counter-claiming that the cleaning has revealed the hands of as many as 13 assistants working on the fresco with Michelangelo. According to Wallace between 25 and 30 per cent of the ceiling is by other artists.

I put this to the chief restorer who snorts angrily and goes all Italian on me, waving at this head and that among the lesser portions of the frescoes where you would expect the work of assistants to be. '*Tutto, tutto,*' he dabs the plaster, 'unmistakable. The work of Michelangelo.'

I find myself being rapidly convinced. Even among the fresco's spear-carriers there is a remarkably brave touch at work. It is a whisker away from being a reckless touch. With a few swift arabesques that will only make complete sense from 60 feet below it gives God a lionesque head of hair. The same thoroughly audacious hand creates the white of Adam's eye by the simple expedient of leaving an area of plaster unpainted. Adam's famous little penis consists of just two brushstrokes that must have taken all of a second to apply.

The restorer, still indignant, pulls me over to a wickedly funny caricature, one of the monochrome devils squashed into a painted spandrel in one of the ceiling's easily overlooked corners. The little devil's tragi-comic howling anguish has been traced at lightning speed in one totally confident profile.

But if the myth that claims this enormous achievement to be, in all essentials, the work of one man remains basically intact, another has been swiftly dispatched to the art-spike by the cleaners. This is the myth, assiduously promoted by Michelangelo himself, that in order to paint the ceiling he had to lie on his back for four years with his nose pressed to the wet plaster, dribbling and sweating.

Depending on which translation of his poem on the subject you read his discomfort was such that: 'My loins into my paunch like levers grind/My buttock like a crupper bears my weight,' or 'My rump's a crupper, as a counterweight,' or 'I've got myself a goitre from the strain.'

In fact, as the restorers point out, one of the great successes of Michelangelo's brilliant scaffolding system is that it allowed him to work upright and to move from the middle of the ceiling to the sides. There are over 300 figures on the Sistine ceiling.

In the room the visiting art historians taking advantage of a once-in-a-lifetime opportunity come and go, Talking of Michelangelo, and asking whether or not the restoration has irrevocably ruined the painting.

There are pinks up on the Sistine ceiling today where there used to be browns and greys. There is rather a lot of a green, bright as Opal Fruits, that draws attention to itself. This is not the Sistine ceiling of the old art history books, a work of doomy Renaissance prognosis and thunderous despair. This is a bright, light, colourful and uplifting Mannerist spectacle, less of a warning and more of a celebration. And in some art historical circles it has been greeted with howls of despair.

What the restorers seem to have removed from the ceiling – along with the build-up of candle-soot, the discoloured old glues, the smoke from all those papal conclaves that have been held here, the botched handiwork of previous restorers using Greek wine soaked in old bread – is that quality of suppressed anger and foreboding which Michelangelo's contemporaries and scholars since have called '*terribilità*'.

No wonder the revelation of this colourful new Michelangelo has inspired grumpy dissatisfaction, accusation and counter-accusation. An awful lot of important art history careers have been built on the myth of darkness and *terribilità*. It is not just a new ceiling that has now emerged from the Sistine Chapel gloom. It is a new Michelangelo.

In the room the German tourists with bazooka-sized cameras come and go,
Snapping at Michelangelo.

I ask the chief restorer what will happen when work begins on *The Last Judgment* in 1989? Will they remove the loincloths and other pieces of modesty-endowing drapery added to the naked and the damned after Michelangelo's death by his friend, Daniele da Volterra, who thus has the misfortune of going down in art history by the nickname of 'the breeches-painter'?

What offended Michelangelo's contempories seems not to have been the wholesale nudity of his damned souls – the Ignudi on the ceiling are just as naked yet no Pope ever seriously suggested they be girded – but the fresco's overt message that come the Last Judgment all will stand equal before their Maker, men, women, saints, sinners, Vatican officials and popes. That was Lutheran talk.

I ask the chief restorer if the loin-cloths will be removed? He is non-committal and shrugs that it is for the art historians to decide. But most probably the drapery will stay.

Even though the cleaning of the Sistine ceiling has exposed with new vividness just how extensive and sensuous a celebration of male nudity the fresco is, there is once again an awkward and unworthy silence on the subject of Michelangelo's homosexuality. It needs saying very loudly indeed that had he not been a homosexual he could never have painted what is probably the greatest masterpiece of Western art.

In the church of Santa Maria sopra Minerva, at the foot of the altar, is a white marble statue, Michelangelo's *Christ Bearing the Cross*, glowing calm. The last time I saw this quiet Christ he was completely nude, as the artist intended him to be, free at last of an ugly metal loin-cloth, added by the church authorities, that had disfigured him for centuries. When I visited Santa Maria sopra Minerva this time around I found that the ugly piece of false drapery had been put back.

*In the room sour-faced Polish clerics from the papal
inner circle come and go with their heads bent into
their breviaries,*
not looking at Michelangelo.

Today is an obscure but important anniversary. It was on
1 April 1475 that Lodovico Buonarotti's term of office as a
magistrate in the small Umbrian town of Caprese expired
and he decided to move his family to Florence. There is no
record of what his youngest son thought of the move. There
is, however, a record, a glorious, uplifting full-colour record,
of what happened next.

In the room a tape programmed to go off automatically
when the noise inside the Sistine Chapel reaches a certain
decibel level begins the laborious task of asking for quiet
in a long assortment of the world's leading languages.
Everyone stops talking of Michelangelo and starts complaining about the noise made by the infernal blabber-
meter.

When Rome falls, warned Byron in *Childe Harold's
Pilgrimage*, the world falls. Which may be why so much
frantic effort is going into keeping the place standing. The
Eternal City has become the scaffolding capital of the
Western world.

In San Pietro in Vincoli, Michelangelo's famously stern
Moses sits squeezed between the old church of stone and a
new inner church of plastic sheeting like a fly trapped in
the double glazing. If you look down on the Foro Romano
from the delightful Piazza del Campidoglio which Michelangelo designed on the Capitoline Hill you witness the
curious surrealism of chronically ruined arches and colon-
nades being turned into odd-shaped blue plastic parcels.

In the middle of the Piazza itself the equestrian statue
of Marcus Aurelius seems to have disappeared for ever
leaving only a large ghostly plinth. The columns of Trajan
and Marcus Aurelius are both under wraps and stand there
in their respective urban clearings looking like the phallic
handiwork of Christo.

There is no more disheartening experience lying in wait for the enthusiastic grand tourist than the sight of a site under scaffolding. And the modern Romans have developed this particular form of torture into an artform.

But the restoration of the Sistine Chapel does not fall into these clumsy surrealistic categories. The thin and neat scaffolding bridge moves along the ceiling like a very slow windscreen wiper. In front of it lies the old dark Michelangelo, the great tragedian, all basso profondo and crescendo. Behind it the colourful new one, a lighter touch, a more inventive mind, a higher pitch, alto and diminuendo.

It is being able to see both at once – Beethoven turning into Mozart before your very eyes – that has made this restoration such a memorable piece of theatre. And such a controversial event.

The anti-restoration lobby – in truth no more than a handful of enthusiastic American professors soaked to the soul in the *terribilità* myth – has no real case. Their argument that the cleaning is removing Michelangelo's final layer, *l'ultima mano*, the finishing touches he applied when the fresco was dry, is based on gut-feeling not on research.

That the painter emerging from the back end of the windscreen wiper should appear such a complete stranger is a testament not only to the number of candles burned in the Sistine Chapel but also to the corrosive power of the Michelangelo myth.

The all-agony-no-ecstasy image of Michelangelo was built up on a series of misreadings. The massive Moses trapped in the double-glazing at San Pietro in Vincoli would have appeared less of a terrible giant to Freud, less of a projection of parental authority, if he had finished up in the place he was intended for, high up on the tomb of Julius surrounded by scores of sculptural colleagues of the same size. If his slaves had been completed as planned instead of being abandoned emerging, in mid-marble . . . If the Sistine ceiling had been clean and bright all along . . . The new Michelangelo is no longer a troubled existentialist. His ceiling is no longer such a doomy outpouring of religious angst. In full colour it appears to be the work of a much more rational mind. Carefully plotted compartments of colour have replaced the all-over effusions.

Figures that had previously seemed downright scary set deep back in their darkness now emerge solid and integrated. The famous Ignudi appear less acrobatic, more relaxed. The Delphian Sibyl is prettier, less awesome. Even God himself seems a whiter, friendlier sort of divinity, closer to the one admired but not recognized by Michelangelo's earliest biographer: 'Among the most important figures is one of an old man, in the middle of the ceiling, who is represented in the act of flying through the air.'

The new ceiling is thus a long, full-colour critique of the tortured genius myth. And it is not surprising that its loudest critics have been American for it is under the fake vault of Charlton Heston's movie set that the mythical Michelangelo gave his greatest, hammiest performance.

Now the windscreen wiper is nearing the end of its journey across the greatest painting in Western art. In my opinion it has made that painting substantially greater by celebrating it as the work of a rational, hard-working, colourful human rather than some sweaty, impulsive tortured genius.

Waldemar Januszczak
1 April 1988

The Ivory ghosts

Abidjan, the capital of the Ivory Coast, is the soft entry into West Africa. It's the town that foreign correspondents like to stay in while filing reports on the troubles of neighbouring states.

It prides itself on being the centre of an open liberal economy. It has a wide tolerance of foreign merchants, who can get on with their business without all the time looking in the rear view mirror. It has absorbed, for example, up to

300,000 Lebanese, mostly small shopkeepers. Many Ghanaians make a living there. Some 30,000 French colonists stayed on after independence.

This cosmopolitan style is down to one man, M. Felix Houphouet-Boigny, who led the movement for independence, founded the new state in 1960, and has been President continuously ever since. World guides that first expressed concern about his health and the succession have long been remaindered. He is now well into his eighties and not often to be seen, but his name is everywhere – on every page of the only newspaper, on the national sports stadium, on the bridge that links Plateau, the business and government epicentre, with Treicheville, the gaudy, swarming district of the big market and the assault-course night-life.

The people however just call him *'le vieux'* and *'le sage'*: to many it matters greatly that he was a village chief before ever the idea of a nation began to work on the radical country doctor from Yamassoukro. As *'le sage'* he can permit himself gnomic sayings. Favourites of mine include his remark when bidding for more foreign investment that 'France does not have exclusive shooting rights in the Ivory Coast'; and, when asked for gauges of economic growth, 'The only valid economic indicator in the Ivory Coast is the level of rainfall.'

In the Plateau market, an organ fed directly by the main arteries of banks and airlines and travel agents and fashion stores, along with a maze of stalls selling fish and fruit and vaulting heaps of veg, the celebrated carved masks, crafts and trinkets, is a whole great section like battlements of a fortress wall, built of towers of tens of thousands of second-hand – and third- and fourth-hand – books.

As much as the cooking and the language and the voluptuous elegance of women's dress, this depot of print – academic, utilitarian, belle-lettriste and frivolous all jumbled together – makes Paris seem nearer than it is, calls up a whiff of Latin Quarter, of contagious texts passing on intellectual fevers from one dogged autodidact to another. My own cheap purchase was like an exam crib. It was a life of *le vieux*, in comic-strip form. It began 'Once upon a time . . .'

So many well-thumbed books, yet only 20 per cent can read. There are said to be over 60 languages and dialects among eight million people: the schools teach only in French, but in country districts not everybody speaks it. The nearest school may be 15 kilometres away. Even if it is near by, a child may quit while young to help his family. Optimism is an abundant crop of fertile soil; when a seed dropped in the ground seems to emerge as a plant with electronic speed, birth control becomes a joke.

However, it is generally easy for the francophone traveller to learn from the villagers working cocoa, coffee and rubber what is being passed on from research and development stations, in the old capital of Bingerville, or inland at Gagnoa, or where latex bleeds into a million cups in the coastal plantations. One small village can sometimes muster a clutch of experts, who take you through the stages with the zest of Scottish distillers expounding the batch process.

But there is a cloud, emanating from Mali, that spooked my contentment. For six weeks the *harmattan*, a mist of white sand finer than flour, hung about like a shroud among the crystal edifices. It was a shock to stand in the sun by the ocean and see it lurking hungrily, and closing off the beach in both directions.

The oil rigs about 150 miles offshore between Abidjan and Grand Bassam have naturally not yet been able to do much for the country, not even to lower the daunting rate of around £5 a gallon for petrol. But buses are cheap enough, and so they should be when you share your space with an unlimited number of others. Sharing with five or six in big collective taxis makes excursions out of Abidjan along the coast, particularly east, very good value.

Abidjan has been a problem of success. The open city approach to foreign business, and the removal of any threat to its money being frozen, produced a bullish mood and a complex of glittering high-rises and a vast cathedral which have a startling impact on people seeing it for the first time. But the action in this ebullient metropolis drains the interior of people.

A quarter of all Ivorians now live in the capital. It has been beyond the power of the autocrat to prevent this movement. Yet the elders of the smaller towns always say when asked for their development priorities that what they most want is to be '*désenclavés*' – freed from dependence on the capital. A large part of the IMF loans were directed towards improving the secondary roads between them, and laying the good red dust.

I was blanketed with this stuff on a trip west to a village on stilts at Tiagba. My vehicle was a metal waggon without aircon and half windows that wouldn't shut. It reminded my French companions of a police *pannier*, with its grill dividing us from our driver, Yaya, and guide, Mamadou. '*Petit à petit*' read a legend outside, and within: '*I djigui ke Allah-ye*' – 'Nothing can be done against the will of God.'

The Lord allowed us a safe run, and purchase of pineapples, and scrutiny of cocoa pods, and other good stops. He vouchsafed too a meal of rice and cassava, and carp from the waters we had to cross to reach the village. The frustration, once over there, was that we were so wholly possessed and mastered by scores of imploring children that it was impossible to approach, much less speak to, their elders (who may have preferred it that way). Talking of tourism *le sage* called it 'the fount of peaceful confrontation between peoples'. Who would not endorse this pious wish? The chances are there – in the splendid wildlife scenes of the national park, the relaxations and sports offered along the developing 'Riviera', with its beaches fringed by casuarina and palm, in villages like Tiagba, in the remainder of the depleted forests, as much as in the seething gigantic market of Treicheville, where the arms of vendors reach out and pluck at you like the branches in Snow White's forest.

On the city outskirts is a classic natural tourist call. The River Blanco acts as city laundry. In the shallows scores of big truck tyres, encircling hefty stones, are used as coppers. The job is all done by men, though women can wash their personal effects.

In fact, anyone can, if they can find a place to park their tyre. Laundrymen on holiday will rent a tyre out. When beaten clean, with the help of a sap boiled down and mixed with palm oil for soap, the garments are spread across acres of grass in colourful motley. The trouble, some say, is that insects lay eggs in them, and unless they are carefully ironed, the wearers will find themselves hosts to jiggers.

Perhaps most appealing of all is the remarkable acceptance by animist villagers of foreigners who want to witness such private rituals as the dramatic dances of the *fêtishistes*. Sadly, their hospitality is sometimes abused, and there are stories of thefts by tourists of religious emblems and figures that preside over them.

The movements of the dancers and the percussive rhythm of the music that incites them as they call on the help of the spirits of the dead to favour the *rites de passage* of the living, and the seeming indifference to pain of the witch-doctors, soon dispose of fancies that Paris is just over the horizon.

Grand Bassam, another former capital which lost its position when visited by a shattering plague but is now gradually being restored as a picturesque resort, makes a fine excursion. The comforts are obvious enough, but there is a sensational historical background often neglected by those captivated by the Assouan Resort, with its immense beach.

There is a certain melancholy about some relics, like the Monument des Morts, a lugubrious specimen of French funerary art with a woman standing over a corpse in white, and some derelict civic buildings, and a long low flat-roofed prison which is still full of convicts.

But this building and other old colonial residences were at the centre of a stirring episode in the struggle for independence. A great gathering of women marched the 40 kilometres from the capital to protest against the gaoling of many of the men leading the movement and stood up to a heavy beating from the army. The crisis came, after three days of pent-up anxiety and fury and petty confrontations, on Christmas Eve 1949 when over 2000 women tried to force the military cordon at Grand Bassam to demonstrate before the prison. Some 50 were seriously injured in the riot that followed, an astonishing phenomenon to the men engaged, as if the myth of the Amazons had been realized. It made at least a partial contribution to the eventual release of the men, but it is a detail of the battle that for me fires the whole scene. And this is the moment when Marie Kore rallied her followers after the first impact of the water cannon and cried 'My sisters of the Beté, the Baoulé, Dioula, and from all about, do not be afraid! We are not afraid of water and mud, because we are used to working in water and mud . . .'

My personal taste in Africa is not for golf and ice-skating though these can be had in Abidjan, nor much for swimming pools, though the Hilton International has an endearingly eccentric one built through a design oversight in perpetual shade. Contrary to a widely held belief, Hiltons are all different, and this one is utterly unlike such awesome palaces as the Rome and Tokyo colossi, being a modest low-slung affair overlooking the lagoon.

It is in the downtown section, with easy walking access to the wheels of commerce and the levers of power. This is useful, and the sight of the lagoon conjures up images of good seafood, which are realized with skill (in fact always opt for fish rather than meat).

But just as a country needs a ghost in the machine like its President, a hotel has only as much character as its manager gives it. Here the Hilton is lucky in André Charrière, a Frenchman as tubby and unpretentious as his establishment, with a great curiosity about the country. He would fit well into a Tintin adventure and to see him bouncing behind the wheel of some rough vehicle ready for an expedition up-country whets the appetite for the exotica ahead.

When I remember him heading on such a trip I think of it as Operation Bonbon, because of his precaution of taking a large stock of sweets for children, and his remark that tourists often spoilt it all by throwing them instead of handing them out, changing smiles to scowls among the elders. These *nuances* are invaluable in a hotelier, especially when, presiding over a formal occasion, he can look as if he had just received a *bonbon* himself. Given, not thrown.

Alex Hamilton
13 February 1988

Terms of reference

Everyone is entitled to the occasional brainstorm. It could take the following form:

With us in the studio is the Right Honourable Nigel Lawson, Chancellor of the Exchequer. Mr Lawson, what do you think will be the consequence of the Indian forces' occupation of Jaffna?

'I was not expecting the question, but since you ask I would like to broaden it out and say that throughout the past uncertain week I have never for a moment doubted that a treaty on intermediate-range nuclear weapons would be concluded. After that I should very much hope to see further progress towards a ceasefire in the Gulf War.'

Alan Beith, would you agree with that? Just one moment. I see Mr Lawson has another point to make.

'Yes, simply to say that the referendum in South Korea was in the end a bold initiative by President Chun and that by extension all of us who enjoy a democratic system of government must hope that the Anglo-Irish Agreement will not be jeopardized by factional interests of which examples all too readily spring to mind.'

Mr Beith, before I ask you to comment on those very interesting points may I ask ... I'm sorry, you wished to say something, Bishop?

'I see in this week's *New Scientist* a composite photograph of five million galaxies taken at random from the many more presumably available for observation. Each of these galaxies contains many thousands of millions of planets. The writer is kind enough to observe that there may be more to the universe than meets the eye. But perhaps you don't wish me to enter upon metaphysical questions at this stage?'

You have raised a very far-reaching and indeed challenging proposition, but first let me ask Mr Beith: I imagine you will have something to say in anticipation of Mr Gorbachev's 70th anniversary speech, but before we come to that I wonder whether you wish to comment on the community charge, or poll tax?

'Well, naturally you won't expect me to comment on individual cases but in general I would say that the taxation of site values has been Liberal policy for many years. Had you asked me about David Alton's abortion Bill . . .'

I was coming to that.

'. . . I would say that David and I have been close colleagues for some years and I have followed with great care the development of his ideas on Namibia. But if you asked me about wider share ownership that would be a different question altogether.'

Mr Benn, you were Secretary for Energy at the time the first BP shares owned by the government were put on the market. What, in your view, is Colonel Rambuka trying to achieve?

'As you know, the government is ultimately controlled by the CIA . . .'

Er . . .

'Oh yes. You only have to look at Mr Peter Wright's book, pages 273 and 274 for example, where he says . . .'

'Forgive me for interrupting . . .'

Yes, Mr Heseltine?

'. . . but the Westland affair is past history. In any case it became confused in everybody's mind with the constitutional status of the Solicitor-General. If I believe anything I believe that the two issues should be treated separately and not regarded somehow as an extension of the argument about the chairmanship of the Conservative

Party, which is essentially a come-day go-day job.'

Mrs Williams?

'I don't think the first part of what Mr Heseltine said can be denied.'

'You see, there are difficulties there, but no greater than we faced in Liverpool when I was at the Department of Environment. And while all that was going on, remember, the stock markets were steady, the problem with Aids had barely been recognized, and the drastic reduction of milk and cereal quotas was only just beginning to be an issue. You have to have a certain perspective in these matters. The Burnham Committee, after all, was never intended to be the be-all and end-all.'

May I now come back to you, Cecil Parkinson, and ask whether you have never had any doubts whatever about the Youth Training Scheme? Are there not times when you wake up in the night and say to yourself, 'My God, the Ayatollah is at it again?'

'May I interrupt?'

Yes, Mr Beaumont-Dark?

'Simply to say that there is another dimension to this which I don't think we have fully explored. I found that when I was in my constituency.'

That's very interesting. But what do your constituents make of the world in general? Are they optimistic, would you say? Are they well-informed? Sorry, you were about to say something, Mr Meacher?

'Your reference to the poll tax was lacking in one respect, and I . . .'

Sorry, I think Mr Beith has a point, or was it Mr Gould?

'Simply about the Korean referendum. I think there is a danger of being too simplistic in our attitude, just as I think the Prime Minister was worse than simplistic about the ANC.'

Dr Owen?

'I agree with that, except that we had the same problem with Quemoy and Matsu many years ago and the difficulty was . . . I wouldn't say solved, but at least made containable. In the long run Gibraltar must inevitably follow the same pattern but I don't pretend it's easy because it isn't.'

Ambassador?

'How is it you say? There is more than one way of skinning a cat and many a mickle makes a muckle. In principle I would agree with previous speakers but I would like to make the point that the Shatt al-Arab frontier has been in dispute not only for years but for centuries and that, as in the case of Trieste just after the war, patient diplomacy may be the ultimate resort.'

Those are very wise words.

'I agree.'

A fitting note to end on.

'I think that is true up to a point, but I don't think the convulsions we have been witnessing can be entirely divorced from the resolution of the Arab-Israeli conflict. After all, the Wars of the Roses are not, historically speaking, all that distant in time, and although I don't want to get into a chicken-and-egg argument, the partial recognition of the Peking government by Taiwan must in the end influence French policy towards New Caledonia.'

Douglas Hurd, Ken Livingstone, Paddy Ashdown, thank you very much.

Geoffrey Taylor
2 November 1987

Unhinged by a handbag

A well-loved 92-year old classic comedy was seized and seriously interfered with on Monday night when two middle-aged men dressed in women's clothes invaded the stage of the Whitehall Theatre. The men, known as Dame Hilda Bracket and Dr Evadne Hinge, who enjoy an undercover reputation as drag artistes, took the comedy by surprise and then went on to commit a series of gross theatrical assaults upon the play, which lasted for more than two hours. An audience of hundreds, many of them well-dressed, was forced to watch helplessly. Some of them even laughed occasionally during the ordeal in which several non-transvestite actors were also obliged to take part.

Later, the severely shocked play, *The Importance of Being Earnest*, was reported to be as well as could be expected and recovering from the experience. Critics were reported to be looking for Mr Lou Stein, named in the programme as the 'adaptor and director' of the onslaught.

The ordeal began when the lights went down and one of the men, known as Dame Hilda Bracket, advanced upon the stage, wearing a barefaced leer, dressed in a cropped grey wig, and what appeared to be a flowered tapestry concoction, surmounted by heliotrope. She gave us to understand that she as Lady Bracknell and Dr Hinge as Miss Prism would be performing an amateur 'tea-time performance' in their living room, aided by two young men and their girlfriends.

An evening of lumpen satire upon the theme of amateur dramatics was about to be launched. For since these aforesaid girlfriends fail to arrive, delayed by their own missing handbag at Victoria Station, Hinge and Bracket were given the chance to slip heavily into the roles of Gwendolen and Cecily – the Dame Bracket done up in golden curls and a falsetto simper, the Hinge person demure to the point of dullness.

Dame Hilda's Bracknell, swaying on high heels, trembling with affronted hauteur, looked every inch a drag queen, flaming in pink and green. It was a performance very much in the vocal and physical mould of Edith Evans and Fabia Drake, a clever, utterly confident piece of theatrical mimicry. Dr Hinge as Miss Prism and Cecily emerged almost identically in both roles, missing almost completely the dimensions of either character. One forgave Robin Kermode's Algernon and Simon Dutton's desperately sweating John Worthing in this hothouse, cooly pacing amidst Norman Coates's design of hideous, chintzy rural suburbia. The play is expected to survive.

Nicholas de Jongh
4 November 1987

"My husband and I think it best to take separate flights. I do believe I spotted him just now in the plane that suddenly came alongside us."

24 February 1988

Khomeini City

In the early hours of the morning at Tehran airport a long queue of newly arrived passengers from London and Paris shuffles forward in the painfully slow process of passport control. Suddenly, a young woman detaches herself from the line, and walks across the cavernous arrival hall to an isolated corner.

Dressed in the black chador of the strict Islamic woman, she pulls its hood around her face so that she is completely obscured by the costume. From the ground to the tip of the hood she is a motionless, black statue. Attracted by the spectacle, three small Iranian children leave the queue and stand transfixed some yards from the woman. The children, dressed in bright, colourful Western clothes, exchange furtive grins as the black spectre bends down first to her knees and then until the hood touches the ground.

Apart from the three children, no one else in the queue of some 300 Iranians is watching the woman's act of religious devotion. They know it is happening but they do not see it. It is a contradiction which runs like a motif through contemporary Iranian culture.

Outside the airport the roads are jammed with traffic by 5 a.m. The Tehran day begins early and within two hours the shops, offices and government buildings are staffed and trading. The relentless dry heat will have exhausted the inhabitants by late afternoon.

The road from the airport passes walls covered with anti-American slogans. Uncle Sam is caricatured as a war-mongering monster clutching bombs and missiles to his Stars and Stripes costume. Similar vilification is aimed at President Saddam, of Iraq, while on the first intersection of the airport road another hideously depicted warrior grim-aces over the written injunction: 'Israel Must Be Destroyed.'

Inside Tehran, it is difficult to relate the city with its worldwide reputation as a centre of religious fanaticism. It is also difficult to remember that a brutal seven-year war with Iraq is being directed from this city where many families have relatives among the half-a-million Iranian soldiers killed in the conflict.

There are few military personnel to be seen and those that are on the streets are clearly not on duty. Neither, again, is there any overt championing of the Ayatollah. Most shops, offices and hotels have a picture of Khomeini on prominent display but the pictures are modest, some-times only postcard-size.

Shops are well-stocked with mostly Japanese-manu-factured appliances and fashion for both men and women. Many Iranian women have still not adopted the chador, although the wearing of a headscarf is now obligatory. Even among those women who do wear the chador, it is not uncommon to see an ankle clad in Levis beneath the black hemline.

In the hotel where the city's affluent go to sip Pepsi or

iced coffee (alcohol is strictly banned) Iranians sit side-by-side with Westerners. In one of Tehran's most expensive and luxurious hotels, the statement 'Down With America' has been carefully assembled on a wall with tiny porcelain tiles. But again nobody seems to notice.

But the war with Iraq enters every home with a television set. Daily broadcasts are dominated by it. Film of the troops at the battlefront is repeated endlessly over martial music, and there are regular discussions between mullahs and senior army officers. Film of Revolutionary Guards holding exercises in speedboats in the Persian Gulf is beginning to supplement the daily viewing.

One thing which must worry people is the recent pronouncement by the authorities that the war with Iraq will continue for another 20 years if necessary. Will the brightly-dressed children of Tehran have to change into military fatigues in the future?

Paul Keel
15 August 1987

The history man

In the steep and usually leafy streets that border Hampstead Heath, where half a hundred writers and historians still ply their ancient trade, lives Britain's most distinguished – and, for the past decade, most controversial – Marxist intellectual.

The house is far from austere, a comfortable and well-off family home, the sofas arranged for conviviality, the great kitchen windows designed to bring light and garden green into a potentially gloomy interior. Only the bookshelves give a hint that this is other than an ordinary middle-class London environment. Volumes of Mörike and Lessing, the works of Goethe and Heine, books by Block and Sartre, suggest a European – even a Central European – background that the very English William Morris curtains cannot altogether efface.

For Professor Eric Hobsbawm, though born not altogether by happenstance (as he explains in his most recent book) in Alexandria, is essentially a product of the Austro-Hungarian empire and in particular of the post-imperial socialist Vienna of the 1920s, a city long famed as a cradle of culture, learning and the arts – and one of the great charm schools of all time.

A tall, thin, stooping, cadaverous man, with a great mane of white hair, Hobsbawm is extraordinarily hospitable, courteous, and polite. Acid in argument, outspoken in debate, and often intemperate in language, he is a scholar of great good humour and wit, a man who relishes the excitement of controversy and polemic. He belongs to that brilliant generation of British Marxist historians, now for the most part emeritus professors, which includes Christopher Hill, Edward Thompson, Victor Kiernan, John Saville, and Rodney Hilton. Of them all, Hobsbawm is the most fluent and most versatile, the most subversive and the most cosmopolitan, a man whose magpie mind produces the most dazzling patterns from the kaleidoscope of the recent past.

Though fame and recognition have come to him late in life, he remains something of an outsider, a man who writes beautiful English but still speaks with traces of a foreign accent, a Jewish refugee who still retains an affection for the European culture from which he springs, a Communist who tries to understand the world as much as to change it, an English patriot who has never been properly used by his adopted country, an historian who is also (as Francis Newton) a famous jazz critic.

Born in the year of the Russian Revolution, Hobsbawm has remained for the past half century the chief and principal intellectual adornment of the British Communist Party – a vantage point from which to view the world and its foibles not altogether dissimilar to that of a Jesuit seminary. Unlike some of his contemporaries, he has never disowned his secular religion – indeed he uses it to great advantage – but he wears his black robes lightly, and treads delicately but surely along the invisible line between faith and heresy. He is a popular figure at the Massachusetts Institute of Technology, yet his many books have never been translated into Russian. And in Britain, given the intellectual vacuum at the heart of the Labour Party, he has been drafted in to fill a role as the political philosopher of the Left. His political interventions, usually published in the columns of *Marxism Today* (and given a wider readership in the *Guardian*), have become an annual, controversial, event. Though a Communist revolutionary with a lifetime of struggle behind him, he is now one of the most cogent voices in the land, not for revolution, but for reform.

How did this happen? I asked him. How had a retired professor suddenly found himself in the political limelight? 'Initially, it really wasn't my intention to intervene, though obviously over time I've sort of got myself much more involved.' It all started ten years ago, in 1978, when he was invited to give the Marx Memorial Lecture. He decided to talk about the British working class 100 years after Marx. His initial statement (subsequently much quoted) was on the surface unexceptional: 'The forward march of labour and the labour movement, which Marx predicted, appears to have come to a halt in this country about 25 to 30 years ago' – sometime around the collapse of the Attlee government.

Hobsbawm argued in his lecture that there were all kinds of external reasons for this stagnation and crisis which it might be necessary to understand and analyze, but in the end the cause would have to be found within the Labour Party and labour movement itself. 'The workers, and growing strata outside the manual workers, were looking to it for a lead and a policy,' he wrote. 'They didn't get it. What they got was the Wilson years – and many of them lost faith and hope in the mass party of the working people.'

Such sentiments were music in the ears of some who heard or read them, but by no means of all. 'It hurt the feelings of a number of left-wing trade union militants in the Communist Party, and provoked quite a lively discussion on the Left,' Hobsbawm recalls.

The whole thing became generalized later, he thinks, 'because of the row within the Labour Party. People like Kinnock found it extremely convenient to be able to point out some support for their position from chaps with an unanswerable track record on the Left, and therefore Kinnock went out of his way to start quoting me.'

But given the crisis in the Labour Party, why, I asked, had he seemingly come down on the right-wing reformist side of the debate? After the defeat of 1979, could not a good case have been made out for supporting the radicals?

'At one time, indeed,' Hobsbawm recalls, 'I had considerable hopes of Tony Benn. But I gave them up as soon as I saw the completely ridiculous way in which he behaved when, for all practical purposes, he'd won the game. All he had to do was wait and he *would* have been leader of the Labour Party. Whether this would have been a good thing is another matter. But looking at his behaviour, I thought this just isn't serious, especially as he then proposed actually to split the Labour Party down the middle – and to do the same sort of thing that is ruining the Social Democratic Party.'

It would not be surprising to find that Hobsbawm's understanding of history informs his political judgments, or it may be the other way round. But reading his new book, *The Age of Empire: 1875–1914*, the final volume of a magnificent trilogy on the nineteenth century, there is some suggestion that the erstwhile champion of labouring men, of bandits and revolutionaries, and of rebels outside history, now has a rather more sympathetic and understanding eye for reformers and reformists, and for Cassandras with disagreeable messages that turn out to be true. Keynes and Kautsky come out well. So too does Nietzsche.

So what is the trajectory that has brought this life-long Communist to the position of a reformist elder statesman? Until he was a teenager, Hobsbawm lived in Vienna, where his mother's family came from. Somewhere he has written that if you came from a well-off Jewish household in Central

Europe between the wars you didn't have much choice in life except to be a Zionist or a Communist. The cause of reform, of bourgeois liberalism, and of capitalism of the pre-1914 variety seemed at that time to be doomed. So before becoming a Communist, had he considered the Zionist option, or been attracted to the Zionist youth movements of Central Europe?

'One knew about them, of course, but my Viennese family was a completely emancipated – and therefore an areligious – family. Except for the occasional wedding, I was never inside a synagogue in my life, in those days. So consequently the attraction of Jewishness as such was nothing special. The main thing – and this is very important – is that one was keenly aware of anti-semitism. The one thing my mother impressed on me was that under no circumstances was I ever to do anything which might even suggest that I was ashamed of being Jewish. That was enough as far as I was concerned. Besides, in the 1920s, there weren't that many middle-class Zionists in Central Europe, yet.'

So the alternative was Communism? 'Yes, but of course if I'd stayed in Austria it wouldn't have been to become a Communist but a Socialist. This is what tempted me as a boy, joining the Young Socialists. In a sense, though, the choice was to be Left or Nationalist.' And the siren voices of National Socialism were powerful too? 'Yes. I do remember, as a schoolboy, understanding how my non-Jewish mates, so to speak, could be attracted by Nazism, and thinking, "Well, of course, I can't, I'm not a bloody German", but one could see how they would be attracted by this hope of theirs.'

There was a further possibility, of course, and one that might have been open to Hobsbawm when his family moved to England. He went to King's College, Cambridge, the intellectual home of John Maynard Keynes, and Keynes was one of the few men who found a way of transforming liberalism and adapting it to a new era. He gets his meed of praise in *The Age of Empire*.

'I'm not particularly favourable or unfavourable to Keynes,' Hobsbawm says defensively. 'I merely point out that what Keynes did was the only thing that Liberals could do, namely, to stop being a pre-1914 Liberal, as he had been, and become something completely different. I'm contrasting him with Liberals who were overwhelmed by Fascism because they really did not see that the old-fashioned kind of political finagling would no longer do. And Keynes did. And I stress Keynes because in fact Keynes never stopped being a Liberal or calling himself a Liberal.

'The point I'm trying to recall – and it's very difficult for people who didn't live through this period to grasp it – is the sense in which everybody believed that the old order was dead. One's elders, even though they were business-men, would say, "Well, my boy, of course I know Commu-nism's bound to come, but it'll be a long run thing." The fact is people were certain they were living on borrowed time. Now clearly since the 1950s this is no longer the case in most parts of the developed world – though in many underdeveloped countries it still is.'

Hobsbawm, it seems in retrospect, was one of the few Communists at Cambridge in the 1930s who was active in the Communist Party and not in somebody's secret service. 'From the beginning,' he recalls, 'I was so public a Commu-nist agitator that nobody dreamed of recruiting me for anything. But I was certainly right in the middle of "Red Cambridge". I was a little bit younger than Burgess and Philby, and I overlapped with Blunt. I don't think anybody in any of the spy literature has ever mentioned me in this connection. Perhaps I'm a really deep agent.'

When war came, Hobsbawm was content to go along with Communist support for the Nazi–Soviet pact. 'I was an orthodox Young Communist. I accepted the line. Later I got very worried about it because it seemed absolutely clear, from the German invasion of France on, that one couldn't do anything with this line, and anyway I didn't think it was right anymore – or at least it no longer con-vinced me.'

With the German attack on Russia in 1941, the line changed, and Communists could dutifully support the war effort. 'I had a very boring war in the Engineers and then in the Education Corps. Politics may have got into this simply because I undoubtedly had a file – I was told on one occasion that I did have one – particularly at the time when one was a premature Second Fronter.'

He never got near any kind of wartime intelligence work. 'I was interviewed occasionally for things like interviewing prisoners – I was bilingual in German – and people said "No thank you", that kind of stuff. No one would have dreamed of recruiting me for Bletchley, for instance, even though 17 dons at King's went there, including my own teachers.'

After the war, many Communist academics found it difficult to get university posts commensurate with their talent. Hobsbawm considers himself lucky to have got in at Birkbeck, in London. He got a job as a history lecturer – and has been there ever since, ending up as an emeritus professor.

'The test was when you got in,' he says. 'If you made it before the Berlin Crisis of May 1948, well, you didn't get promotion for ten years, but nobody threw you out. I got in within about a year of getting out of the army – on my graduate record. So consequently I was OK. But if I had waited, say until after my PhD, I might never have managed to get in. During the Cold War there were some tough moments, and even relations with one's colleagues could be very tense.'

At the age of 70, Hobsbawm has now completed what will probably prove to be his most popular and lasting work, a history of the present era that will survive well into the twenty-first century. So how does one set about writing a huge three-volume history of this kind, and what does he see as his own special skills?

'In the first place, I didn't set out to do it – it developed. I wrote the first book, and that turned out to be successful, and then they asked me to do the second in the same series, and after that, the third. So in effect it wasn't really until I did the second one that I said to myself, Jesus, maybe I'm actually writing the history of the nineteenth century – or the long nineteenth century from the 1780s to 1914.

'This particular book I'd been chewing over for an awful

long time, one way and another, and writing bits and pieces, and taking vast numbers of notes. In the end I decided the only way to write a book which actually flows – not to be muscle-bound as it were – is at a certain stage to put the files away and just start writing; as though one were in a prison-camp, you might almost say, which is the way, you may remember, that Pirenne wrote his *History of Europe* and Braudel the first draft of his *Mediterranean*.'

Hobsbawm lays no claim to a textual memory of the kind that Macaulay is alleged to have had. 'I can't memorize passages. But I can remember lots and lots of different bits and pieces which have accumulated – though I very often remember them wrong. Memory is very misleading, obviously, so you have to check on a lot of it. But on the whole it's a sort of magpie memory which I try to structure by fitting it in to an explanatory or theoretical scheme. It's one of the advantages of being a Marxist, you see. Things which might otherwise be a "trivial pursuit" actually get fitted into a pattern – or you think you can fit them into a pattern.

'In some ways the real problem is to write in such a way as to try to make it all hang together in your own mind, or at any rate if it doesn't hang together in your own mind to try and pretend to readers that it looks as though it hangs together so that they feel maybe that something has been explained. But really I'm trying to explain it to myself too.'

And does the study of the nineteenth century help one to understand what's going on at the moment? 'Well, it's what we've inherited. The nineteenth century in some ways is where we all come from; the "dual revolution", the industrial revolution and the French revolution, you don't really have to go much further back than that. To that extent, it is directly relevant to today . . . If one spends a good deal of time thinking about a particular period, one tends to get rather fond of it as such. And I must say I've got rather fond of the nineteenth century. It's a peculiar place, but today, looking back on it, I think in spite of all the awful things, it was an era, if you like, of hope and progress – in the sense of people being confident that they could overthrow the evil system and replace it by something better. In the nineteenth century everybody was utopian, not just the Marxists and the socialists. Freetraders were utopian. President Ulysses Grant was utopian. Whereas today, when no one is utopian, the evidence for progress is actually rather stronger.'

Yet against this there is the witness borne by Nietzsche, a somewhat disparaged and neglected nineteenth-century figure who makes an intriguing guest appearance in Hobsbawm's book. 'Yes, I've got on to Nietzsche, in a sense, late. It's not that I like him. On the contrary, I rather dislike him. It's a bit like Wagner in some other ways. There's no denying he was somebody. He wrote marvellous language.

'I think I put in a lot of Nietzsche in this book simply because he seems to me in some ways, and was at the time I think felt to be, articulating the sort of peculiar dilemma of the bourgeois world, the need somehow or other to revalue all values at a time when, superficially, everything seemed to be, so to speak, rolling along nicely, moving forward – progress – and here was this guy saying "it isn't really like this at all, we're working up to some enormous catastrophe". That's why I keep quoting Nietzsche, because in a sense, this is the theme which from a different way I see in this golden and progressive and hopeful era. And I suppose you must say that a man who intuited these things is somebody that's to be taken seriously. I mean I wouldn't like to have people like that around, but you've got to admit that he's an important – in this instance even a key – figure.'

One looks, inevitably, in Hobsbawm's writings for some key to his political outlook, and I thought perhaps I had found it when I came across a passage highly critical of Modernism. The artistic avant-gardes of the era immediately preceding the First World War are effectively dismissed as 'the various small minorities who asserted their status as dissident anti-bourgeois rebels by demonstrating admiration for styles of artistic creation inaccessible and scandalous to the majority.' I suggested to him that this hostility to Modernism was now part of the 1980s Zeitgeist.

'Well, not to my Zeitgeist. I have taken this view for quite a long time, although I'm beginning to modify it a little bit in the light of looking at the 1920s a bit more. I have a feeling, looking back, that the time when really great works were being done in the Modernist idiom was the 1920s, the Weimar period. It's really since seeing a thing like the Brecht–Eisler *Massnahme* that this has kind of hit me. Nevertheless the point I'm making is that the basic idea of Modernist high culture and high Art was misconceived. The real revolution in the arts was something else, through things like movies, which did everything that the manifestos of the Cubists and others said they were going to do, but only did, at best, for a relatively small number of people. And I believe that this is the critique even of the greatest achievements of Modernism, that they very rarely reached out to the masses, except by this curious side way, via advertising and design.'

Hobsbawm has always had his followers as well as his critics within his profession, but over the decades he has found an ability to attract readers far beyond the practitioners of his craft. 'I think it's one of the nicest things about the British tradition of history writing,' he reflects, 'that they've always paid the right kind of attention to communicating to ordinary people. The idea of writing not for other people's footnotes seems to me to be terribly important.'

Though certainly a well-known and respected historian in Britain, Hobsbawm abroad has almost the reputation of a guru. 'My fortunes have been very largely made by progressive intellectuals. My books have been translated into an incredible number of languages. I've actually had a book translated into Persian. I discovered when I went to Korea that five of my titles have been translated into Korean – pirated I need hardly say.'

In Italy he is an honoured guest, in Brazil they flock to interview him. 'The moment my books do really well is when a military government or some old authoritarian regime is beginning to loosen up. In Spain, for instance, it was from the late sixties to the mid-seventies that my kind of thing started absolutely taking off. Everybody who was being, as it were, trained for the post-Franco period came out of the universities, and in the universities they wanted to read stuff which was both respectable and progressive, and there aren't that many people around producing that sort of material. The same thing happened in Brazil in the seventies.'

And Britain? 'The peculiar thing is that this doesn't happen in England. In so far as it does, it is also obviously the Left which reads my books, and some others too – I hope.' And it doesn't happen in Russia either. 'I've never really been taken up by the Eastern bloc – with the one exception of Hungary. The Russians have never known what to do with me at all. It's an interesting fact that not a single movement has been made to translate any of my books into Russian – ever.'

Hobsbawm himself of course has steered well clear of the great Communist revolutions of the twentieth century. 'For many years, being a Marxist and a Communist, I wasn't anxious to write about Russia – because you'd get into trouble. You couldn't write without actually deciding that the official line on most things was horseshit. We know that. So it was easier to keep off it.' China is a more intriguing omission. 'From the point of view of my interests – like bandits and popular movements and peasant rebellions – China would be an absolutely central subject for me.' But he lacks the language. 'I do have a fairly strong conviction that if you don't talk or read the language you'd better go easy. I'm too old to start learning Chinese now – and so I just have to shrug my shoulders about it.'

So what is he going to do now? 'I think I've finished with the nineteenth century. Some people say, "Well, why don't you do something about the twentieth century?" That's a possibility, although it can't be the same kind of book because personal memories and being "a participant observer", as the anthropologists say, comes in. I'm personally quite interested in pursuing my older things, the sort of line of Primitive Rebels, and I suppose I'll carry on being on the margins of politics, too.' And what about the world?

Is capitalism going through another system-endangering crisis similar to that of the 1930s?

'The system on a world scale is obviously extremely stable. On the other hand it has in fact saved itself by very dramatic changes. This is the point of my book – here was the great nineteenth-century Liberal bourgeois system which generated its own collapse. The years from 1914 to 1945 were a time of catastrophe and cataclysm, generally speaking an apocalyptic era. And in fact if capitalism had not managed to adapt itself quite fundamentally, in ways which practically nobody would have been prepared to envisage, it wouldn't have lasted.

'I think there will need to be other equally fundamental adjustments. I think they are likely to be adjustments in some sense within capitalism simply because the challenge to capitalism which existed at one time – and was represented by Labour and Socialist movements – does not at the moment exist in that form, and with that global homogeneity.

'So while I think there's going to be enormous numbers of revolutions, and shifts within the capitalist system, the major danger at the moment is for the whole thing to collapse under its own contradictions and create – whatever it may be – a nuclear holocaust or the destruction of the ozone layer.' But in these circumstances isn't there a parallel, not with the 1930s, but with the situation described in his book before 1914 when revolutionaries were faced with the problem of how to bring about a new society 'in times when the collapse of the old system looked far from imminent.' Wasn't Hobsbawm's position akin to that of Karl Kautsky, the German Social Democrat who called himself a revolutionary but didn't seem over-enthusiastic about making a revolution?

'Well actually to be fair to Kautsky, he really did worry about how to get power, only he didn't quite see how under German conditions you could do it. "It's no use all this barricade stuff," Kautsky argued, "it's no use even talking of this stuff that Lenin and the Russians are doing because we're not in Russia."

'This is why I mention this peculiar business about them saying "We are a revolutionary party, but we don't make a revolution."' At this stage, I smiled gently.

'It isn't a joke,' said Hobsbawm, almost upset. 'It's actually what a lot of Communist parties have been facing since the war. The Italian one is a case in point, isn't it? "We're a revolutionary party, but what do we do?"' There is in his voice, for the first time, a note of the twentieth-century pessimism from which prolonged study of the nineteenth has allowed him for the most part to escape.

Richard Gott
26 February 1988

The Minister for Poetry

Kenneth Baker, our misnamed Minister of Education, has two gifts which should disqualify him from sitting in a Thatcher Cabinet – a sense of humour and a readiness to take risks. And if this tribute should be thought too flattering altogether, I will offer at the conclusion of this article some irrefragable evidence which, if there is any pretence to dignity on either side, should happily break the Cabinet wide open.

Meantime, we must make the best we can of Mr Baker's latest offering, a history of England presented in an anthology of poetry. A first hasty glance at the index and elsewhere suggests some sharp conclusions: an excellent idea too sycophantically executed; too much war, too much royalty, too much Kipling, too much Chesterton, not enough Milton and Pope and Swift, not enough Byron and Shelley and Blake, not even his hymn to free love, 'Jerusalem'.

But wait: do not be misled by these impulsive strictures. Reading between the lines in the anthologist's own guide to what is happening, reading some of the poets themselves who have made their own forcible entries into these pages, a different picture can emerge. I would gladly send my own marked copy to Number 10, to assist Mr Baker's career.

Quite early on he seems to stumble on the right approach when he quotes the deathless lines: 'When Adam delved and Eve span/Who was then the gentleman?' Mr Baker seems to imply that the author was giving expression to some strange, forward-looking doctrine which he himself did not fully comprehend. Don't be deceived: the Reverend John Ball, the Bishop of Durham of his day, knew exactly what needed to be said and how his words would perform a special service whenever ignorant latter-day politicians might seek to suggest that ideas of socialist equality were not natural growths from English soil. The man of Kent knew what was right and feasible 500 years before Karl Marx was born.

Alas, our well-intentioned author does miss another opportunity here. With John Ball's blessed invocations still ringing in his ears and with all the proper attention he does give to the horrors of the Peasants' Revolt, why the omission – suppression might not be too strong a word – of much the most famous poem of Wat Tyler, the one by Robert Southey in which he showed what the root of all the trouble was? Yes, they called it by its proper name in those days: the simple heading, 'The Poets and the Poll Tax', would have made a nice section all on its own and might even have caught the eye of some of Mr Baker's least literate colleagues.

But again we must be fair. Quite often he does turn aside from the central theme of our rough island story, the defeat of Frenchmen and Dutchmen and Spaniards and such men, to see what was happening to some of the others – the Luddites, the African slave ships, the Peterloo demonstrators, the Chartists, the Tolpuddle martyrs (downright lawbreakers, every man Jack of them), the factory children. Indeed, do I properly detect a deliberate touch of irony when he chooses the bold, brass capitals: VICTORIANA? Immediately below we are offered, somewhat incongruously, a brilliant modern poem by Sylvia Townsend Warner on 'Mr Gradgrind's Country' in which little place is found for the 10 Downing Street interpretation of Victorian values. How I wish Mr Baker, in this rebellious mood, could have found space for the Idris Davies classic on this same theme.

> In gardens in the Rhondda
> The daffodils dance and shine
> When tired men trudge homeward
> From factory and mine
>
> The daffodils dance in gardens
> Behind the grim brown row
> Built among the slagheaps
> In a hurry long ago.
>
> They dance as though in passion
> To shame and to indict
> The brutes who built so basely
> In the long Victorian night.

But again we must adjust the balance. Too much royalty, too much pageantry, too much deference, did I say? Not so; not even in the year of the Armada celebrations and such-like triumphs of our once-numerous seamen and our once-nationalized dockyards. The same wide-eyed Mr Baker does not omit to mention that this 'teeming womb of royal kings' could somehow develop the extraordinary taste of falling in love with male favourites. Without a single Thatcherite hand raised in remonstrance, he recalls the escapades of Edward II with Piers Gaveston, of James I with his Somersets and Buckinghams, walking more warily when he comes to more modern times, with Dutch William and his ambiguous, unbecoming tastes. Has Mr Baker here fallen foul of Clause 28 or 29? Who will tell us, who knows?

Our intrepid author can hardly have been aware of all these hazards when he set out on his task. Indeed, the nearer to our present age, the more reckless he becomes. The prime ministers and their peccadilloes seem to have for him a peculiar fascination. Thus Asquith is dismissed in a George Robey couplet:

Mr Asquith says in a manner sweet and calm
Another little drink won't do us any harm.

Or a few others by Hilaire Belloc:

Of all the politicians I ever saw
The least significant was Bonar Law
Unless it was MacDonald, by the way
Or Baldwin – it's impossible to say.

Which brings me at last to the afore-promised masterpiece or mistresspiece, if you wish, which Mr Kenneth Baker included in an earlier anthology at the time when he was still a devoted follower of Mr Edward Heath.

The unforgettable lines which Mr Baker himself has somehow forgotten are of course by Robert Burns. Readers of the *Guardian* are advised to make two copies: one to paste into this most agreeable English history in verse and the other for despatch at a suitable date to Number 10:

Extempore Pinned to a Lady's Coach

If you rattle along like your mistress's tongue,
Your speed will outrival the dart;
But a fly for your load, you'll break down on the road,
If your stuff be as rotten's her heart.

Michael Foot
18 April 1988

Escape with an ape

This is a story of how a simple, kindly doctor suddenly and mysteriously sprouted hair all over his face and went round terrorizing people. This is a story of the lord of the primeval jungle; of Conan the barbarian; of the mad scientist; of the man who could tell all with his penetrating eye; of the urban superman and the thief in the night and the fiendish . . .

But we had better go back to the good doctor. He is at the centre – and at the wings – of a 26-year cycle of anniversaries which mark the creation of Nine Heroes or Worthies whose fame (for shame!) now eclipses that of the three Paynims, three Jews and three Christian men listed by Caxton in his preface to the *Morte d'Arthur*. (Can anyone name all of them? And who was Godfrey of Bouillon anyway?)

The simple kindly doctor sprouted hair all over his face exactly 75 years ago. No, it wasn't Dr Jekyll. That was 101 years ago. It was Dr Arthur Conan Doyle, who was so pleased with his latest creation, Professor Challenger, that he kept dressing up as him, pasting on a black beard and false eyebrows and saying ferocious things. One biographer, John Dickson Carr, says that Doyle enjoyed George Edward Challenger more than any other of his creations: he could make Challenger say or do things which social usage forbade, like bite his housekeeper on the leg to see if anything would upset her composure, or take a reporter by the seat of his pants and run him half a mile down the road.

Doyle actually posed as Professor Challenger for a photograph that the *Strand* magazine never used: he was delighted with his own zestful glowering ('the scowl of the Conans'). Later, so as not to waste the costume, he sped to the home of his brother-in-law, E. W. Hornung, claiming to be a friend of Herr Doktor Doyle, and harangued the creator of Raffles in German for several minutes, to be shown the door in disgrace.

Professor Challenger first appeared in print in 1912. In fact, Conan Doyle delivered the manuscript to the editor of the *Strand* in December 1911, saying 'My ambition is to do for the boy's book what Sherlock Holmes did for the detective tale. I don't suppose I could bring off two such coups. And yet I hope it may . . .'

Sadly, it didn't. *The Lost World* is one of Doyle's finest works; the imagery of even its title worked its way into the popular imagination to join Ruritania and (to a lesser

extent) the Blue Lagoon, Green Mansions and the Never-
land as features on the landscape of innocence. The book
had prehistoric monsters, ape-men, two arrogant batty abs-
ent-minded professors, the jungle and even a lord of it: Lord
John Roxton, sportsman, crack shot, traveller and cool
head. ('Our learned friends were just stirrin'. Hadn't even
begun to argue yet. Suddenly it rained apes. They came
down as thick as apples out of a tree . . .')

Alas, this superb story was ultimately to be eclipsed: that
same year, deep in the urban jungles of Chicago, an idea
stirred. 'This story business is all new to me but I like the
work provided I can make it pay,' wrote an ex-cavalryman
who managed the stenographic department of Sears,
Roebuck in 1911. He had, in fact, just sold a story about
adventures on Mars to a magazine, using the pseudonym
of Normal Bean. He too had just devised a jungle tale of
apes, two batty, absent minded savants and an English
lord. The two scholars were Professor Archimedes Q. Porter
and Mr Samuel T. Philander, but hardly anyone ever remembers them. They remember the lord, Lord Greystoke,
better known as Tarzan of the Apes.

It ought to be one of the great riddles of literary history:
how and why a tiny coterie of second-rank (or in some cases
third-, fourth- or fifth-rate) writers came to create, within
the space of one generation, nine figures who have achieved
mythic status – that is, who have become known the world
over, who have passed into popular speech ('Who do you
think you are? Sherlock Holmes?') and out of the hands of
their creators to occupy a space in the popular imagination
that credits them with a reality independent of a literary
origin.

Their position really is curious: Mrs Gamp is an unforgettable character, but you have to have read *Martin
Chuzzlewit* to be unable to forget her. You don't need to
read Bram Stoker – or even see a Peter Cushing movie –
to know who Dracula is.

The figures are in order of appearance, Jekyll-and-Hyde
(1886); Sherlock Holmes and Watson (1887); Svengali and
Trilby (1894); Dracula and van Helsing (1897); Raffles and

Bunny (1899); The Virginian and Trampas (1902); Peter Pan and Wendy (1904); the Scarlet Pimpernel (1905); and Tarzan, not forgetting Professor Archimedes Q. Porter's daughter Jane (1912).

Their creators, and men with whom they rubbed shoulders in the inns and cafés of late Victorian and Edwardian London (Edgar Rice Burroughs being the odd man out) also devised and perfected a number of forms and genres and creations of fiction which fall only just short of world domination. Rider Haggard devised She-Who-Must-Be-Obeyed; Oscar Wilde dreamed up the Portrait of Dorian Gray; H. G. Wells invented the Time Machine and, with it, I suppose, real science fiction, and H. de Vere Stacpoole came up with the idea that everything would be all right if only we lived naked and innocent upon a desert island with a Blue Lagoon. Jerome K. Jerome put three unforgettable men, to say nothing of the dog, in a boat. Kenneth Grahame rediscovered everybody's lost childhood messing about in boats with Ratty and Mole and Toad and Badger. George and Weedon Grossmith put Mr Pooter down on paper: the Nobody that lives forever.

In the same 26-year span a House of Commons clerk who worried about German military superiority and Irish independence (he was against one and for the other) perfected, in the same book, the spy story and the yachting novel: Erskine Childers's *The Riddle of the Sands* (1903) contains both a young espionage chappie called Carruthers and a mysterious boss back at the Foreign Office called simply M. The spy yarn was beaten, so to speak, to the draw by the Western (yes, even that came from the coterie – it was written by Henry James's nephew Owen Wister) in 1902. *The Virginian: A Horseman of the Plains* is a somewhat tedious book but on page 29 a hand lays a pistol on the card table and a voice 'that sounded almost like a caress, but drawling a very little more than usual' issues the immortal words 'When you call me that, *smile!*' and a star is born, not to mention a couple of feature films, an interminable television serial and a prototype who pops up in almost every film, novel and illustrated comic from

Zane Grey to Sergio Leone and back to the White House.

All these heroes, like their creators, were born in a world which was closing fast. Livingstone and Stanley and Mary Kingsley had marked out the real jungles: even the earliest of the progenitors could expect adventure only by courtesy of Thomas Cook. By 1900, life was ordered by the 8.15 from Surbiton. The first paper clip and the first hamburger were already on sale; it was possible to route a call through the first automatic telephone exchange; the secret agent could rely on his first Browning automatic; the politicians at the beginning of the Edwardian age had already begun to step delicately through the minefields of Islamic nationalism and Zionist aspiration (although for a few years Zion was to have been established in Uganda: O what an alternative history of the world there might have been!) and customs officials were already watching out for drug smugglers.

The world rumbled with dubious imperial adventures in Manchuria and South Africa and while Peter Pan was but an infant there were serious books on the arms race like *Germany and the Next War* and even *Why Modern Warfare is Impossible*. Winston Churchill was already Home Secretary and the thinking world had begun to divide into socialist and capitalist camps. There were indeed new frontiers, but pioneers like Freud and Einstein brought no comfort to any normal household. The cities were rich, but not safe: George Cadbury and others had to raise a subscription for the relief of famine not in Ethiopia but Canning Town and West Ham.

There was no radio, nor of course, television: there were only the magazines. *Pearson's, Pall Mall, Strand, Harper's, Windsor, Blackwood's, English Illustrated* ... the list is long. These magazines had, for the first time in history – indeed they existed because of it – a universally literate population. The 1870 Education Act provided the means of learning to read and write for everybody. By the time Shaw and Conrad and Chesterton and Arnold Bennett and Henry James (all of whom dealt with the magazines) were ready to write, a nation hungry for print as never before or since was in search of them. Quite possibly popular journalism was never so richly endowed with Good Writers. (And never more appreciated by the readership. When in 1899 Rudyard Kipling lay seriously ill with fever and Pope Leo XIII hovered near the point of death the *Pall Mall Gazette* simply splashed on its posters the words 'Kipling and Pope'.) But there are times when even Good Readers don't want Good Writing. They want escape. They got it.

The most intelligent of them understood this need. Blood-and-thunder literature, Chesterton pointed out vividly was 'as simple as the thunder of heaven and the blood of men'. It might, he conceded, be a very limited aim in morality to shoot 'a many-faced and fickle traitor' but it was a much better aim than to be one. Arnold Bennett, ever practical, examined the work of his contemporaries and set down, in *How To Be an Author* (1903) a sensible guide to writing 'sensational and other serials'. He wrote: 'Avoid all truthful subtlety of characterization and dialogue. Draw characters broadly. Make the heroines beautiful, the heroes brave, the villains villainous and the conversation terse and theatrical.'

And they did. Oddly, though, the cycle starts not with literary escapism but the inescapably literary. In 1885 Fanny Stevenson interrupted her husband in what she took to be a nightmare. 'I was dreaming a fine bogey tale,' complained the sickly RLS. In three days he had finished the story of Dr Jekyll and Mr Hyde. Mrs Stevenson, however, dismissed the manuscript as 'merely' a story – a magnificent bit of sensationalism which missed the allegory and therefore could not be a masterpiece. RLS burned the first version and in three days wrote the masterpiece we all know instead.

This may have been a pity: the world is not rich in sensational stories which are also magnificent, and master-pieces are not quite as much fun. Subsequent authors tried not to be too talented. Sherlock Holmes, for all the fuss the Baker Street Irregulars make about him, is the creation of a broad theatrical brush: an actor can play him as anything except fat and stupid. Bram Stoker's Dracula is magnifi-cently sensational – and as theatrical as you would expect from the pen of the manager of Sir Henry Irving. Stoker took care to make his heroines toothsome, but then he had a thing about people's teeth. He remarked upon Lord Tennyson's canine and he met the explorer Sir Richard Burton and descried within him the unborn visage of Christopher Lee: 'dark and forceful and masterful and ruthless. I have never seen so iron a countenance . . . as he spoke the upper lip rose and his canine tooth showed its full length like the gleam of a dagger.'

If George du Maurier had acted upon Arnold Bennett's advice ('incident must be evenly and generously distributed') people might today still read *Trilby*: even so, the word Svengali has entered the OED supplement and millions know him for one under whose mesmerizing, malevolent eye and hoarse, rasping voice ('we will make music for them to dance to! Boum! Boum!') yet another star is born. *Trilby*, like the source of Mrs Grundy and the Gay Lothario, is another example of the redundant book: a strong, provoking idea, a memorable name and the character takes wing.

Raffles took wing (he's in the OED too) because he provided a form of shorthand for headline-writers. Raffles is short for 'the short of chap you don't expect to go round breaking into people's houses and stealing from his own class, dash it!' He still pops up two or three times a year in the courts of England and Wales (and has been known to get the sympathy vote from the Bench, ever reluctant to send 'our sort' to the clink). Hornung's Raffles the amateur cracksman, in case anyone has forgotten, is of course a gentleman, an England cricketer, a social asset and a thief in the night. He conducts stylish robberies with great daring, usually with the help of his snivelling ex-schoolboy friend Bunny. 'Why settle down to some humdrum uncongenial billet when excitement, romance, danger and a decent living were all going begging together?' he explains, and he's not talking about keeping a straight bat in Faisalabad. 'Of course it's wrong, but we can't all be moralists.' Raffles has probably never been quite out of print and Radio 4 has been serializing him only this month.

He remains, alas, a gentleman who grows tiresome but not up.

But never to his friend Bunny, whose jaw always drops and whose mouth blubbers adoringly at the fiendish skill with which Raffles disguises himself. But then Holmes was fond of astounding Watson with his disguises. Baroness Orczy's Sir Percy Blakeney, the fop who leads a double life rescuing aristos from the tumbrils of the French Revolution (another anniversary approaching fast) actually manages to deceive his own wife by his metamorphoses.

At the heart of the appeal of these characters lies the capacity to astonish the companion – but never the reader. No, that would not do, for the reader derives his comfort from the assurance, the certainty that Dracula will be there the second they throw the garlic away, that the policeman who arrests Bunny will always be Raffles himself in disguise, that Tarzan will always spring from the trees with a keen blade in his hand and primeval anger in his throat; that van Helsing has a stake, as it were, in getting there in the nick of time. Somewhere in such stories, there is a place for the reader. They are for the most part the icons of triumph illuminating the dreams of failures. Just as the stories of Homer were told and retold and refashioned by the Homeridae, and the legends of Arthur and Charlemagne and Robin Hood underwent a hundred re-shapings from the balladeers until they lodged indelibly in the hearts of the trudging and the oppressed, so have the new myths arisen to nourish the daydreams of the prisoners of the 8.15.

Chesterton called the penny dreadfuls of his era the gaudy diaries of the soul. Edgar Rice Burroughs put it more simply. 'Tarzan was, in a sense, my escape from unpleasant reality. Perhaps this is the reason for his success with modern readers.' Not everybody can accept escapism for what it is. There are, notoriously, people who cannot accept that Sherlock Holmes is fiction, and if not fiction, then by now long dead anyway. The letters still arrive. But then two years after the publication of Doyle's *The Lost World*, the University of Pennsylvania Museum organized an

expedition up the Amazon. Oh yes, they were going in search
of the Lost World.

Tim Radford
24 December 1987

An eagle is lauded

It will come as some comfort to wets of all persuasions that,
while Mrs Thatcher was thumping her uncompromising
win, win and win again philosophy at the Brussels summit,
thousands of miles away across the Atlantic, an anti-hero
more in tune with changing times emerged. The man who
came last. If you were to add up the column inches in
newspapers around the world it is a fair bet that Eddie
Edwards, Mr Magoo on skis, would have swamped anything
the Prime Minister could have mustered. The 24-year-old
plasterer from Cheltenham, reared on the plastic ski slopes
of Gloucester (when his myopia permits him to see them),
brought up the rear with such style that the 46,000 crowd
watching the Winter Olympics embraced him as their own.
Someone called Matti Nykonen hardly got a look in. He
made the mistake of coming first.

It wasn't just that Eddie the Eagle's reputation had
preceded him to Calgary: the way he has to ask passers-by
whether there is anything in front of him because he can't
see; the night he slept in a mental hospital to cut his costs;
the time he broke his neck, tied a scarf round it and carried
on. They all know the problems of our health service over
there. What they liked was a rare example of true grit from
a country where the snow usually comes unfrozen; a more
honest reflection of the spirit of the Olympics than the 57
forgotten competitors ahead of him who jumped further,
much further, than he did.

The Canadian papers are full of Eddie. In Calgary the
local journal has a daily column featuring 'Eddie the Eagle'.
People thrust money into his hands at airports. His

sweetheart, whom he – literally – bumped into on the plastic slopes back home, is flying out this weekend. She declares: 'He's not nuts. He's my hero and I love him.' Even the French, forgetting little local difficulties about agricultural surpluses, have risen to the occasion. A full page spread in *Liberation* lionizes '*le Benny Hill du ski*' with the manner of Stan Laurel. The article notes that, having roared down the precipitous approach run and soared seemingly into eternity, Eddie sometimes can't see where he is supposed to land and has to guess when to put his feet down. He also confessed to them: '*J'ai en horreur toutes les sortes de vent. Particulièrement celui qui souffle de derrière.*'

But hold your praise. Fast Eddie, the devouring eyes of the world's media upon him, has still to prove himself in the Big One. So far it has just been 70 metres. At the weekend the 90-metre jump begins. That will really separate the men from the boys. As Britain holds its collective breath, the unthinkable is already being thought about. He might not make it. It is at least possible that he will not come last again. The advice now can only be crude and to the point. Don't blow it, Eddie. History can be very hard on penultimates.

Leader
17 February 1988

I spy: the *Petersaga*

As the light faded and all around the court eyes glanced up at the hands edging towards four, Lord Donaldson suddenly jerked his head. 'Just a minute,' he demanded: 'How come this is the third time round?'

Mr Robert Alexander QC drew breath and began. Long ago, in misted history, there was an appeal against the judgment of Mr Justice Millett. Then there was a leave of appeal granted to the House of Lords, as well as an appeal against an interlocutory injunction. Which was before the separate contempt action and the discharge of the injunction upheld by the Court of Appeal in July 1986, which in turn . . .

'Yes, I remember,' said Lord Donaldson. 'I ought to have remembered. I suddenly became puzzled.'

Sagas are like that. In the tradition of the great Norse sagas – *Egilssaga, Crislasaga, Grettissaga* – we were witnesses to *Petersaga*, a story of intrigue and drama about an old man in a faraway land which has been told time and time again all over the world.

Like the great sagas, the story has been written down, but lives on – in this country at least – in its oral form. Like the great sagas, the origins of the legend have been all but forgotten.

Like the great sagas, this one is immensely long – 14 volumes of legal documents so far. Like the great sagas, there are frequent disputes about authorship and whether or not the story is true.

Mr Alexander is a relative newcomer to this legend. 'I have only been involved in this saga for some little time,' he apologized yesterday. 'Some of this is very old history.'

Lord Donaldson, also a comparative new boy, complained: 'This whole case is very difficult. It is all *very* difficult, isn't it?' Finally, his patience snapped. Arguing the rights of the saga's hero and checking with Mr Alexander whether what he said was right, he exclaimed: 'I wish to goodness the man had a different name from Wright.'

The meaning of the rites at the Appeal Court yesterday is best left to lawyers or Norse folklorists. The difficulty the learned judges were having became apparent as they fumbled for analogies for the story, which Lord Donaldson admitted he, for one, had not read.

'What happens if one assumes – and this is totally fanciful – Mr Wright were to mount a sufficiently powerful radio transmitter and get everyone in the country assembled around their radios so that everyone was given the information in Mr Wright's confidence?' asked Lord Donaldson.

'A bit like Radio Luxembourg,' suggested Lord Justice Dillon.

'One could go back to Lord Haw-Haw,' chipped in Mr Alexander.

'I'm not sure he had any confidential information, did he?' inquired Lord Donaldson, then returned to his point. If Mr Wright did broadcast to the entire country in this fashion then everyone would have received that information in confidence. 'Does it follow that no one could discuss it with anyone else?' he asked.

Mr Alexander thought for a moment and said it did.

Lord Donaldson pondered further and thought it would be all right, 'or a very minimal wrong', to tell one's wife. A wife was one thing, said Mr Alexander. Telling a newspaper was 'vastly different'.

Lord Justice Dillon joined in. 'Any ordinary person who is hearing these allegations is not in contempt of court discussing them with his wife or over dinner.' An alarming thought struck Lord Donaldson. 'It would be if you held a dinner party for four million people.'

Lord Justice Dillon agreed. 'Or a dinner party with only members of parliament.'

What, asked Lord Donaldson, if Mr Wright were to reveal his information at Speakers' Corner? Could someone watching him go home and tell his mate what Wright had been on about? Could a newspaper editor also stand at Speakers' Corner handing out newspaper reports of what Mr Wright was saying?

On these and other questions we will have to await their Lordships' ruling. Copies of the original saga lay in front of them, for the most part untouched.

Lord Donaldson characterized the proceedings as a 'whole hog case'. He said to the newspapers' lawyer, Charles Gray QC: 'You have been going the whole hog. The Attorney-General has been going the whole hog. And the little intermediate hogs have got crushed.'

The Saga continues.

Alan Rusbridger
19 January 1988

Stoppard's secret agent

Tom Stoppard recalls that during the run of *Rosencrantz and Guildenstern are Dead* on Broadway a woman rushed up to him outside the theatre and asked if he was the author of the play. With becoming modesty he said, 'Yes'. 'Well,' she said, 'I want you to know that it's the worst play I ever saw in my life.'

Nothing like that has happened to Stoppard outside the Aldwych since the opening of *Hapgood*. All the same, Stoppard, 36 hours after the first night, seems ruefully pensive. He envies the breezy *élan* of Cole Porter who, just before his own Broadway premières, used to set off on a world cruise. In contrast, Stoppard is still fine-tuning the text of *Hapgood* and seems less than gruntled at the tone of some of the reviews.

'The play,' he says, 'has been written about as though it were incomprehensibly baffling. It doesn't seem to me to be borne out by experience. After all these years one thing you learn is what's going on in an audience and by God you know when you're losing them. It's like getting a temperature: you can't miss it. My impression is that your ordinary punter has less trouble with it than some of our critics.

'But critical response is like a branch of natural history. It's a cycle as inevitable as that of the sea anemone. It's nice to be discovered as a bright young man but then the playwright gets older and the critic becomes the bright young man who's not going to be taken in. It's nothing to complain about. But the truth is you get over-praised when you're young and sandbagged a bit when you're older.'

Hapgood, on reflection, strikes me as taxing but penetrable: an engrossing theatrical equivalent of David Mamet's *House of Games*. The problem is we are so used to up-front, single-issue plays we tend to get thrown by a multi-layered, hydra-headed animal like *Hapgood*. I counted half a dozen issues whirling through it. Was it finally saying that if the laws of quantum physics are not susceptible of proof, then everything else is treacherously uncertain?

'No,' says Stoppard. 'That's too sweeping. If there's a central idea it is the proposition that in each of our characters – yours and mine are doubtless exceptions – the person who gets up in the morning and puts on the clothes is the working majority of a dual personality, part of which is always there in a submerged state. That doesn't seem to me a profound or original idea but I still find it interesting.

'The play is specifically about a woman – Hapgood – who is one person in the morning but who finds that, under certain pressures, there is a little anarchist upsetting the apple-cart. The central idea is that inside Hapgood One there is a Hapgood Two sharing the same body; and that goes for most of us.'

In that case who is Stoppard Two? Who is the sleeper lurking inside the genial, ironic, surprisingly boyish 51-year-old playwright, expensively accoutred in a brown suede overcoat and, give or take the overnight reviews, pretty much at ease with the world?

A pause.

'I haven't considered revealing my other side to more than one person at a time. But I suspect the genial interviewee is a sort of cover. I do have periods when I'm extremely cross with life. My metabolism is much higher than it ought to be for a professional playwright and, as I get close to a first night, I try to do 18 things an hour. If you go on like that, you blow the circuits. I am a very emotional person. People wish to perceive me as someone who works out ideas in a cool, dispassionate way but I don't think that's my personality at all.'

Stoppard's double identity, even as a playwright, is territory that has been too little explored. His plays, from *Rosencrantz and Guildenstern* to *Hapgood*, have been analysed as if they were intellectual conceits: I suspect they only work because of their emotional ground-base.

That first play is anchored in what John Wood once called the 'bravery' of those two attendant lords whistling in the Elsinore dark. In *Jumpers* – more in the Aldwych revival than the original Old Vic production – you felt the pain of a marriage audibly splintering. In *The Real Thing* – more in the New York than the London version – you were aware of the torturing self-abasement that stems from the knowledge of infidelity. Stoppard reveals that his regular director, Peter Wood, is always on at him to up the emotional ante.

'Imagine,' says Stoppard, 'I write a play about astronomy because I've got all these fascinating things to say about Neptune and Ursa Major and that I also feature a married couple. Peter will say these people are married and can we take their relationship out of the fridge. He always bullies me and says I am stingy about this side of things.

'For instance, there's a scene in *Jumpers* where George recalls the first day Dotty walked into his class and, because her hair was wet, he called her 'the hyacinth girl'. These lines give the play emotional leverage and make it a play about marriage rather than moral philosophy.

'Peter tries to get me to put a hyacinth girl into every play including *Hapgood*. I always think I've done it and he says I haven't. Peter is an advocate for the audience and tries to make the plays work for an imaginary spectator called Rupert who he believes was the bear of little brain. It's no good my telling him that was actually Pooh.'

Stoppard, I would claim, has a dual political as well as emotional identity. On the one hand there is the Stoppard who regretfully says, 'We live in an age where the leper is the don't-know.' On the other hand, there is the Stoppard of *Professional Foul* and *Every Good Boy Deserves Favour* who has taken a clear stand on the question of human rights in the Eastern bloc. But even now Stoppard is wary of being dubbed a committed playwright.

'With Eastern Europe I don't feel I am carrying some kind of torch for the causes that might crop up in this or that play, because what I do – which is write plays – is something whose problems are empirical. With *Professional*

Foul, I didn't sit down to sound off about human rights. It happened to be Prisoner of Conscience Year in 1977 and Amnesty asked if I could write a play to mark the event. Well I obviously couldn't do a play about a couple who go *Come Dancing* in Prague. What happens is you sit down in a practical, level-headed way and you end up with *Professional Foul*.

'If you're writing plays or painting pictures, whatever your public postures, what you're trying to do is write a good play or paint a good picture. I still believe that if your aim is to change the world journalism is a more immediate, short-term weapon. But art is important in the long term in that it lays down some kind of matrix of moral responsibility. It's on that one pins one's hopes of the thing lasting. I mean can you think of a play that has helped to change anything?'

I suggest that *The Normal Heart* did an effective job of raising consciousness about AIDS.

'Fair enough. But will it last as long as *Ghosts* which hardly even mentions directly the subject of a transmitted sexual disease? My point is that plays work through metaphor. In the end the best play about Vietnam will probably turn out to have been written by Sophocles.'

If there is a moral touchstone in Stoppard's work it is probably to be found in children: the boy Sacha in *Professional Foul*, the son in *Hapgood*, and now the 11-year-old hero of the film *Empire of the Sun*, directed by Steven Spielberg, which Stoppard has adapted from the J. G. Ballard novel about a boy surviving the 1941 Japanese invasion of Shanghai. Why this enduring faith in children?

'It's to do with their innocence which isn't something they acquire but which is something they haven't lost. I do have an idea which crops up all the time which is that children are very wise because they don't know how to be taken in. You can fool people if they are very clever but it's quite hard to fool a child. I think children start off with a sense of natural justice which is obscured through a process of corrupting sophistication.'

But although *Empire of the Sun* endorses the idea of the

moral wisdom and survival capacity of children, Stoppard does not see it as essentially a writer's film.

'It was a happy experience but on a film like that the writer is there to serve the director who himself is serving the narrative. It's nothing like the theatre which is the other way round. I didn't write *Empire of the Sun*. J. G. Ballard did. It's not supposed to be Stoppardian. But the cinema is a wonderfully madcap world in that you're writing 18 months before a camera turns and so the whole thing is quite leisurely. Then when they are shooting you get a phone call from Seville at eight in the evening asking for a new speech to be shot at seven the following morning.

'What I acually wrote was more modest than the film turns out to be. When I started, it wasn't a Spielberg film and I was a little wary of putting in World War Two aeroplanes flying about and shooting at each other. In the event there were Mustangs and Zeros flying around the south of Seville and it was highly exciting. But writing for the movies is a technical challenge. If I had tried to express my personality and favourite leanings it is doubtful if Steven would have shot it or that it would have been in the finished film.'

Stoppard actually seems to enjoy the nuts-and-bolts side of writing as much as the high-flying ideas. This week, for instance, he has inserted four speeches into *Hapgood* because he knew something was missing: the precise point at which the heroine moves from entrapment to warning and realizes that the technical traitor is also the person most anxious to help her son. Stoppard the brain-box is also the practical mechanic.

But that is just another symptom of Stoppard's double identity. He is the intellectual firecracker who writes about emotional havoc. The apostle of non-commitment whose stand on human rights is unequivocal. The thriving playwright (and ex-hack) still gnawed by thoughts of the public prints. The wordsmith who admires Ayckbourn because 'I have a predilection for plays that don't depend on lines you can quote.'

If he were not Tom Stoppard, who would he like to be? 'Someone who sings or plays a musical instrument well. It causes me intense grief that I can't do it or even tell good from bad. I'm not talking about being Placido Domingo. I'd just be happy to be someone who plays piano in a pub.'

As we finish talking we make our way down Carnaby Street with its extraordinary hungover sixties aroma. 'I feel it should be in the V and A rather than out here,' says Stoppard. As he sets off in a taxi to do a television interview, his parting shot is that he can't wait to get the Sunday reviews over and done with as if he were a tyro playwright undergoing ordeal by criticism. I feel as if I've had a sudden, touching glimpse of Stoppard Two: the anxious, self-doubting Thomas that still lurks under the poised, equable figure of the success-wreathed, acclaimed public playwright.

Michael Billington
18 March 1988

Letters: Changing the *Guardian*

It's lovely. It's clear, modern and readable. The same quality reporting in a readable format. Only one criticism, though. Could we have the spelling mistakes back? I believe in modernization but the *Guardian* is not the *Guardian* without the mistakes.

Simon Manchip
Southampton

When I was a young girl I was fortunate enough to get to know Arnold Bennett. He gave me much good advice, part of which was that I must always read the *Manchester Guardian* – that was in 1916 and here I still am, doing as I was told. I think I must be amongst your longest established readers – I am now in my ninety-second year.

As a life-long member of the Labour Party, I am, of course, intensely conservative. But you might have done much worse. On the whole there is not much to complain about.

Janet Marston
St Albans, Herts

Got the comic. Where's the newspaper?

Patricia MacLeod
Fife

15 February 1988

Taming the Angry Bird

Lashed to ice screws on the tiny ledge we had hacked from the face with our axes, Lindsay and I were shivering. The snow poured down the mountain like a mighty river, a torrent of cold, suffocating, endless, piling up inches thick on every non-vertical suface.

Invisible through the cloud, inaudible from the wind, 150 feet above us at the other end of the ropes, Victor, Doug, and Sharu were making the crucial decision of the *Guardian* expedition to Bhutan.

It was two o'clock in the afternoon on the fifth day of our attempt on the summit of Jitchu Drake, which had never been climbed, and we had been on the face for nine hours, three of them in the storm, climbing from camp two at the top of the glacial shelf to a longed-for, unknown bivouac above.

If we began to retreat, abseiling back to our camp of the past two nights, we had just enough time to get down before nightfall. In the Alps, none of us would have climbed on in such conditions. In a Scottish winter, one would probably go on: but then there would be an easy way off, a cheery pub, a warm bed.

Victor was for descending, but to do so, as Doug pointed out, meant almost certain failure. We would have to abandon most of our precious stock of ice screws to fix the abseil ropes and would be left with insufficient to return. In our waterproof jackets and dungarees, he went on, we were still just on the right side of hypothermia, and if we carried on climbing diagonally to the right, we must in the end hit the south-east ridge, where at some point above, the Japanese expedition of 1984 had found an adequate campsite.

At last it was Sharu who provided the necessary impetus. 'We've come so far. We can't turn back now.' 'As the only woman,' Doug said later, 'her determination was enough.'

Jitchu Drake wasn't giving up easily. Two days earlier, climbing from camp one, established during an exploratory foray the previous week, we had become lost amid a bewildering maze of crevasses. We were forced to pitch our tents where we stood, in what seemed to be a spot safe from avalanche, without a clue where we were.

Only next day, during the clear weather of early morning, could we see that somehow we had ended up directly below the line of the next portion of our intended route, the 55-degree ice of the south face.

The following morning we were supposed to 'go for it'. It was a disturbed night, punctuated by Victor's perambulations to check the weather. At 3 a.m. it was clear, the face glinting in the almost full moonlight. We left at seven, climbing four 'pitches' or rope lengths before the massing clouds in the valleys far below brought warning of the inevitable late morning storm.

That day we retreated, leaving our four ropes in place to speed progress on the morrow. 'Basically we've got to write off the afternoons,' Doug said that evening, 'they just don't exist for climbing.' The pattern seemed set: after a few hours of clarity and intense heat from the reflected sun on the ice, the cloud would surround us from 11 o'clock, to be followed within minutes by gales, hail and snowfall, intensified on the face by the phenomenon of 'spindrift' –

the constant cascade of new snow slipping downward from the slopes above.

Now, as Sharu brought resolution of the team's dilemma, the pink rope went tight on Lindsay. He moved off, a lanky beetle in a blue nylon shell, crawling his way towards the next boot-sized resting place with the sharp points of his crampons and ice axes. After 30 feet, he too was invisible.

At last, the red rope was taken in and came tight on me: my turn. As fast as I tried to clear the snow from the ice screws in order to remove them, they were buried again by the spindrift. I had to take off my gloves, fingers sticking to the freezing metal.

I cranked the screws out with the blade of an axe and climbed, isolated in space by the mist and wind, blindly following the line of the rope, panting with the altitude – now well over 20,000 feet – and sheer fear.

There was still a long, long way to go. At dusk, Lindsay and I found ourselves tied to yet another pair of ice screws on yet another tiny ledge, utterly miserable, when a lull in the wind brought down a shout from Victor, two pitches above: 'I've reached the ridge.' Hope flared: bed and a brew might not be far beyond. We had not eaten nor drunk since 2 a.m., 17 hours before.

It was another two hours before I too, last man on the rope, reached the ridge. The moon was beginning to shine fitfully through the clearing storm: a good thing too since I had just dislodged my head torch and watched it plummet to the bottom of the face, while there was still a further double rope length of 300 feet to climb along the ridge.

But up there, torches bobbed merrily: surely home at last. A few feet below Victor, who stood taking in the rope, I rested one last time, beyond exhaustion. I pulled over the top. There was a ledge about the size of a single bed on which Doug had pitched a two-man tent. Above, a wall of snow where Lindsay crouched in a little hole. 'Our only hope,' he said, 'is to enlarge this cave.'

After two hours hacking, there was just room to lie down. At each end of the cave, entrances opened directly onto the great precipes of the south and east faces. That we could cope with, by tying ourselves to ice screws driven in the wall. The through draught was less pleasant. With each gust, loose particles of snow and ice blew down our necks. Round midnight, we crept into sleeping bags, too tired to make tea.

Morning brought slow rehydration and bowls of rejuvenating muesli. Somehow, Doug and Victor found the energy to climb a few pitches, returning at lunchtime to announce that they had found the bivouac site used by the Japanese, not far beyond along generally easy ground. We packed and left.

Our new campsite, camp four, lay at about 21,500 feet, below a short vertical step of rock and hard green ice. There was no flat ground, but a steep bank of soft snow was easily dug to make platforms for the tents. Doug chose a spot about 30 feet below the step. Unwisely, Lindsay, Victor and I excavated our ledge next to it. That night we had the worst storm of all. The spindrift poured into the gap between the vertical step and the tent, creating great bulges that took up half the tent and threatened to send it and us spinning down the south face below.

We were up half the night, digging away the snow or trying vainly to sleep, squashed by the bulges.

The three of us heartily cursed Bhutan and its weather. Unknown to us, earlier that day, our base-camp manager Karma Tenzing had hiked up to advance base at 16,000 feet and held a Buddhist puja for our safety and for an end to the storms. There could be no question of a summit bid next morning, 30 May, although Doug had tried to interest Victor in the idea sometime after midnight. But the next day dawned more promisingly than for more than a fortnight. There were only exiguous wisps of cloud in the valley bottoms, and the storm, when it arrived at its usual time, was markedly reduced in its ferocity. For the first time in days, we began seriously to think of reaching Jitchu Drake's summit.

For me, it was a day of agonizing decision-making. Doug, Victor, and Sharu used the morning to fix three rope lengths beyond the bivouac: they, at least, would certainly be in the summit team. As I dug a new and lower platform for the tent, I fretted endlessly over whether I should join them.

Lindsay had barely slept for three nights, and while he protested that he lacked nothing but a good kip, he was far from well. He hardly spoke, and had almost stopped eating – a fact that made him covertly popular, at least with me, since our rations were clearly going to have to stretch to double their intended three-day span. He suffered from severe headaches, despite taking a variety of pain-killers. There were strong reasons to suggest that he should not be left alone.

Doug and Victor were obviously going to be the lead climbers in the 1500 feet of steep ice remaining. Like Sharu, I knew I would be capable of following them on a rope. But as our ordeal on the ice face had shown all too clearly, the greater the number, the slower we moved. If the weather cleared – for the first time since we had begun – it was possible that four might reach the summit. But it was more likely that my presence might jeopardize the team's success, or worse. With a heavy heart, I decided to stay behind.

The evening was still and clear. After going to bed about seven, the only climbing expedition leader in the world without a watch kept waking up with excitement to yell across the narrow gap between the tents to ask what the time was. At midnight, Victor, Doug, and Sharu began to get up.

Victor made do with a pint of warm water and a grain bar: Doug and Sharu managed to make tea. Doug's lips and fingers were sore, 'but when I saw how good it was outside, all the aches and pains of the past days began to go away'.

Karma's prayers had worked. For the first time since our arrival in Bhutan nearly six weeks before, there was no cloud at all in the valleys, nothing to build up later in the day into a storm. As Lindsay and I bade the team farewell at 2.30 a.m., we believed they might make it.

They were travelling light: just spare gloves, torches, batteries and a bit of food. Victor had argued that rather than carry water bottles, they should take a stove and pan and brew tea: lighter and more refreshing. At the top of the fourth pitch, one rope length beyond their highpoint of the day before, Doug realized he had forgotten the pot. This would be a summit bid without drink.

As they climbed, odd traces of fixed rope left by the Japanese expedition of 1984 appeared under the ice.

They had reached Jitchu Drake's south summit, but had been unable to make the traverse to the main north peak, some 300 feet higher. Doug found the last shred of Japanese fixed rope just eight feet below the south summit.

High on the ridge, conditions worsened underfoot. Firm ice was replaced by loose, aerated snow. In places, holes appeared in the ridge up to 12 feet from its crest, and through them, the team gazed down the 4000 feet of the east face. 'It was nice,' Victor said, 'to have three on the rope: if one fell through, the chances were that the others could hold the fall.'

They reached the south summit at 10.30. After so long on the south side of the mountain, the view suddenly changed: Tibet, brown and flat, like Saudi Arabia, a high altitude desert, level with the very tops of the rolling Bhutanese hills between the mountains. The spine of the Himalaya on either side of Jitchu Drake seemed impossibly thin, a single great divide: the snow line on the northern side far above that on the south. Not far from Jitchu Drake were three finger lakes, the source of an illicit trade in dried fish with Bhutan, and beyond, a vast inland sea.

Below and left was the south-west ridge of Jitchu Drake, tried by teams from Austria and Italy, where two Italians had died – the other wing of Jitchu Drake's 'angry bird', the meaning of the mountain's name in the language of Bhutan.

For once, its anger was stilled. 'There were a few clouds around but they didn't strike fear into your heart,' Doug said. Descending 100 feet from the south summit, they made their way along the 900 feet of ridge joining it with the north peak, traversing by the side of huge, billowing rolls of snow. All the time, the panorama grew: beyond the northern peaks of Bhutan, the easternmost extremities of the Himalaya, the forbidden area of strife-torn Arunachal

Pradesh on the Indian north-east frontier; and finally there was the 25,000-foot Namche Barwa, the highest unclimbed mountain in the world, its base lost in tropical forest where the Tsangpo bends from Tibet to become the Brahmaputra.

As they climbed, Karma was again at work. He had sent Sonam and Passang, two of his staff, to the ridge above advance base with a pair of binoculars. Shortly before noon, they saw Sharu, Doug and Victor reach the summit. 'We stopped about two feet from the very top in deference to the gods,' said Doug. 'In the snow just below, we carved the holy mantra with our ice axes, *om mane padme hum.*'

All felt a mixture of elation and worry. Victor said: 'My thoughts almost immediately were with my loved ones. I was very keen to get down, and I knew how far it was: we'd dug ourselves into a sort of hole by getting there. There's almost nothing more frightening than being on the top of a big peak.' Most climbing accidents occur during the descent: 'If all you can think of is being back in base camp,' said Doug, 'you've lost it.'

Without food or drink for many hours, their exhaustion was palpable. The descent of the ridge involved a long and difficult series of diagonal abseils. But shortly before dusk, at about 6.30, Lindsay and I – who had spent the day making coffee, restoring Lindsay's health entirely – heard their approach as the summit trio dislodged material on to our tent from the slopes above.

The elation and worry continued into the night. Supper was a few noodles in a thin soup squeezed from a tube: we had a handful of muesli for morning, some glucose tablets, then nothing. If the normal weather pattern were to return, descent would become a nightmare.

But the weather held. On the ridge between camps four and three, which we had climbed in enveloping cloud, Lindsay and I too had our view of Tibet, marvelling at its limpid light.

The descent of the ice face, which we had all dreaded, proceeded effortlessly. At the end of each abseil, Doug found perfect ice screw placements for the next 150 feet, and for 12 consecutive rope lengths we slid down towards the glacier plateau and camp two, pulling the doubled ropes down behind us.

We had left food at camp two and enjoyed a lunch of wild gaiety, tossing what was left into a crevasse, imagining future archaeologists discovering our leftovers at the glacier's snout in about a thousand years' time. Beyond, we saw something we had never seen before: the dark greens and purples of the Bhutanese foothills in afternoon sunlight, and behind, the south face of Jitchu Drake lit up like clotted cream: in six weeks in Bhutan, we had never seen a sunset.

A last tricky snowslope: then we were on the dry scree before advance base. Before we left for base camp and egg and chips, making a descent of nearly 8,000 feet in a single day, we shook hands on it. There was a bottle of malt whisky. The toast was: 'Happy endings.'

Next day the storms were back.

David Rose
10 June 1988

Under the clouds

Glasnost, whether or not it will ever reach these shores, has reached back 20 years in an attempt to explain the deaths of Yurii Gagarin and his co-pilot Vladimir Seregin, whose MIG-15 dived out of low cloud into the ground during an approach to landing.

Yurii, first man in space, had taken the US by storm in a triumphal tour and his banter, good humour and modesty convinced a space-struck US that maybe the Russians were human after all. This gift for getting on with folk in the West did not please all strata in the Soviet hierarchy at that stage of the Cold War. In any case, Yurii was fond of the vodka just like most of the service pilots I recall from the rather earlier days of the hot war. When Yurii crashed the pundits concentrated on his state of mind, the possibility of political pressures and a few snide references to booze.

It had always seemed odd to me that (unless the sandbaggers were around) any competent pilot should simply dive out of low cloud into the ground, booze or no booze, and even odder that a warm chap like Gagarin should do something like that deliberately and take one of his mates with him. Which is why the latest analysis of events during the final few moments of that fatal flight are very interesting.

Yurii was making his approach from between two cloud layers and had been told that the base height of the lower layer was 900 metres. This was correct in general for the region of airspace served by Gagarin's control, but it was seriously wrong for the immediate region of the airfield. There, we now learn, the cloud base was less than 500 metres. On a normal approach this would hardly matter. He would simply break cloud rather later than expected and carry on to make a normal visual final approach and landing.

But before this final approach Yurii was struck by something unexpected.

I happen to know about these things because something like it once happened to me. Sounds a bit like Pilot Officer Prune ('Ever been inverted in cloud, old boy? Why only the other day . . .'). Nor was it, thank goodness or the benign gremlins, on a final approach. But it seems relevant that once, in the dim and distant past and in a rather larger than usual formation of clapped-out Spits absurdly celebrating victory over a beautiful Austrian valley in which the airfield and village of Zeltweg huddled quietly, disaster stalked.

We were 15 aircraft, formatting fairly closely and practising changing from a V to an arrow formation. I was one of the outer four aircraft of the V which had to move inward to form the arrow shaft. Down a few feet, across and up again, neat and quick.

We were getting quite slick at it. Until, that is, local turbulence and a formation wave struck at the instant of change. After a few moments of amazing wrestling in the close slipstreams of two or three aircraft, I and another went down like rocks in high-speed stalls that needed the best part of 1000 feet to rectify. Fortunately we had the height.

A casual in-house inquiry never wholeheartedly believed that such an event was possible. Booze, they said: plain old finger trouble. A bit bruising, that.

The latest assessment of Yurii's final flight eases the sting. It is now revealed that, as his MIG-15 was descending into the lower cloud layer, a much larger aircraft – a MIG-21 jet – which had come down through the upper cloud layer, passed over the top of Yurii and crossed down through his flight path only a short distance ahead. He did not even see the MIG-15.

Yurii, just entering the lower cloud, would have hit a jetstream wall of turbulence that would have knocked him temporarily for six. Knowing that he had 900 metres of clear air below cloud and with instruments tumbling, he would have held a dive on airspeed and altimeter ready to pull out when he saw the ground. But when he broke cloud, probably at Mach point eight or more and nearly vertical, he would have had less than 500 metres to go.

It takes a second or so, emerging from cloud, to assess height from visual clues especially if it is hazy as seems to have been the case. Yurii had neither the time nor the height. Like many others, when luck runs out, he just went straight in.

This explanation is believable. The odd thing is that it has taken 20 years to emerge. The original inquiry, they say, contained no expert group able to assemble the facts that had been unravelled by separate working groups. It may be easy to ask why not: but thinking back to Zeltweg, expert groups can be pretty cynical when they think that someone has carelessly spoiled their image.

Anthony Tucker
30 January 1988

Down in Cardboard City

Cold and hunger. These are the two predominant feelings when you're homeless on the streets of London. I know because I've been there.

Desperation, wondering where it will all end, doesn't come into it very often, because most of your time is taken up with the problems of day-to-day survival – where you will get your next cup of tea (never mind your next meal – you're lucky to get one or two of those a week) and whether or not you'll be able to get into one of the overcrowded day centres to get warm and maybe even have a shower.

There still exists in London the myth of the intentionally homeless. But while the people who dwell in cardboard boxes under the arches by the Embankment or in the Royal Festival Hall car parks may appear defiant to outsiders and may reject what they perceive as often patronizing offers of help, this is largely because they are a proud breed, who want desperately to stand on their own two feet.

None of them wants to be there. Few are drug addicts or drunks. Most are normal human beings, looking for shelter and food, who have slipped through the net of the social security system. If they appear belligerent or confused, dirty or hungry, it is only the result of living on the streets. They don't live on the streets because they're crazy, they are crazy because they live on the streets. These are not people who have rejected society, they are people whom society has rejected.

Keith shares a cardboard box near the Festival Hall with his friend Barry. Keith has been out of work for almost four years; Barry for two. They came to London, where they met, to look for work. It is a common story.

They soon discovered that London is not the Utopia it's cracked up to be. There may be more jobs, but there are also more people looking for them. And there is a definite lack of housing. One of the major obstacles in trying to find a place to live is that most landlords demand a hefty deposit – two months' rent in most cases. If you haven't got a job, or if you're making £2.00 an hour doing casual work in a restaurant, it's almost impossible to get that much money together at one time. Because these people come from out of town, local councils refuse to take responsibility to house them. They are what the government refers to as the 'intentionally homeless'.

But the only reason they became homeless was because they were jobless. And that is where the vicious cycle begins. You can't find a job because you haven't got a home. You can't get a home because you haven't got a job. Government ministers urge the unemployed to 'get on their bikes' and look for work, but when they do, the harsh reality is life on the streets. As Keith says: 'There are four classes in Britain today – upper class, middle class, working class and unemployed.'

Nevertheless, once you've arrived in London, you make the best of what you've got – often a cardboard box and a woollen blanket. If you're lucky, you might have a sleeping-bag.

There is a sense of community among the inhabitants of the Festival Hall car park, and they are suspicious of outsiders. Their community was disrupted when the people from under the arches were moved along by developers.

'The drunks are the ones who fight,' says Keith, who has been there off and on for two years. 'But as long as you keep out of their way, you're OK. The others don't fight among themselves. It's much nicer up here than it was on the Embankment. The drunks would be fighting all night over a bottle, and the trains are going back and forth all night. Here, at least you get a bit of peace and quiet.'

Sitting near the Festival Hall at four in the morning, you can see what he means. You can hear the blackbirds singing, and Big Ben counts the hours. There is a tea van that comes around at 11 at night, and another at one in the morning. If you have 20p you can get a cup of coffee at the kiosk outside Waterloo station, and if you have 10p more you can enjoy the warmth of the station's indoor toilets for a few minutes. But you can't stay there very long. As another Festival Hall resident warned me: 'If you stay in here too long, the police tell you, "You can't stay here, sonny," and you have to leave.'

There is a strong code of ethics in the homeless community. You don't take what isn't yours, no matter how long it is left unguarded. A newcomer made the mistake of taking another's piece of cardboard in an attempt to shield himself from the wind. He was told, politely but in no uncertain terms, to put it back immediately. The others laughed. 'Stealing someone's bed already!'

Recent research by Centrepoint Soho, a night shelter for people under the age of 19, indicates that there are 50,000 young homeless people in London. The centre has beds for 32 people a night, but it is taking in 34. Countless others, turned away from the capital's few night shelters because of lack of room, are left with no choice but to sleep rough.

One such person is Bruce, a 23-year-old labourer who came to London two years ago to look for work. He has managed to get casual work here and there, but he hasn't found anywhere to live. He recently injured his feet in a building site accident, and the bridge of one foot has collapsed. The pain was so bad that he had to cut the tops off his boots. One morning it was so severe he couldn't walk. When he went to hospital, he was told to see his doctor. Because he was homeless, he wasn't registered with a GP. He didn't know where to turn.

He tries to find work every day, but it's difficult without a home, without a phone, without clean clothes to go to job interviews in, without an address to give potential employers, without being able to have a shower and shave beforehand, without the benefit of breakfast (or lunch, or dinner), and in Bruce's case, with the additional problem of holes in his boots – without which he would be effectively crippled.

There is sometimes casual labouring work for one or two days a week, but as Bruce said: 'Sometimes when I look for work, it just isn't there.' It's not as though he hasn't tried, but economic forces are often greater than any amount of willingness. When he has found a few days work, he sleeps on or near the building site to save on shoe leather and because there doesn't seem much point in going anywhere else. One doorway is more or less like any other.

The problems and stress of unemployment are great enough when you do have a home, but imagine the strain of not having anywhere to go back to except a cardboard box in a concrete block that you share with two or three others every night. No television to help you unwind; no music to calm you down or drinks to help you relax; no family to reassure you or feed you or help you out. No wonder there is bitterness in their outlook. And yet, sometimes their compassion is astonishing.

'I don't mind going hungry sometimes, because I know there are other people who are hungry as well,' said Bruce. 'Whenever I get some money, I always end up giving it away to someone who needs it.'

Bruce never uses public transport, preferring instead to walk, sometimes covering up to 20 or 30 miles a day on foot, despite his injury. It's not an economy measure in the sense of saving money. The money isn't there for him to save.

Steve, 29, came to London from Glasgow two years ago because 'London has more colour'. He hasn't been able to find work either. He spends his days looking for jobs when he can, but like the rest, the problem of survival is more pressing. He sleeps in youth hostels when he can get in, and when they're full he curls up near the Festival Hall with the others. Keith and Barry allow Bruce and Steve to sleep on their bit of cardboard when they need it.

Their days are spent in pursuit of warmth, food and drink. There are places you can go, but they fill up quickly. There are the friendship rooms at St Martin-in-the-Fields in Trafalgar Square, and St Botolph's Crypt in the East End. There are the railways stations, which offer shelter if not warmth, and you can always sit in the Festival Hall itself for a while. During the week I was there, videos were playing and you could sit in the warm room for as long as you liked, until the centre closed around 11 p.m.

Another favourite spot is the Imperial War Museum, because it's free, warm, and interesting. 'Every time I go in there, I come out a different person,' said Bruce.

You learn very quickly about when and where you can get food, tea or coffee, where you can shower, and where there are free public conveniences.

Keith figures you can 'get just about anything you need for free in London'. If you smoke, you collect the butts of cigarettes tossed away by others, or cadge what you can from passers-by. No one likes to beg for money, but the desperation and hunger drives you to it. You begin to resent those who walk by eating packets of crisps, or carrying bags of groceries from Sainsbury's. You begin to crave fresh vegetables, and dream of fruit and hot meals.

Every Wednesday night, the Hari Krishna van comes round to the Festival Hall and distributes free food – paper plates heaped with vegetable curry and rice. Other groups like the Salvation Army and Bronzeway Charities also bring around hot food, usually soup, but there is never enough to feed everyone. You have to get what you can.

One of the worst feelings is being dirty. Even if you manage a shower you still have to put back on the same dirty clothes, so you don't feel clean. Few people have the luxury of a spare set of clothes, and even if they do, they can't afford to do the laundry even once a week. Try wearing the same clothes for a full week, including sleeping in them, with maybe one quick shower if you're lucky, and you will understand how demoralizing it is. Don't fancy trying it? Imagine living it as reality for 365 days a year.

People treat you differently when you're scruffy, too. Bartenders pretend they don't see you. People stare at you in the streets, move away or pretend not to see you at all. In some ways you feel invisible, in others you feel like a sideshow freak. It's very difficult to deal with.

'I wish I had some nice clothes. I've got to get a new pair of trousers and some new boots,' said Bruce, after a particularly trying day. We had walked from Kennington to the Festival Hall, then over to Guy's Hospital, where after a desperate plea, they finally agreed to X-ray Bruce's feet and give him some treatment. Then we walked up to Tower Hill station, to St Botolph's, and then back to the Festival Hall.

Bruce had seen an ad in Earl's Court for a bed and breakfast place in Kennington where you could stay for £3 a night. Since he had done some work the week before, he decided to go there and paid for two weeks.

For three pounds he got a bed in a room with six other people (three bunk beds and a single bed), a few blankets and a cooked breakfast the next morning. There was also a television room with 12 beds in it and, at a guess, seven other rooms with between six and 12 people each. In all, there must have been close to 100 people staying there – all young and all homeless.

The conditions weren't exactly luxurious, but it was better than the Festival Hall. The rooms didn't look like they'd seen a vacuum cleaner or a bottle of disinfectant for a few years. There were mice scurrying across the floor of the TV room; some of the windows were broken; the blankets were dirty and the rooms were freezing cold. But to many, including Bruce, it was as close to a home as they'd had in years.

The young homeless are not stupid; they are not incapable of work; they are not lazy. They are young and they are disillusioned. They are people who, because the system has failed them, have given a lot of thought to the way this country is run. Quite rightly, they blame the government for much of their trouble. The new Housing Bill and benefit changes will make their lives even more difficult. The story is always the same. They have come to London to look for work and they haven't been able to find a place to live.

Out of the six others in Bruce's room, none had been able to find steady work or accommodation in the time they had been in London – anywhere from three months to two years. As one person said: 'I want to find somewhere [to live], but they always ask too much for the deposit. I don't have that much money.' He makes £50 a week making sandwiches seven hours a day, six days a week, in a restaurant. Another says all he wants is a place of his own 'where I can make myself a cup of tea'.

One person who came down from the north of England has found a job with a mailing company, but only makes £2.50 an hour and can't afford to stay anywhere else. And yet, their optimism remains. One had applied for a job with a travel agency, and was full of hope and plans if he gets the job. He will get a nice flat, he says, one that is bright and clean, because 'I don't like the dirt'.

They still hold on to their dreams. They believe in fairness and in sharing what little they have. If someone in the room has food, he shares it with the others. None of them drink, but those who smoke share cigarettes.

The one moment which touched me more than any other was when, during a chat, one young man said, with tears in his eyes: 'Make sure you tell them this is what Thatcher's Britain has done to young people.'

Michelle Beauchamp
18 May 1988

Country diary: Machynlleth

On fine nights my wife and I like to sleep with our bedroom window wide open, but for several days last week there were problems. Soon after dawn a pair of swallows came flying in to perch on the curtain rail, twittering happily as they discussed which end of it to build their nest on. We might have been prepared to accept this invasion if our bedroom did not face south-west which means that on wet days we have to shut the window to keep out deluges of rain. So I am afraid the swallows have had to make do with the cowshed though they have to share it with a family of barn owls. After the swallows the swifts arrived. Not that they have the slightest interest in any part of our house. They have always nested under the eaves of the vicarage a mile away and never anywhere else. Compared with the simple lives of the swallows, the swifts are strange, remote birds that belong to the sky and would make their nests up there if only they could. No birds are more sensitive to the elements. If the weather is good we can see them catching flies from dawn till dusk. But during depressions it seems they go far away in search of the sunshine, their nestlings evidently able to survive days without food. It is known that swifts can live at least 21 years and that they may spend their nights as well as their days on the wing. So I wonder how far does the swift fly in 21 years?

William Condry
28 May 1988

No room for Mickey Mouse

Terry Davis, harness maker and saddler, lives below Wart Hill by Wenlock Edge. The biggest thing to have happened recently in his neck of the Shropshire woods was a strike at the Chuckie Chicken factory farm, two miles away in Craven Arms where the pay, say the picketing workers huddled against the wind by the gates, is atrocious; as bad as farm labourers', the work soul-destroying.

Fifty years ago the Chuckie workers would have been on the land, with horses. There was one for every 12 people, says Terry, but mechanization and then the war came and the shires, the percherons, the Suffolk punches, the Ardennes and the Clydesdales disappeared almost overnight, those remaining to be overbred by the few and paraded like dogs round agricultural shows.

But the legacy of the working horse remains, even in Terry's own village of Wistanstow. The blacksmith's old forge stands opposite the wheelwright's old workshop, which is just down the road from the farrier. Next door, Terry points out from his kitchen, still lives an old driver, and on the opposite side of the valley is a shire horse breeder.

At this point the new face of the countryside drives up in

a BMW. Enter from London, in full regalia of walking boots, billowing scarves and anorak, Dr Sara Lunt, of English Heritage, who comes to Wistanstow to inspect two full harnesses Terry has been making for their latest venture, a working farm museum at Boscabel House on the other side of the county near West Bromwich.

Boscabel is where Charles II hid in an oak tree from the Roundheads. An otherwise unremarkable house, it became a romantic shrine for the royalists and, unwittingly, a precursor of the current British obsession with the past. The old oak was pollarded by seventeenth-century entrepreneurs who lopped off boughs, even roots, to turn into memorabilia. It was finally felled, but not before an acorn was taken for the sake of future generations. On 29 May, Oakapple Day, English Heritage will reopen the estate as a new shrine of profitability, and the model farm will be central to this instant tourist attraction.

'Pretend' farms, as Terry likes to call them, are all the rage in Shropshire at the moment. Down the road from the Craven Arms is the Acton Scott farm museum where busloads of families, women's institutes and schools come to watch heavy horses (in Terry's harnesses) plod with antique ploughs up and down over old fields. Ironbridge, 20 miles away, has become a centre of Victorian excellence with its industrial museum and Victorian 'township' of Blist Hill. Terry, like many another English craftsman, has worked for all of them.

'One can really only justify it as information leisure,' says Dr Lunt, who trained as an archaeologist. 'How can it be relevant to today? I think it's a 1980s yearning for the 1960s, with all those people who didn't quite go travelling returning to their own roots and saying this is how we were. I quite like packaging it for the public and seeing them all trail round and come out at the end with a smile on their faces. It's mainly for adults, but I like to think that one child in a hundred will take it in and even pursue it as a career.'

Terry's daughter disagrees. About one in a million, she mutters, 'I think it's all boring.'

The tradesman's point of view is different. On the one hand this commercial obsession with the past provides Terry with the most interesting work around. As one of the very few working horse harness makers in the country he has had to research and learn the intricacies of the trade from scratch. There are old books but next to no one he can exchange ideas with. It's leatherwork on a grand, hand-made scale. One harness can take six weeks of cutting, shaping and stitching. It involves wood and metalwork which he contracts out, and when finished the whole thing, weighing many hundredweight and shining bright with brasses, is like a bespoke tailor-made suit, a job to last two generations or more.

The dark side is that like so many craftsmen Terry feels he is regarded as a museum exhibit himself. If he demonstrates his skills – which he is often asked to do – 'they almost poke me to see if I'm real'. Besides, he says, the word 'crafts' has become a tourist thing, associated with little old ladies crocheting. 'Crafts for me is wheelwrighting or hurdle making, anything which performs a real function in the rural community.' Everything else, he implies, is Mickey Mouse work. 'I prefer the word tradesman.'

And the new interest in old farming methods? 'It's all part of the leisure factory. Anything to do with horses is a growing industry. Round here there are trekking schools opening everywhere, and more children than ever have horses. It's an automatic response to all this new technology. People can't keep up with it.' There's a security in looking back, he says, like an anchor point. 'It gives people something to hold on to. The future is a black hole.'

Terry's future is less precarious than it was when he came to Shropshire seven years ago from London after learning the trade at the Cordwainers College. He chose Craven Arms because there was no other leatherworker around and the Acton Scott museum could give him immediate work repairing and making harnesses.

Meanwhile he battles with grant bodies and the council, who are happy to use his harnesses on their glossy brochures promoting the county as a storehouse of all that is good and wholesome in the countryside, but who are not prepared to help him build decent workshops.

In the quieter winter months he turns to making bellows and leather buckets for the Boscabels of Britain. In a bad year he'd do better at the Chuckie Chicken factory.

John Vidal
19 March 1988

The return of the cannon fodder.   *13 November 1987*

Saint Joan and the Queen

There were always two intriguing opposites at work within Joan Baez. Something to do with the mixture of the big, sad eyes, and the brilliant, ready smile.

One came to be called 'Saint Joan'. She sang folk songs and spirituals, she adored her parents, she led protest marches, she worked with Martin Luther King, she married an organizer of draft resistance and they lived in a Californian commune, she was jailed twice for her commitment to pacifism, she watched the bombing of Hanoi from below. Latterly, she worked with the Mothers of the Disappeared in Argentina, she sang to Solidarity strikers in Poland, she organizes her own human rights group, Humanitas. She campaigns for Soviet dissidents and she calls herself 'a dissident in my own country'.

The other became known as 'Queen Joan'. While writing his book about the *Rolling Thunder* tour with Bob Dylan in the 1970s, Sam Shepard watched her dance, 'doing a pre-bop boogaloo. She's incredible to watch. I never used to think of her as sexy before, but she's definitely that. No more folksy peace-licking Scottish-folk-ballad stuff. She's transformed into a short-cropped, shit-kicking Mexican disco dancer,' he noted.

The Queen to Bob Dylan's Jack had lived on the edges of the hard drug scene in New York, she flirted, she loved jewellery. Latterly, she dined with President Mitterand, she found herself a companion who owns a castle in Normandy, she says she couldn't live without dancing, she picks up a tanned German in an airport lounge and takes him along with her on a tour.

Today, an autobiography of both these Joans is published, a story bursting with an almost vulnerable passion for the causes of peace and freedom, for which she is best known, and for a life of FUN (her capital letters) which was lived more privately, and more equivocally, behind the scenes. The dichotomy – indeed, the conflict – between Saint Joan and Queen Joan is the theme which drives the book, and the relationships between Baez and her music, her politics, her lovers, her brief marriage, and just about everything else.

Following the book will come her first album in six years (and one of her best), on which both Joans, inevitably, feature: a tumultuous jam-session with an 80-piece black church choir from LA throws up rousing accounts of 'Let Us Break Bread' and 'O Freedom'; but then comes the Aretha Franklin song that goes 'If you want a do-right all-night woman, you gotta be a do-right, all-night man'.

Queen versus Saint began in youth. She was chirpy and

confident, but also pensive and haunted by what she calls 'demons' – fear of flying, fear of vomiting, a recurrent, disturbing nightmare, nerves and nausea. 'And,' she says in conversation, 'I still am.

'I think all our phobias and demons are replacements for the real fears of disintegrating, disappearing and dying and vanishing – death of one form or another.' She has been in sporadic psychotherapy and analysis for over 20 years, 'building up to combat that craziness, building up an adult within me which was strong enough to reason with that.' At the outset of her career, she is torn between the reclusive intensity of her first love, Michael, and the first flattery of success as a singer. She is both scared and thrilled by the dinginess of Albert Grossman's night club in Chicago, and she cannot stay . . . and so it goes on.

In conversation, it becomes clear that one Joan feeds the other – that Saint Joan is spurred on by the guilt of being Queen Joan, and that Queen Joan is a dare, a challenge laid down by Saint Joan. 'I suppose I would have fewer demons if I really worked out a relationship between these elements of me,' she says. 'Demons have to come from guilt and fear mostly . . . And the guilt around being Queenie is always causing me problems, and the tendency is to go over into the other camp. I think the trick is to – I love the British expression – "bash on regardless". You have to. If I started analysing motives . . . well, I'm sure we all have terrible motives.'

And so it comes as a relief when, for instance, she finds that Martin Luther King, too, gets drunk and had a woman in his room one night on the campaign trail. 'It kind of cleared the air. It meant we could go on in that way without trying to be saints,' she says. Queen Joan, it seems, is a fallen angel cast out by Saint Joan; and so the demons are like Lucifer – not the thoroughbreds reared in the nether regions.

It's fairly clear where she gets the guilt from: 'Look, there are two grandfathers who were ministers, and ministers beyond that – all varieties of churches in Spain and Mexico. On my mother's side the Victorians . . . Her mother always said: "You're a worthless human being, and on top of that sex is wicked" – so, thanks for the legacy, everybody.' Brought up as a Quaker, she is as religious as she ever was. It is 'a curious relationship with God'.

Joan Baez, now 47, is the most enduring image of the innocent outrage and dogged idealism of the 1960s. Hers was always the strength of honest simplicity, of a kind that has lost some of its potency in both the lasertronic-stroboscopic rock culture and the current politics of selfishness. But her pacifist and humanitarian message is unchanged. 'All this just makes me specially grateful that I can still fill a reasonable size hall with that relatively simple message.' Her popularity is nowadays mainly in France, Germany and Italy, rather than her old Anglo-American stomping ground. In 1983, she sang to 120,000 for a free concert 'dedicated to non-violent struggle' in the Place de la Concorde, which, she says, gave her 'the feeling that, after all, the courage is just as contagious as the fear'.

But she berates 'the nostalgia I see rampant' for the sixties. 'It won't come back as it was,' she says, 'and neither will I. I don't miss those times and I don't go to sixties parties. The other day I saw a *Twenty Years After Avalon* show – Mick Jagger and the levitation of the Pentagon and stuff – and I thought, "Where was I during all this? I was in jail." And I thought that, except for the intensity, which sometimes we lack now, I don't have nostalgia for the details of what went on in those years, and for my general grimness. Now is fascinating, and now is important.'

Joan Baez has shed the financial profits of her career with a willingness which contrasts with her wealthier peers in the music business. Now, most of the money goes into Humanitas – her own creation. The organization is an unapologetic challenge to current cynicism and sprang from her establishment of a branch of Amnesty International on the West Coast. It is concerned with 'the constant business of getting people to see with both eyes that oppression is oppression, wherever it is'.

Humanitas works with people like the Greens in Germany, and on behalf of political prisoners, 'wherever possible, fusing a human rights issue with disarmament'. It involves Baez and her delegates talking relentlessly about abuses of power across the world, talking about Argentina in Poland, about Chile in the USSR, and about the USSR in the USA. Over here, Baez has worked with the Irish Peace People and the Greenham Common camp.

Baez calls these times 'the meantime years' of Western politics, insisting that 'the pendulum is about to swing right over', pushed by 'those for whom the yuppie dream isn't quite as substantial as they're told'. It is as though her radical pacifism was sitting out a siege laid by the years of what she calls 'Ramboism'.

'I think that what we have to keep doing in the meantime years can be anything from organizing on a visible scale to simply keeping sane, especially if one lives in the States under a constantly heartless administration like ours. Just keep any values at all against what people tell you to believe or encourage you to believe.

'And depending on how we have conducted ourselves during these times, that will determine the nature of the next movement, if there is one. It won't come out of a vacuum. It will be built on the structures that people manage to hold together and even build a little during these times.'

In a sense, the Baez dichotomy is now lived out between her home in California, which is all politics and music, and the castle in Normandy owned by her part-time sort-of-boyfriend, the young and rich French secretary of Médécins Sans Frontières, whom she met in Cambodia.

'If I were to be a little less hard on myself, I would spend more time at the castle,' she says. It's like 'stepping into a film like *La Belle et la Bête.* 'The castle is absolutely pure Queen Joan. It's where I'm a gypsy countess.' In California, she lives mostly alone. Ira Sandperl, the pacifist who has been the Baez guru since the 1960s, observed that 'Joan has more women around her than men, but she seems to be most genuinely comfortable with men.'

'The curious thing is that that's true,' says Baez. 'I wish I could say I have this wonderful person stashed away and that's who I go home to. But I'm absolutely awful at working out a reasonable relationship. I've sort of given up, anyhow. Picnics – I'll just have to settle for picnics with men. It's the best I can do.'

For all her consistency and commitment, Baez sometimes comes across as a leaf that is more or less content to blow around on zephyrs. But zephyrs sometimes turn into gales – and the most momentous and celebrated of those pre-picnic relationships was at gale-force, with Bob Dylan. The book affords some pretty extraordinary insights into both Dylan's behaviour (sometimes ludicrous, sometimes callous, brilliant and always self-indulgent), and into Baez's miserable attempts to cling on regardless. It comes across as addiction rather than love.

Dylan two-times her, refuses to let her on stage time after time; he drinks, shrugs and shambles through his enigmatic haze. In a hotel room, on the *Rolling Thunder* tour, a truly bizarre scene: a hopelessly drunk Dylan attempting to cut his wrist with a filthy blade so that he and Joan can swear blood brotherhood/sisterhood. Amazingly, Baez changes the blade, and goes along with it.

In the book she is quite harsh, addressing Dylan in the second person singular: 'You were mantled with praise, sought after by hysterical fans, appealed to by liberals, intellectuals, politicians, the press, and genuinely adored by fools like me, and I don't think you ever really recuperated.'

In conversation she is more reflective: 'Writing it all helped me to understand it. Don't you think that if somebody is just out of reach, you keep grabbing for it? Even the most stable person has that, even without whatever intricacies I had in my nature. You think, "*Damn*, that's the one who got away." I suppose I'd say, "It's not that I was in love with you, it's just that nobody had ever been able to kick me around like this."

'Basically, I just kept wanting to go back and wanting to stand up to it and prove that I was . . . I don't know quite what . . . as good as, or better than, or as big as – because it certainly wasn't any fun being there. But that's what couples are like – you just shred the thing to death and when you look at it there's nothing that makes you want to be in the room with that person. It's just that you can't bear them having walked out of the room first.'

The affair did however produce the one song that equals anything written by Dylan – 'Diamonds and Rust', opposites again.

Baez is, above all else, a child of the idealist romantic movement at its most determined. For her *Desert Island Discs*, she would choose Wagner's *Tristan und Isolde*, 'So I'd have years to try and figure it out, particularly the last movement [Isolde's *Liebestod*], and die happy.'

Romantic opposites again. What is all this about a link between love and death? 'Listen, the way I've conducted my life, I've got to see a link between love – and beauty – and death.'

Ed Vulliamy
25 February 1988

And a Voice to Sing With by Joan Baez (Century Hutchinson)

Diary: *Pianissimo*

The performance of Beethoven's *Missa Solemnis*, at Acton Town Hall, was reaching its most profoundly beautiful moments. The conductor, Professor James Gaddarn, of London's Trinity College of Music, was gathering Ealing Choral Society, the soloists and orchestra to plunge into the final movement. The audience was hushed. You could have heard a pin drop. Crash. The door. Prof. Gaddarn, on the rostrum with his back to the hall, felt a prickle of anxiety. 'I heard this commotion. It was like a horse coming down the aisle,' he said. 'I heard footsteps behind me coming towards the rostrum. I turned round and there was this apparition.' A spaceman. In a glittering, silvered helmet, black leggings, chains, heavy gauntlets and big boots. 'What on earth do you want?' hissed Prof. Gaddarn. 'I didn't know if I was going to be attacked. It was one of those nightmares.' Mumble, mumble, said the spaceman. 'I wasn't able to understand a word he was saying. It eventually tumbled out that he was sent on behalf of some kissogram. By cross-examining him very quickly I was able to discover that he had come to the wrong hall.' Clank, clank. Away clumped the spaceman. The baton was raised again. Eyebrows in the audience weren't. There was an absolute stillness. 'Only the English could have stayed so calm,' said the professor.

Andrew Moncur
1 April 1988

The second mourning

Belfast:
It was impossible not to keep glancing behind you. It was impossible not to look away from the grave back down the hill. Everybody in the cemetery was doing the same. Every so often they looked over their shoulders and scanned the scrubland between them and the motorway for any move-ment.

It was exactly 24 hours since they had been there last. Exactly 24 hours since someone had crept up the slope and announced himself with a volley of fragment grenades and gunfire.

Many of the 5000 mourners were the same people who had been there on Wednesday. Then they were mourning the three IRA volunteers killed in Gibraltar. Yesterday they were there to mourn Kevin McCracken, the 31-year-old gunman shot by soldiers on Monday.

The RUC had stayed away again, but the atmosphere was tense. As mourners entered the cemetery there was a suspicious movement in some bushes. Instantly scores of young men tore across the graveyard.

That was a false alarm. So was that over a car parked in the cemetery entrance which had its back window punched in by an investigating Sinn Fein steward.

The stewards were everywhere: young men mostly dressed in jeans and black bomber jackets with green and orange armbands. They commanded respect.

Kevin McCracken was 11 when the Troubles started. He lived in a terraced house in Norglen Parade, Turf Lodge, West Belfast. It is just round the corner from the home of young Sean Savage, one of the three buried the previous day.

McCracken was shot barely 100 yards from his own home. It was a dismal landscape in which to grow up. The local shops have all been bricked up and sprayed with H-Block graffiti.

He joined the IRA at 18 and spent eight of his 31 years in prison. His parish priest, Father Aidan Denny, told mourners at his funeral mass yesterday that his membership of the IRA was not wholly surprising, given his background and the area he came from.

McCracken's world, said Father Denny, was one without hope. He found it hard to convince the young men in his parish that non-violent resistance was the better way.

Earlier, as we waited for McCracken's coffin to be carried out of his house we saw the next generation budding. A little boy – he can only have been four – came up behind pressmen and shouted 'I – I – IRA'. Another boy, perhaps seven, was hanging about outside McCracken's house when Gerry Adams arrived.

The boy looked up at Adams in open-eyed admiration. Adams looked down, ruffled his hair and chatted to him, all the time puffing on a pipe. He gestured to Martin McGuinness, standing near by, and said in conspiratorial tones to the lad: 'That's the head of the IRA.' The little boy's eyes grew round in wonder. Picture him in ten years' time.

While we were waiting for the coffin, an IRA guard of

honour was firing a volley of shots over a temporary 'shrine' in Rockville Street. A Reuters photographer had been invited.

The coffin came out shortly before midday, followed by sobbing members of his family. For the fourth time in two days, a tricolour was draped over the coffin.

For the fourth time, hundreds of journalists and TV crews from around the world were there to record the ritual. The pictures would reach Boston, New York and Chicago just before the St Patrick's Day parades.

The church was packed. We asked God to receive McCracken into his loving embrace. There was a reading from Luke instructing us: 'Let your first words be "Peace to this house".'

Father Denny's address also took in the Gibraltar killings. 'Murder is murder is murder,' he said. 'Christians cannot condone murder, no matter by whom it is done. But it has an even more sinister dimension when it is done by state security forces.'

By the time the cortège reached the gates of Milltown cemetery it was being followed by about 5000 mourners.

In the cemetery, stewards were checking the perimeters and marshalling the gathering crowds. Near the IRA Volunteers' plot the grass was churned up and headstones knocked over from Wednesday's panic. Where one of the grenades had landed the tarmac was scorched and pitted.

The loudspeaker system was not working properly and only snatches of the graveside oration could be heard: 'A patriot who attempted to lead his country . . . collusion of RUC . . . shoot to kill . . . actions of hypocrisy.'

The crowd started drifting away well before the oration was finished. The ceremony had been peaceful and dignified, but anxious. Many mourners were still glancing toward the scrubland as they made their way out into the Falls Road.

Alan Rusbridger
18 March 1988

Mr K's unbearable certainty

I can never read two pages of Milan Kundera without trying to remember who called Matthew Arnold Mr Kidglove
Cocksure. Or, for that matter, who said: 'I wish I could be
as sure of anything as that man is about everything.'

Part of the trouble, I know, is that even after Nabokov
we are still not used to novelists as aggressively intelligent
as this; not used, at least, to novelists who flourish their
cleverness like a matador's cape. What really irritates me,
I suppose, is that having spent a decade or so comparing
the English novel's provincialism unfavourably with the
inventiveness and fantasy of the historically and politically
literate writers of Central Europe and Latin America, I
now find young England making a cult figure of a Czech
whose work sometimes reads like a parody of those virtues.

Too clever by half would be an older English verdict. But
then Kundera *is* clever; in these short pieces which cover
much the same ground as the speculative or didactic inter-
ludes in the novels, he is at least as often thought-provoking
as just plain provoking. Like the novels, they're worth
being irritated by, for in spite of the showing off, Kundera
is usually pointing to something interesting.

He proposes a noble work for the novel. It is to protect
us, afflicted by the global electronic racket and a crudely
reductionist post-Cartesian rationalism, from 'the forgetting of being'. From Cervantes on, the novel has become
our most subtle tool of ontological inquiry. Every novel says
to the reader: 'Things are not as simple as you think.' And
Kundera paraphrases his master, Hermann Broch, to add:
'The sole *raison d'être* of a novel is to discover what can
only be discovered by a novel.'

That's close enough to Pound's requirement of poetry –
anything that can be said as well in prose can be said better
in prose – and the Kunderan novelist means to be a poet,

with a poet's intent reaching for the essential. Not, however, a lyricist. This is a bad word in Kundera's later books, connected with revolutionism and other forms of infantile malady or dangerous innocence. (Remember the damning picture in *The Book of Laughter and Forgetting* of Paul Eluard joining in some Party fiesta and dancing in the streets of Prague to honour the revolution the day after his friend Zavis Kalandra, the Czech surrealist, had been hanged.)

He proposes the equation Novel = anti-lyrical poetry, and to prove it calls up the novelists of the other modernism: not the modernism of Apollinaire or Mayakovsky or the various avant-gardes, nor schematic university modernism, 'establishment modernism' as he calls it, but the anti-romantic modernism of Kafka, the sceptical modernism of the other great Central Europeans, Musil, Broch and Gombrowicz the remarkable Pole. This tradition has the further advantage of not repudiating its forerunners, or at any rate those Kundera approves of, and looking back over the form's brief history he has a sudden endearing vision that brings together Cervantes and Kafka, a rare moment combining perceptiveness, affection and humour. 'Isn't that Don Quixote himself,' he wonders, 'after a 300-year journey, returning to the village disguised as a land-surveyor?'

Some of this general argument about the novel comes in the first essay which takes Cervantes as its point of departure. Another analyses in some detail Broch's deeply pessimistic trilogy *The Sleepwalkers*, and a third offers as lucid and painful an account of the Kafka situation as you could find anywhere in half a dozen pages.

The two pieces Kundera calls dialogues are edited interviews in which he mostly glosses his own novels, the second making elaborate musical analogies of their construction. They are polyphonic and serial, based on 'key-words' said to function like Schoenbergian tone-rows. With one exception, *The Farewell Party*, they come ineluctably in seven parts ('a deep, unconscious, incomprehensible drive, an archetype of form that I cannot escape'), each of which could carry a musical tempo (he gives them); and we are asked to notice the *seven* movements, of similarly irregular length and pace, of Beethoven's Opus 131. This goes a bit far, even for the son of the Director of the Brno Conservatory. Another section is a variant of the 'Words Misunderstood' chapter, or movement, of *The Unbearable Lightness of Being*, a set of 63 aphoristic definitions, some of which are simply or largely quotations from the novels, and many of which are revealing. '*Beauty* is the last triumph possible for man who cannot hope,' for example. Or take 'Elitism', not so much a definition as a deft deflection of what's clearly a familiar charge. Czech propaganda used the term never to designate politicians, bureaucrats or athletes, 'only the cultural élite: philosophers, writers, professors'. And now there's 'an amazing synchronism. It seems that in the whole of Europe the cultural élite is yielding to other élites. Over there, to the élite of the police apparatus. Here, to the élite of the mass media apparatus. No one will ever accuse these new élites of élitism. Thus the word "élitism" will soon be forgotten.'

Which brings one to 'Irony', Kundera's favourite key and the novel's essential mode, he claims, going on to quote with relish the woman revolutionary in Conrad's *Under Western Eyes*: '. . . women, children and revolutionists hate irony, which is the negation of all saving instincts, of all faith, of all devotion, all action'. (Incidentally, in all his multitudinous reference, Agatha Chistie is the only woman writer to win a mention.)

The seventh and last section (this little book being subject to the same deep structural drive) is an address on receiving a prize in Jerusalem, which includes the assertion that 'Novelists who are more intelligent than their books should go into another line of work.' That's brave or rash depending on how far you think Kundera's own novels deserve the same respectful criticism he offers of Hermann Broch to whom he owes so much, notably that the diverse elements of *The Sleepwalkers* – narrative, essay, aphorism, reportage, very much Kundera's own mix – seem more juxtaposed than truly 'polyphonically' synthesized. I think it recurrently true of both the later novels, though *The Book of*

Laughter and Forgetting, is pulled together by its greater emotional energy and general élan, less burdened by characters like Sabina and her tedious symbolic bowler.

Clearly, as *The Art of the Novel* and the novels which talk so artfully about themselves demonstrate, Kundera knows very well what he intends: 'To bring together the extreme gravity of the question and the extreme lightness of the form – that has always been my ambition.' But there seems to me something relentless and driven about his ironies and provocations that doesn't in fact make for lightness. (Can this be a male form of the female malady now identified as 'Look At Me'?)

Similarly, his writing about sex is so cerebral and voyeuristic, so struck with the discovery that sex can be funny, that it usually misses the lightness of the erotic for want of tenderness. Even the pessimism and the oddly punitive existentialism from which it proceeds seems willed, as though his art needs bad news and wouldn't thrive on better.

It may be that Kundera's considerable talent was frostbitten by the bitterness and abiding mistrust of history and man-in-history with which Stalinism's betrayal afflicted his Central European generation. ('*Central Europe*: . . . a premonitory mirror showing the possible fate of all Europe,' runs the bitter definition in this book. 'Central Europe: a laboratory of twilight.')

Or perhaps knowing too much, too precisely, about what you are up to is problematic in creative work, inhibiting some growing principle, some integrating touch of the organic. More painfully still, of course, it may be that for all Kundera's wit and speculative intelligence, he is simply not a Master, not a magus of the art of the novel, as Nabokov was, and may not therefore be forgiven his sins by Time.

W. L. Webb
10 June 1988

The Art of the Novel by Milan Kundera (Faber)

Diary: Dig deep

Hard times in New York are reportedly forcing the people of the streets into greater inventiveness. They have been spotted carrying placards saying 'Help support research on the impact of wine on the human body' and 'Due to inclement weather, we will not be washing windows today. We will accept donations, however.'

Stephen Cook
30 October 1987

Booted up

Evelyn Waugh summed up the most crucial equipment for any amateur explorer when he chose the name Boot for the hero of *Scoop*. Wellies or trainers may be fine in the Lake District (whatever the 'Tsks' from passing wardens) but the tropical traveller demands boots.

My own experience is limited to the jungle, but I've no doubt that the rule applies wherever today's William Boots roam. And most of them, unless they managed to conjure sponsorship from a bootmaker, will have shopped at Silverman's warehouse in Mile End, East London.

Run by a cosy East End family, who constantly brew tea in a muddle of military kit, this is the biggest surplus outlet in the country. After a pallid skinhead had bought some obscure rank badges, I quoted hesitantly from my list: 'Have you any self-draining US Army boots?'

They have thousands, although most of them are actually the cheaper Korean model, which means an alarmingly large size-number for Western feet. Trying them on is a chore, with endless lace holes to thread and a tendency among the short-sighted Silverman aunts, or possibly daughters, to bring you the wrong size. But, of course, it is important to get a comfortable fit.

Their great advantage which gives them the edge over Doc Martens, fellboots or the British Army rival, are the Heath Robinsonish self-drainers. After you've paddled through the rainforest equivalent of a puddle, metal valves in the instep squirt out jets of water with every step you take.

Silverman's offers hundreds of other crafty Army inventions and you could end up, like Carruthers in *The Riddle of the Sands*, burdened with portable stoves or an SAS 'bergen' (the explorer's codeword for a rucksack). But unless you're going solo, your expedition's quartermaster should be dealing with the heavier stuff; and don't forget, airline baggage limits apply to explorers as well as businessmen.

So concentrate on baggy cotton everything, topped by a sunhat, to complete your tropical trousseau. Shopping around in the High Street may be enough for this, but why not visit the tropical outfitters, Airey and Wheeler of Piccadilly, if only to savour the lingering air of Empire days?

'Who will be doing your washing, sir?' inquired my expert assistant, explaining that native women always boil everything so socks one size too big are in order if dhobi wallahs are involved. My laundry actually turned out to be a jungle pool, but Airey's long cotton socks – the sort District Commissioners used to wear – are admirable and almost impossible to find elsewhere.

I have to add that they are also South African made, which may explain their effect on Third World leeches, especially if you ring them, at the top of your self-draining boot, with smears of Autan insect gel, one of two essential extras to your basic First Aid of paracetamol and sticking plasters, etc.

The other is a store of water-purifying tablets, which don't improve the taste of sludge from a buffalo wallow but kill off the bugs. Communal tab-unpackaging, from the foil wrappings, is a feature of any expedition, but the pills can get overlooked on a day's trek. So get your own (from chemists or the Youth Hostel Shop in Covent Garden).

Dextrosol tablets are the lightest and most efficient food extra, while the most inspiring maps, to psych yourself up rather than for practical use (because there won't be accurate maps if you're really exploring) are the Tactical Pilotage Charts from Stanfords (also in Covent Garden) with stimulating details like 'Elevations and contours in this area unknown'.

For your one luxury, the umbrella is popular – as walking stick, climbing hook, tent pole or weapon, as well as defence from sun and rain. But I chose my ornate London Transport Travelcard, whose stamps, photograph and signatures proved a talisman in that other Third World jungle – bureaucracy. When I gave it to an Indonesian colonel on leaving, his look of purest joy was the greatest discovery of my trip.

Martin Wainwright
2 April 1988

The eyes say so

Moscow:
This may be a sign of a curious perversion, but I find Russian winters rather erotic. It is something to do with women's eyes, which are usually the only feature you can see as they wrap up against the cold in thick fur collars and hats.

Russian women tend to have plumply rounded cheeks, pale skin and delicate small noses, and their eyes flash in a quite remarkable way. To trudge through the snow is to experience a constant barrage of their twinkles and gleams and mysteriously penetrating looks.

It is all quite harmless, a matter of the briefest eye contact that is in no way an invitation to stop and converse, still less to plough through the layers of winter clothing to the woman underneath. But there is something more sensual, more exciting, in these bright eyes flashing through the snow than any number of bikinis on beaches.

Eyes are ageless. These bold visual challenges can come from grandmothers and schoolgirls alike, from women whose waddling walk suggests an ungainly dumpling, to the sveltest of Svetlanas.

There is something quite magical about this. Many Russian girls, when you see them indoors, have a characteristic colouring of white skin, very pale blue eyes and blonde-white hair that makes them look seriously anaemic. But wrap them in fur and clap a winter *Shapka* on their heads, and the eyes suddenly blaze out fiercely, dark and strong.

Russians will tell you that there is a reason for the celebration of Russian eyes in poetry and prose. They say it comes from the habit of tightly swaddling Russian babies, wrapping their limbs so closely that they learn to communicate with their eyes alone, flashing invitations from the very cradle.

There are other sensual pleasures of winter. There are few sensations that so combine heat and cold as kissing the super-chilled cheeks of a woman who has been walking in temperatures of minus 20°C.

But the great mystery to me is what on earth the Russians do about this constant current of deep-frozen eroticism. The Soviet Union is officially a rather straitlaced society. Casual sexual encounters are not encouraged by the system.

Amorous Russians cannot quickly check into a hotel, not without showing the papers that say they are married. And the Soviet housing shortage is a far more effective prophylactic than any passing worries about AIDS.

Human nature being what it is, solutions have been found. One, or rather two, can take a night train to Leningrad or the Baltic city of Tallin, booking one of the soft class two-berth cabins. In summer, there are the river steamers, again with two-berth cabins.

This can be fun. The bunks are so narrow and the train ride so bumpy that anything more than the most casual amorous dalliance requires a sense of balance and a readiness to undertake physical contortions that put the *Kama Sutra* to shame.

But tickets for two on a night sleeper cost over 60 roubles, or an average week's pay. It is not, therefore, a common resource. And that great standby of Western courtship, the car park, is less than attractive in a society where cars are few and the outside temperature low enough to freeze the locks, if not the passions.

From my own strolls through parks and countryside, I can confirm that the Russians are among the world's most enthusiastic practitioners of the splendid art of love-making in the open air. Indeed, in the long grass of Izmailovo park last summer, a friend of mine was flying a kite and broke his leg when he tripped over one enraptured couple.

But a superhuman degree of passion is required for al fresco frolics between November and March, and so the perennial lovers' question of finding somewhere to be alone has a particular intensity in Russia. They are not a prudish people. They could not be, speaking a language so marvellously rich in earthy jokes and bawdy oaths. So flats and spare rooms and dachas are made available and borrowed among friends almost as a matter of course.

But probably the majority of young Russian single people, whether students or young workers, tend to live in hostels and dormitories, where real privacy can seldom be found.

Interestingly, there is no single Russian word that can be translated as 'privacy'. There are circumlocutions about the state of being alone, and privacy of thought has to be expressed in Russian as one's secret thoughts.

And so I was not over-surprised when a straw poll of those friends to whom I am close enough to ask about this sort of thing found that only one in four had not at some point made love in public, or with only a thin curtain around the bed to shield them from others in the same room.

This must mean silent love-making, I observed to one chum. Who needs to speak, when it can all be said in the eyes, came the unanswerable reply.

Martin Walker
20 February 1988

The teeth have it

Some observers of Tory revolts have developed a useful barometer of how serious they have been for the government. Down to a majority of 80: trifling. A majority of 50: embarrassing. Of 30: humiliating. Of 25 or under: Edward Heath smiles.

Last night, as the tellers recorded the division on the poll tax, we had a long and agreeable flash of Ted's front teeth. In recent years they have seen little daylight, skulking in that dispossessed mouth, grinding and gnashing at Mrs Thatcher. But yesterday they had a pleasant day out, gleaming in the warm light of Mrs Thatcher's worst night of this parliament.

The teeth had reserved judgment as the debate began, firmly closed behind Mr Heath's lips as Michael Mates raised the standard of revolt from the Tory back benches.

The House was packed. Michael Heseltine, fingered by forces loyal to the government as the *éminence blonde* behind the enterprise, sat in one of the small two-seaters at the end of the Chamber. Mr Heseltine was later to make a very effective speech, deploying all his rhetorical assets in greatly mocking the government. At the beginning of the debate, to even greater effect, he was deploying his principal physical asset, waving his hair vigorously to urge his ally on.

Colonel Mates, tall, dark, stiff of bearing and economic of speech, made an unlikely rebel. His *Who's Who* entry – with its highlights of service in the Queen's Dragoon Guards and on the Defence Staff – reads like the true-blueprint for any aspiring officer and gentleman. On almost any other issue, he is a man so sound he might be set in concrete. It is that, perhaps, which made his rebellion all the more effective.

The colonel was fortunate in his enemies. As he made his methodical way through his speech, a succession of the younger Tories, of the type who probably first saw life as a culture at the bottom of a Central Office test tube, rose to intervene.

Simon Burns, the member for Chelmsford, was particularly instructive about the quality of support for the government on its own backbenches.

'May I say to my Right Honourable Friend,' said Mr Burns, exquisitely word-imperfect, 'that I find his argument rather disingenious.' What, perhaps, the son of Stamford school meant was disingenuous. Kenneth Baker, unfortunately, was not listening; nor, after Mr Burns's unfortunate preamble, was the rest of the house.

Colonel Mates was generous with other interventions, playing out the rope to any Tory foolish enough to offer his head for size. Winston Churchill queried a statistical detail in the speech. 'I cannot say precisely,' replied the colonel, 'because the government cannot tell me precisely.'

The colonel sat down to a reading of appreciation from Mr Heath's mouth.

The speech by Nicholas Ridley, the Environment Secretary, in defence of the government, need not detain us for long, for nor did it Mr Ridley. The same speech has been travelling up and down the country for the last year and has neither improved with age, nor travelled well. The Environment Secretary read it out with the panache and spirit of a Mongolian newscaster. Experienced observers claimed the first sighting of Mr Heath's teeth.

But it was at the vote that we got a definitive reading: in a blinding flash of white from the end of the Chamber, Mr Heath told Mrs Thatcher more about her humiliation than any mere reading of the votes.

Andrew Rawnsley
19 April 1988

The reluctant diva

Joan Sutherland is a prima donna unmatched in our time, and her singing career is already as long as those of Adelina Patti and Nellie Melba. Even her arrival as an international star was unique, the achievement of total success in a single performance.

No one who was present at Covent Garden on the night of 17 February 1959, the first time she sang Donizetti's *Lucia di Lammermoor*, can have been in any doubt that a major operatic figure of the first flight had arrived, as it seemed overnight, in full command.

Dame Joan now returns to the Royal Opera House for what might well be her last operatic appearance there, singing the title role in Donizetti's *Anna Bolena*. Though the voice has not come through the three intervening decades unscathed, it is still the Voice of the Century, presenting a combination of distinctive sensuous beauty, virtuoso flexibility and sheer size that is hardly credible in one singer.

One of my favourite memories of Sutherland is from the late sixties. Walking down the road in Montreux (I was a judge in the first International Record Critics' Award) with an American colleague, we suddenly met Joan, who lives not far away, wearing an old raincoat and carrying a shopping bag. When we asked what her plans were, she mentioned 'a few *Sonnambula*s at the Met'. Candidly suggesting that she was getting 'a bit long in the tooth' for the part, there and then, in the middle of the pavement, she did a parody of herself, shopping-bag held like a posy, tripping lightly on stage in the Bellini opera.

The jolly, extrovert side of Sutherland is not the full picture, though it helps to explain her enjoyment of singing, the exuberant exploitation of a god-given voice and a phenomenal technique. The technique did not arrive suddenly or by accident. Her career may have been fortuitously timed, and she has certainly had her strokes of luck, but the purposefulness has always been remarkable.

With the family impoverished on her father's sudden death, it was not an easy girlhood. She was dogged by ill health, and as she reached her teens she was acutely conscious of her height and physical clumsiness, regularly trying to hide herself in any group. But Scottish grit inherited from her Highland father, tight family bonds, the courage with which from her earliest years she had to face physical pain, all gave her the tenacity to overcome obstacles.

Initially she had difficulty believing in herself as an operatic heroine. Even when, under the guidance of her husband, Richard Bonynge, she was developing a coloratura technique, she could not associate herself and her physique with that repertory and its frail heroines. She was helped by the acting lessons given her at Covent Garden by Norman Ayrton, but it was Franco Zeffirelli, coaching her as producer for the first performances of *Lucia*, alongside the veteran Tullio Serafin as music director, who more than anyone helped her to overcome that inhibition, 'making me feel that I was minute, giving me confidence, courage'.

Sutherland's native purposefulness also helps to explain how, with Bonynge, she developed a technique and range few would have predicted from the original qualities of her voice. When Bonynge first heard her in their native Sydney, where both trained at the Conservatorium, she was still in her teens. It initially struck him as a cold voice, and Sutherland herself talks of 'illusions of becoming a second Flagstad', aiming for a steel-edged Wagnerian quality.

Sutherland's mother was a fine contralto who could readily have become a professional, and in fact kept her singing voice into her seventies, but firmly chose to be a housewife and mother instead. What Bonynge realized was that Sutherland, with her remarkable ear and ability to imitate, was unconsciously trying to sound like her mother.

With a voice that was loud even in childhood, she was at first thought to be a mezzo. The mistake took some years to correct, and it was only when she reached London in 1951 that she went to a teacher, Clive Carey, who 'fattened up the top of the voice'.

Bonynge, fascinated by vocal technique, was encouraged by Carey to attend her lessons, and the collaboration worked. Bonynge's love of the *bel canto* repertory of Bellini and Donizetti influenced his wife towards it, and she resisted pressures, when she got into the resident company at Covent Garden, to develop as a Wagnerian soprano.

It was almost seven years after she joined the Covent Garden company that she had her big success in *Lucia*, but the London musical world had already been alerted to her potential. I remember hearing her as Pamina in *The Magic Flute* in 1957, and marvelling at the beauty and poise of the performance. Earlier that year, she caused a sensation taking the title role in the first production since the eighteenth century of Handel's *Alcina*. (For two performances at St Pancras Town Hall, she recently revealed, the Handel Opera Society paid her £10).

Maria Callas attended the dress rehearsal for the famous *Lucia* performance with Elisabeth Schwarzkopf and her husband, Walter Legge, and the Covent Garden press officer shrewdly arranged for a photographer to be present when they all went backstage afterwards to congratulate Sutherland. The photograph that resulted, reproduced in *The Joan Sutherland Album*, shows the two divas both laughing, very rare for Callas, very common for Sutherland.

The meeting was symbolic. Callas was just bowing out of intensive opera performance, newly caught up in the circle round Aristotle Onassis. Her stage career was virtually over, even though she was less than three years older than Sutherland, while Joan's was really only just beginning.

Where, then, does Sutherland stand in relation to Callas, the other prima donna of our time who similarly sets herself apart? The contrast, and what has often been thought the conflict, between them has obsessed commentators ever since. Far from conflicting, Sutherland has been the singer who over 30 years has more than any other reinforced the great achievement of Callas in re-establishing *bel canto* opera as a viable dramatic form. Sutherland may have learned from Galli-Curci, Melba and Tetrazzini, the supreme and dazzling exponents of coloratura, who cared relatively little about acting. But she learned fundamentally from Callas, too, not to mention from Rosa Ponselle.

Callas has been quoted as saying that Richard Bonynge – and by association Sutherland herself – had set her work back a hundred years. That is the opposite of the truth. What Bonynge did in drawing out Sutherland was to make sure that, as well as dramatic relevance, the performances had essential vocal and musical qualities.

Sutherland may never have been a natural actress in the way Callas was – though curiously both had physical inhibitions to overcome before they achieved stardom – and her musicianship (more sensitive and responsive than has often been thought) does not have the quasi-creative quality that puts Callas into the imaginative category of a Casals or a Kreisler. But never has she represented the world of canary-fancying.

Anyone who saw Sutherland in those 1959 *Lucia*s, let alone the many she has given since, must know that dramatic integrity, total involvement, is as much a concern for Sutherland as it always was for Callas, if not at the expense of purely musical factors.

Conscious of her strength – a voice bigger and more beautiful, more secure in production and technique – Sutherland nevertheless sought to avoid direct rivalry with Callas, both in her live performances and in her recording career, which, after beginning fitfully, suddenly took off in 1959. Important as Callas's congratulations were after the *Lucia* dress rehearsal, those of Walter Legge, Schwarzkopf's husband and recording impresario, were of more practical value.

Legge told Sutherland not on any account to sign any recording contract until he had spoken to her. He promptly signed her up to sing Donna Anna opposite Schwarzkopf's Donna Elvira in what remains a classic recording of Mozart's *Don Giovanni*, with the Philharmonia Orchestra conducted by Giulini.

It was her first complete opera recording, but with Callas as the principal prima donna on the regular EMI roster, Legge was clearly barred from ever going on to record Sutherland in any of the *bel canto* repertory where she was having her international success. The Decca company stepped in but were initially shy of recording the new diva in complete operas. Instead – and this quickly proved a shrewd move – she made recital records designed to show her virtuosity and versatility. The first included the two big solo scenes from *Lucia*, done with unparalleled freshness, Verdi and more Donizetti.

Then Decca broke new ground by developing a format for Sutherland not used before, the two-disc recital album: in 1960 she produced what in many ways is her most spectacular recording achievement, *The Art of the Prima Donna*, 16 substantial scenes or arias, each dedicated to some great soprano of the past – Jenny Lind, Patti, Melba and so on.

Attending one of the recording sessions at Kingsway Hall, I was struck, as I have been since, by her total professionalism, the absence of tantrums, her ability to turn on at full intensity like an electric light before the microphone, and not least her sense of fun.

During an astounding performance of a Meyerbeer *cabaletta* of almost unimaginable difficulty, she pretended to strangle herself with her pearls, rather like Gracie Fields doing an operatic parody. Listen to the record now, and marvel still.

Bonynge has always encouraged Sutherland to be teamed with the singers most likely to challenge her, something she positively enjoys. One of the few singers in the world who in the same generation have been able to match Sutherland in coloratura brilliance is the American mezzo Marilyn Horne, and for many years they regularly performed together.

And when in August 1972 she was persuaded to go well outside her usual repertory and record the title role of Puccini's *Turandot* the Liù opposite her was a direct rival among sopranos, Montserrat Caballé. Everyone was apprehensive, but thanks to Sutherland's sense of humour and her insistence on yielding to Caballé the central place on stage, it was a delightful, even relaxed occasion.

The sheer length of Sutherland's career as a supreme prima donna has been a tribute to sound training and technique, but also to natural stamina. With extreme partisanship bedevilling the operatic world, her very dominance since 1959 has encouraged criticism. Certainly Sutherland has had her faults. Within two or three years of her first success she was beginning more and more to indulge herself in a mooning manner, using exaggerated *portamento*, smoothing over consonants and reducing many vowels to an 'oo' sound.

She has never totally eradicated the habit, though it was always more obtrusive in Italian than in French or English. More serious, to my mind, a question of vocal quality rather than of style or technique, has been the development of a pronounced beat in the voice, where a creamy, even quality always marked the distinctive Sutherland sound earlier on.

One might question, too, just what her musical contribution has been. Her central repertory itself, however, revalued, can never convey the weight or depth of the supreme masterpieces. Yet as Violetta in Verdi's *La Traviata* – one of her three favourite roles – she gives a portrait of exceptionally deep involvement. One has only to think of her renunciation duet with Germont in Act 2 or Violetta's death scene in her 1979 recording to register what dramatic weight she has developed in her vocal acting over the years.

Important also historically has been her encouragement – thanks to Bonynge – of authentic ornamentation, not only in the *bel canto* repertory (Callas and Serafin hardly touched on it) but in Handel too. There may have been quips about 'famous mad-scenes from the Messiah', but, quite apart from earlier recordings, you have only to hear Sutherland's contribution to Christopher Hogwood's 1985 period performance of *Athalia* to appreciate her continuing mastery.

Over the years an enormous list of recordings, not to mention live performances, bears out the breadth of her repertory. She has helped to bring back long-buried operas,

from Graun's *Montezuma* and Bononcini's *Griselda* through
rare Bellini (*Beatrice di Tenda*, now firmly re-established)
to Massenet's *Esclarmonde*, and even Leoni's *L'Oracolo*.

No one would claim that Sutherland's voice today is as
fresh or firm as it was 30 years ago, but it remains a glorious
instrument, even weightier than before in the middle and
lower registers, and latterly the beat has been less obtrusive
than it was ten years ago. And whatever criticisms have to
be made of '*La Stupenda*', they weigh little against the
unique combination of qualities that make up the Voice of
the Century. Happily, there is no talk of retirement yet.
Nor should there be. Joan still enjoys her singing too much
for that.

Edward Greenfield
20 May 1988

People: Bride price

Lao Tzu, the Chinese sage, fell for a dancing girl. Paul the
Apostle was smitten by the virgin Thecla. Carl Jung was
infatuated with the young Antonia Wolff. And 19 months
ago Sylvester Stallone, then 39, married a statuesque 23-
year-old Danish model named Brigitte Nielsen.

This week the star of *Rocky* and *Rambo* announced a
separation from the six-foot beauty, forcing the American
press to tear their gaze from Olliewood to the rift in Beverly
Hills. Was this, lawyers wondered, a divorce made in
heaven?

In a recent survey conducted by *Glamour* magazine
among 350 American brides, 69 per cent placed a high
priority on a man's sense of humour.

No problems in that department, although it was not
Stallone's celebrated repartee, delivered in the whiplash
tones of Marlon Brando, which first entranced the 11-year-
old Brigitte as she watched 'Sly' punch through his first
Rocky role.

Ten years later she caught up with him, sending her photograph and telephone number to his hotel. She had abandoned her young son and songwriting husband in Copenhagen. It was, by all accounts, business at first sight.

Soon they were starring together in *Rocky IV* and more recently *Cobra*. A critic wrote uncharitably of the latter that watching their relationship was like waiting for pandas to mate.

There was no shortage of bamboo shoots. He planned to give his bride £300,000 a year, with a bonus after five years. He explained: 'I'm paying my wife a salary. The longer she stays with me, the more she makes.'

When an earlier Duke of York tried to buy Kitty Fisher's favours for £50, she threw him out of bed, had the note baked in a pie, and then devoured it. If reports are to be believed, this is what happened to Stallone.

She is said to have blown her allowance in four months, asked for more, conducted affairs with actor Eddie Murphy and director Tony Scott, not to mention having a lesbian relationship with her assistant.

While Brigitte's 'friends' speculate what percentage of his estimated £70 million fortune she will sue for not withstanding a pre-nuptial agreement, many blame Stallone's indomitable mother.

From the outset she denounced Brigitte as a gold digger and predicted the marriage would last 'just about as long as a cheap facelift'.

'I'm the bravest guy in the world until she lifts her hand – then I'm a mouse,' the Italian Stallion admitted of Brigitte. But a show of dominance might not have worked, either: 'It was partially my fault we got divorced. I had a tendency to place my wife under a pedestal.'

Stuart Wavell
16 July 1987

A world safe for Coke

Ollie North's unabashed portrayal of embattled American patriots struggling to sustain freedom in a wicked or indifferent world may have done great things for his standing at the box office this week. But it has also uncorked the genie of covert action in a manner so public that it will be hard to bottle up again, despite the colonel's protestations that he did no wrong.

It is not simply that the malevolent and conspiratorial political extremist, Lyndon La Rouche, was able to blame his cheque fraud problems on an Ollie North plot when he appeared in a Boston court. Far more significant is the casual reference to 'the parallel government' which such a sober and Establishment commentator as the ABC TV anchorman Peter Jennings began dropping into text about the same time.

It is as if the American media, having for so long been squared or squashed by the Teflon presidency of Ronald Reagan, is finally swinging wildly off in the opposite direction again. Having pronounced the emperor fully clothed, or at least properly dressed, for nearly seven years, the press and television are now ripping the shirt off his back with a gusto increasingly reminiscent of the last days of Nixon. Colonel North's testimony fans the flames.

Of course the conspiracy theorists have always insisted that Reagan's benign public image was a fraud. Throughout the Reagan presidency there have been recurring scandals of unusual frequency, ranging from hands in the till (not all have proved true, but seven special prosecutors are currently at work), to the mining of Nicaragua's ports by the CIA, and last summer's calculated disinformation against Gadafy. *Guardian* readers are familiar with the Christic Institute's lawsuit against 26 alleged conspirators (including Messrs Secord, Tom Clines, Albert Hakim, Robert Owen, etc) arising from the 1983 bomb plot against the charismatic Contra leader, Eden Pastora, who wouldn't play ball with the CIA. The *Washington Post* carried a version of the story at the weekend.

Most American voters, preoccupied with their own affairs and insulated from the world by two great oceans, tend to see such incidents as aberrant excesses by a great power 'walking tall' again. Now, suddenly, many blinked at the near-ubiquitous presence in such company of the world's most incorruptibly energetic Marine. It is as if Graham Greene's *Quiet American* had landed a White House job to make the world safe for Coca-Cola and democracy, and for Coca-Cola if democracy proved elusive.

It has reached the point where Ollie's name is being tenuously tied, so far mainly in left-wing magazines like the *Nation*, to such near-forgotten incidents as 'debategate'. Remember that one? It was the theft of President Carter's preparation notes before his televised election debate with Governor Reagan on 28 October 1980 (Carter lost).

According to the 1984 congressional inquiry the theft was the work of a special team, the 'October Surprise' team, put together by Reagan's campaign manager, the brilliant ex-spook turned venture capitalist, William Casey, and – ominous phrase – 'retired military officers'.

Actually the kind of guys Casey and the inevitable Edwin Meese were dealing with included the very unretired head of Strategic Air Command, General Richard Ellis, who requested a request (for form's sake) for a session with candidate Reagan so he could help 'blow Jimmy Carter out of the water', as put in a memo headed: 'To Ed Meese – what think?'

Like Casey (CIA), Meese (White House and now Attorney-General), and Secord (deputy assistant secretary of defence until driven out under a financial cloud), Ellis was promoted by the new administration. Ollie North, a military observer on the Turkish–Iran border during Carter's abortive hostage rescue mission, has since got a better billet.

From here it is a leap more plausible by the day to the theory that the 'October Surprise' team's determination to prevent Carter springing a pre-election surprise – the release of the Iranian embassy hostages – took it to the lengths of dealing privately with the then Iranian president Bani-Sadr and the speaker of the Iranian parliament Hashemi Rafsanjani (the link man this time round) to prevent the premature release of the hostages – they took off for home only moments after Carter ceased to be president.

There is a precedent: the Nixonian 'backchannels' to ensure that South Vietnam did not boost the 1968 Humphrey campaign by agreeing to peace talks in Paris.

'We don't have to worry about an October Surprise. Dick cut a deal,' one Reagan campaign staffer recalls someone saying one night. Dick was Richard V. Allen, Reagan's first NSC chief, said to have been present at the meeting with the Iranians at the L'Enfant Plaza Hotel in Washington along with a chap called Bud McFarlane. So reported the *Miami Herald*, one of the second rank of great US newspapers (Donna Rice notwithstanding) behind the *Post*, the *Wall St Journal* and the *New York Times*.

The *Herald* does not go as far as the *Nation* in suggesting there was a pay-off: the Argentine CL-44 Turboprop plane which crashed on the Soviet–Turkish border on 18 July 1981, full of weapons in transit from Israel to Iran, with (Israeli officials later said) full US approval. There were no hostages to be traded for arms in July 1981. 'Suppose they were in payment for a hostage release delayed to influence the 1980 election?' the *Nation*'s Washington correspondent, British exile Christopher Hitchens, asked his readers.

Last Sunday Alfonso Chardy, the tenacious Mexican-born correspondent of the *Miami Herald* who stuck with the Contra story through the dog years, got front-page treatment for the story from which ABC's Mr Jennings took the phrase 'parallel government'. It operated without the knowledge or against the wishes of the cabinet officers – though Casey and Meese were on board. So increasingly was Ollie. One well-documented but unexplained incident arising from its labours was the secret 1985 visit to Tripoli of Reagan's chum, William Wilson, US ambassador to the Vatican – who carried the can Ollie is busy declining to carry alone this week.

Ironies abound here. Alfonso Chardy's name, for instance, appears in the three-inch pile of documents released by the Iran–Contra investigators on Tuesday. Chardy, wrote Admiral John Poindexter to Col. North on 3 June 1985, was working on a story alleging 'an NSC connection to private funding and other support to the Nicaraguan resistance'. But someone (name deleted) had warned him off with the threat that, if he printed any derogatory comments about the FDN (Contras) or its funding sources, Chardy would never again be allowed to visit FDN bases or to travel with their units.

Revenge must be sweet for Mr Chardy, for it was all true. The second irony, of course, is that in this most open of societies insiders had a pretty good idea about Ollie's role for years before a Beirut newspaper made it stick last November. The first profile of him appeared in *Izvestia* on 22 August 1985; 60 or 70 US stories named him in the subsequent year.

What is devastating about Ollie as he portrays himself and his chums as defending the Alamo against the commies (Bill Casey is surely organizing the good angels even as we speak) is his assumption that Congress, full of leaky windbag politicians, still has no business to ask the questions it does. His impudence is breathtaking. But, unlike Britain, where many of the same questions arise, in the US the legislature and the media will not take no for an answer – and the courts will probably support them. Mr North's candid admission of past lies to Congress has inflamed them – since they effectively protected him from investigation for so long after *Izvestia*'s opening salvo.

Some, possibly most, of the charges now belatedly flowing may not be true or true only in part. But the question lies as it always has in the control of civil societies. There is a hint in the Tower Report, where that Reaganite establishment figure, Senator John Tower, allowed to stand the line

from Juvenal's *Satires*: *'Quis custodiet ipsos custodes?'* –
who will guard the guardians?

Michael White
11 July 1987

Diary: Hello there!

Here's a private and confidential line on efforts to keep
fragrant the image of British Telecom, after all that adverse
publicity about dial-a-knee-trembler phone services (by no
means all of them BT's) and the Talkabout link used by
randy teenagers, scrapped in February. Incidentally, of all
the complaints, my favourite remains that lodged with the
Advertising Standards Authority by a customer who rang
up to hear about 'Page Three girl's first ride' and found
himself listening to an account of pony trekking on Dart-
moor. Anyway, Dr John Short, who is responsible for value-
added services at BT Enterprises, has been warning his
troops of the dire consequences of ignoring the company's
efforts to keep its name 'irreproachably clean'. His internal
letter says: '. . . audit your activities, adopting the point of
view that could be chosen by the most scurrilous, "puritanical", anti-BT journalist, and identify all activities within
your patch that are unsavoury from any angle whatsoever.'
Lists, please, of all 'danger zones', and '. . . your proposed
actions to clean them up or root them out, and the case for
the retention of anything that represents a time bomb.
Surprises on this score are in danger of becoming a capital
offence.'

Andrew Moncur
1 June 1988

My life with the stars

When the *Guardian*'s arts editor asked the paper's critics to change disciplines for a session around Christmas, he discovered that most of them wanted to write about films. And judging by my postbag, literally hundreds of aspiring journos would like to be film critics too. Where thou art not, there alone is bliss, thought I, pleased to have a go at writing about music instead.

But, of course, it is a good job, particularly on the *Guardian*, where one's brief is wide enough to allow one to write not just about the English-speaking films, but the wares of the whole world too. And that means film festivals, which means travel, which means getting away from those awful new cinemas in Britain through the tunnels of which you can sometimes get in but seldom find an easy way out. I am indeed a very lucky man, though I'd rather you didn't tell the editor, who is a film buff himself and might just take it into his head to switch jobs.

There are, in fact, several 'buts'. And the chief of them is that at least every other film one sees is unutterably awful. Yes, at festivals too, which are supposed to discover the *crème de la crème* of world production.

There is nothing quite so boring as a turgid art movie. Far better to sit through the worst of Hollywood, which usually allows one to giggle away quietly in the dark, or to contemplate how easily one could do better oneself with a good cameraman and editor, and perhaps Madonna as helpmeet.

I see, for instance, that they are finally putting out, on video only in this country, the prize Los Angeles daftie from Cannes last year – disarmingly entitled *Surf Nazis Must Die*. They have just sent me the poster, and it is up in my loo already.

But it is festivals people are most envious about. What glamorous fun they must be, what stimulation to brain cells weary of Wardour Street hackery! Oh, yeah . . .

I once saw eight films in one day at Cannes, starting at 8.30 a.m. and ending at around 1.30 a.m. the next morning. Only the last one was good, and by then I was too tired to give it my undivided attention. My food for that day was a dozen coffees, a doughnut and a bar of chocolate, though I nearly took a bite out of a Yugoslav director's leg when he suggested that I had deliberately avoided his screening that afternoon in favour of a long lunch.

But festivals are not all like Cannes where, the moment you stop going to movies, someone tells you that you've missed a masterpiece.

Some of the smaller affairs, at which you need see no more than two or three films a day, give you time for your long lunches or your hours on the beach or your chats with Yugoslav directors who badly want you to know that the particular film they have just made is the bright start to a new wave.

The three premier festivals in Europe each year are Berlin, Cannes and Venice. Berlin is by some way the most efficient and, on the whole, the most friendly. If you've filled your forms up anything like correctly, you can get a press pass in two minutes flat. You are met at the airport too, and your hotel room is booked for you.

And another great merit is that Berlin hotels give you a damn good breakfast. Spend time eating it, and you won't need any lunch and possibly not much dinner either, which is just as well since, at less than three marks to the quid, a good meal is pretty prohibitive anyway. And no, the *Guardian* doesn't pay for you to have two bottles of wine a night at the Kempinsky Bar.

The trouble with Berlin, as with Cannes, is the number of films on the programme. When I was director of the London Festival, I got slagged off by some churls for displaying around 150. Both Cannes and Berlin would laugh at that number as totally inadequate.

This means that, whatever you see, you have the sneaking feeling that, in a screening room just round the corner, there is probably something better.

Obviously, however, you can't see anything like everything and, even if you could, there's no way of expanding the space provided to write about it. But if you don't look at three times more than you can actually write about, you can't judge the general standard. You could get away with it on some papers, who wouldn't really know Tarkovsky from Wim Wenders. But not the *Guardian*. One's readers are too knowledgeable – Dear Mr Malcolm, How can you possibly say that Schneiderhoffer's fifth film is better than his first? He's only made four, etc. etc. One slip, and they are down on you like a ton of intellectually disposed bricks.

Cannes, of course, is the biggest and best film festival in the world, largely because it is everything to everybody. What you get there is not only the purest of art but the most crass of commercialism, with your *auteurs* rubbing shoulders with hacks and mountebanks they wouldn't be seen dead with anywhere else. It's a seller's market and a buyer's paradise, a home from home for both the pretentious and those merely thrashing about to make a quick buck, perhaps with a soft-porn epic.

Incidentally, you used to be able to see hard-porn too at Cannes, but they stopped it, largely because they found too many international critics getting in the way of potential distributors at the screenings. Well, you've got to relax sometimes, haven't you?

Venice is something else again – a supremely beautiful place but apt to be organizationally hysterical. For years, I never got any messages in my press box there because they couldn't get it into their heads that I was Derek Malcolm, not Malcolm Derek. And once, the chief press officer announced to a packed cinema, some of whom had incorrectly coloured passes: 'This projection will not commence until everyone has left the cinema.'

But there are film festivals all over the world now, and the hegemony of these three old faithfuls is beginning to crumble.

If you want disorganization, try Rio rather than Venice. The people are nicer when they announce that so-and-so's *magnum opus*, to see which was the reason for going in the first place, has failed to turn up but should arrive in a couple of days or so.

The list of festivals is endless, and can carry you from Ougadougou in Africa to Vancouver in Canada, from Hong Kong to San Francisco, from Karlova Vary to Sydney, from Southampton to Cairo. And often what you see are the same movies, hawked round the world with the director in tow, not really knowing which continent he or she is in.

For film-makers lucky or unlucky enough to make the festival circuit, it becomes almost a way of life for a year or so. You arrive, nervously awaiting your performance, you try to watch your film with an audience who only partially understands it, you make a bow on the stage and you answer silly questions at your press conference.

And perhaps you see Malcolm Derek in the street and hail him lovingly. After all, he might go to see your film, and he might even like it. Besides, nobody's taken it for Britain yet. And doesn't he work for the *Guardian*, or is it the *Observer*?

Unfortunately, Malcolm Derek is not quite certain who you are, and what is the name of the film you have made. But he has perfected a good trick to get himself out of trouble.

'Oh, hello,' he says. 'How are you? When's your movie on? Tell me, didn't they change its title recently?'

'No,' you say innocently. 'It's always been *Surf Nazis Must Die.*' That way, Malcolm gets the clue he wants, and can arrange suitable avoiding action. 'I enjoyed your film,' he can always say later. 'But I'm sorry I had to leave it half way through. I had a pressing appointment.' You never know who has seen you leave.

But the worst thing about film festivals is trying to get the prize results before your deadline expires. Nowadays, everything is done for television and the newspapers can go hang. Which means a very late deadline for the morning papers, and you have to get to a juror instead of waiting. They are sworn to secrecy, but there are ways of making them talk.

One of them is to say: 'Thank God you were on the jury.

We might get some sensible decisions. Tell me, how could you stand listening to that American juror talking rubbish?'

This often works amazingly well. 'Oh, my dear,' says the juror (I usually go for a she, if possible), 'it was quite awful. That idiot actually thought the French film was the best. But, of course, I blocked it. Yes, we got the Russian one through in the end. But it was a struggle.' Now you know what has won. And it only takes a few more minutes to gather in the full list. Indiscretion is so much the better part of valour.

But I really mustn't give away any more secrets. Instead, let me just tell you what once happened to me at a very crowded screening at Cannes, just to prove that it isn't all joy.

Well, I got there in time to avoid the usual French-born Alsatian dogs that are set on the press if they are late, and took the last seat available. Happily, I settled down to watch the film. But no sooner had I done so when a very large old lady, with an even bigger carrier bag, entered in the darkness and sat on my lap. I protested in vain, but she wouldn't move. And soon she started getting out sandwiches from her bag, and even a Perrier water.

She stayed there munching and slurping for at least half an hour, while my protests became understandably weaker and weaker. Fortunately, she then got up and left. I'll never forget what she said as she left: 'Bloody uncomfortable seats these. Can't stand it any longer.'

I've still got the creases.

Derek Malcolm
5 March 1988

Angst in Austria

Kurt Waldheim had taken the first tentative step towards resignation even before yesterday's fresh allegations about his wife's Nazi past. That move came when he decided not to speak at the ceremony planned for 11 March to mark the fiftieth anniversary of Hitler's annexation of Austria.

The decision, whch he insists was his own, followed threats of boycotts and walkouts by cabinet ministers and many other dignitaries. Instead, Dr Waldheim will address Austrians on the eve of the *Anschluss* anniversary from the safety of a television studio.

Even many of his supporters are beginning to realize that a head of state who has to melt into the background on a day set aside for national soul-searching about Austria's involvement with Nazism is no longer capable of fulfilling his prime political function.

Of course, there remains a strong school of thought, especially within his own generation, which sees Waldheim as a martyr. But the Waldheim affair is now fatally undermining Austrian self-confidence. It is destroying the consensus politics on which its post-war institutions have been built. It has revived tensions in a society which has not yet forgotten the traumas of the thirties.

Austria's economic miracle is fraying at the edges. The country, still run by an oligarchy, urgently needs to root out nepotism, and embark on reform. Yet an already awkward coalition government spends most of its time bickering over Waldheim, in slanging matches over corruption charges, or trying to defend Austria's name abroad.

The country is being ostracized in the West at a time when its government is making first approaches for Common Market membership. Foreign leaders, Mrs Thatcher included, pointedly avoid Vienna. Already some governments are balking at using Vienna as a site for future East–West negotiations. The Pope has reportedly intimated that he might withhold his blessing on Dr Waldheim when he comes to Austria in June.

Internally, things are getting much more tense. The chancellor, Dr Vranitzky, shows his frustrations quite openly. The Austrian People's Party, which made Waldheim its presidential candidate, continues to defend him in public. But even it now refers to the 'difficult situation' and calls for compromise.

Public opinion polls have shown steadily diminishing support for Waldheim. One newspaper, in what was admittedly an unscientific poll, last week asked about preferences for his successor. Way above the politicians, the man who scored the highest marks was Hugo Portisch, a political commentator whose series of remarkable television documentaries about Austria's history before, during and immediately after the Nazi era has drawn mass audiences.

Abroad, Waldheim is being advertised as a monster and a war criminal. Austrians, not because they shirk the wartime issue, are more apt to condemn him as a liar and a weakling.

The irony about the Waldheim crisis is that such an insignificant person has become a catalyst for an earthquake, commented an Austrian official.

Invariably those who have worked with him refer to Waldheim's 'servility, superficiality, and readiness to bend with the prevailing wind'. There is a consensus among those who know him well that, in one observer's words, 'He is a mediocrity and a coward, who yearned and schemed to become president because he likes the pomp that comes with the job.'

'Throughout his career, he always worked hard; but without exercising the slightest moral or critical judgment,' says one of his former aides.

The former Austrian chancellor, Bruno Kreisky, has only belatedly come to the conclusion that Waldheim 'is a liar and a disaster for Austria'. As chancellor, Kreisky made Waldheim his protégé and eventually his foreign minister precisely because he never questioned orders and carried out the policies defined for him.

One of Waldheim's contemporaries at the UN says he was 'uninformed, and always cared most about protocol'. Foreign trips would be judged a success 'principally by whether he was accorded honours as a head of state'.

Outside Vienna, with its strong Social Democrat tradition, the generation that fought in the war still stands solidly behind Waldheim. Typical of Vienna's coffee society, a well-to-do elderly woman who was a nurse during the

Second World War argues 'that we all experienced terrible things during the war, which we buried in the subconscious'.

But, like many less sophisticated people, she also passionately resents the external pressures that are being exerted against Austria.

She undoubtedly speaks for many when she fears that 'Austria's fate is being determined by outsiders once again. In the thirties it was Hitler. Now it is the United States, Israel, Britain.'

Equally certainly, the West's own convenient post-war image of Austria is now falling apart under pressure.

'We have had a very myopic view of Austria,' says one diplomat in Vienna. 'After the war it suited us to designate Austria as the first victim of Nazi aggression and encourage Austrians to build a stable prosperous country.'

It was a sound investment. Austria, adopting eternal neutrality, secured its State Treaty from the Soviet Union, and has become a bastion of Western democracy in the heart of Central Europe. Many of Austria's accusers today actively connived in the collective amnesia over its citizens' involvement in events between 1938 and 1945. The Allied Powers did not demand war crime trials for Austrians, or insist on reparations for the Jews.

'Even Israel,' the Vienna diplomat recalls, 'never made the same requirement of Austrians as they did of Germans, to declare that they had not been Nazis, when applying for visas.'

By turning the tables on Austria now, he reflects, the West may be trying to salve its own conscience. 'But it has lost all sense of proportion.'

Hella Pick
20 February 1988

Scrap values

Pick a number, any number. Let's pick £250 million, a quarter of a billion, the sort of nice round figure in which only governments usually think. You can play around with the calculations, but £250 million is roughly 'what our government is paying to British Aerospace to take Rover away.

You can react to that in a number of ways. You can say, as the Opposition doubtless will, that a great piece of British industry is being sold by the government at a disgracefully low price. You can say, as Lord Young did yesterday, that the deal is good for everyone and that there were no other firm offers.

You can say, as that apolitical indicator, the share price of British Aerospace, indicated yesterday, that in financial terms the price is extraordinarily advantageous to the buyer.

But if the City scented a good deal yesterday, and duly marked the shares up, its initial reaction was altogether the reverse, for when the deal was first mooted, the BAe share price collapsed. And so you could also say, as we did here, that in terms of industrial logic, the merger is madness.

But perhaps the most important point to ponder today is why, oh why, is this giant company, employing lots of people, making and selling perfectly acceptable cars, worth nothing?

Or, if you accept that £250 million figure, why does it actually have negative value?

Worse, why it is worth nothing when all that energy and money have been pumped into it? Were all Sir Michael Edwardes' efforts to turn BL round, all those crisis meetings with the TUC, the battle with Red Robbo, all that investment in robots, have they all been utterly wasted?

There are three answers to this, and there is a bit of truth in each. The first is that the company is probably being sold too cheap. True, there have been no other firm bids, but it has not been a proper free sale.

Ford or General Motors would have paid more, but they were effectively barred from buying.

It is not the greatest of times to sell, with the strong pound making all UK-based manufacturing difficult. You would get a better price were the group to be further dismantled, rather than selling it as a single lot.

This was a political sale, to a politically convenient purchaser, and so the purchaser had to be bribed to go ahead.

The second answer is to say that being a large employer carries an enormous cost, which has to be entered into the equation when it comes to reckoning a group's worth. The plus comes from the stream of profits which the group can generate. The minus comes from the redundancy costs which overhang any organization which is likely to have difficulty in maintaining a labour force of its existing size.

But it is more than just the arithmetic of redundancy. It is common PR-speak to say that a company's greatest resource is its people. You read that sort of remark in any glossy brochure describing a corporation's operations. But the hard reality is that it is rubbish. People are trouble. Managing a large labour force is extraordinarily difficult anywhere and we do not in general seem to be very good at it in this country.

In reality the key resource is management time, the product of a group of people who have the culture and communications to work together to run something. What Rover needs is oodles of management time.

But that has to be put into it, and one of the things which makes the group not very valuable is the drain it will place on any management's time. Most companies have better fish to fry.

Indeed, that is the best argument against BAe's involvement. It has problems aplenty of its own, including, like Rover, the disadvantage of a UK manufacturing base when selling abroad (watch for currency write-offs of up to £400 million when its figures are published). And it does not have a great deal of suitable management time which can be apportioned across.

The third explanation for the low value put on Rover is that the gap between success and failure in business is often very fine. If you go back over the history of most companies, there have been times when they were flat on their backs, and times when they were booming. This seems particularly common in the motor industry and its suppliers. Go back to the 1960s and Dunlop was one of the key companies in British industry. It was effectively bust when it was taken over by BTR some five years ago. Now the rump earns good profits.

Or look at Jaguar, with its switchback from triumph to disaster and back again – and all with virtually the same product line.

Remember, too, how Rolls-Royce did go bust, though it was never the car side that was the problem.

Look abroad and remember how BMW was within an ace of going under at the beginning of the 1960s. Tell that to the yuppies now. Or there was the plight of Chrysler in the US, or Citroën in France. Even Renault – an interesting test case in terms of what government support is or is not acceptable to the EEC – is worth virtually nothing now.

You could throw in a host of other fine names in the car market, and show how fickle their fates have been. The gap between success and failure is one outstanding model. Alas, it is that one outstanding model which has eluded Rover during the last decade.

It is because of that failure, as much as anything else, that Rover is worth so little.

Those are three rational explanations of the lack of value that is evidently attached to the group.

You can rationalize further, in saying that the economic and industrial future for Britain lies as a service industry country, with a few bits of specialist manufacturing tagged on. But it is disturbing, is it not, that the whole group, with Land Rover, the volume division, and all that property and so on, is worth at best £150 million, and at worst has negative value? Recently the cement company, Blue Circle, bought the lawnmower manufacturers Birmid Qualcast for far more than BAe is paying for Rover.

We can, as a country, make money out of making lawn-mowers. But we find it hellish hard to make money out of cars.

Hamish McRae
30 March 1988

Golden ironies

Every Friday night over recent weeks the comedian Harry Enfield has been strutting on to the set of the Channel Four programme *Friday Night Live*, waving great wads of tenners and proclaiming, in his role as a character known as 'Loadsamoney', that the secret of human happiness lies in lots and lots of what he calls 'dosh'. Now he is going to strut off. To his horror (for in private life Mr Enfield is a politics graduate of impeccable left-wing persuasions), a creation intended to be a satire of the money-worshipping philistinism of Thatcher's Britain appears to be savoured and loved. Real yobs all over the City, according to eye-witness reports, have begun appearing in pubs, brandishing bundles of genuine bank notes and screaming 'Loadsa-money, loadsamoney'. Before long, if present trends continue, the thoroughfares of the nation could be crammed with 'Loadsamoney' lookalikes. Mr Enfield alone has the power to discourage such practices. And, no doubt at great cost to his own load of money, he means to use it.

Meanwhile, across the Atlantic, the writer and director Oliver Stone, who made the Vietnam war film *Platoon*, is said to be equally chagrined by some of the audience responses to his new Oscar-winning movie *Wall Street* which opened in London yesterday. This features a villain called Gordon Gekko (played by Michael Douglas), a creature whose creed is greed and who aims if he can to twist and cheat his way to a million dollars a day. You're not supposed to like him. 'I think the pigs and greedies will be offended by the portrait,' Mr Stone opined as the film hit US screens. Not a bit of it. When they got to the scene where Gekko delivers a hymn to grasping avarice not a million miles from the genuine words of the notorious Ivan Boesky ('greed is all right, by the way') some punters, it seemed, stood and cheered.

Harry Enfield won't lack for company in the pit he has dug for himself. We weren't meant to love Alf Garnett when Johnny Speight unleashed him in a cloud of foul-mouthed racial rhetoric; but millions did. The great cartoonist Vicky thought he could ridicule Harold Macmillan by drawing an Edwardian caped crusader and calling it Supermac. But people loved Supermac too. The media, and especially the screen, have become a kind of philosopher's stone, transforming base irony into gold – loads of it. Tom Driberg used to warn of the dangers of irony. If you've got to use irony in a newspaper, he used to instruct young reporters, make sure you get it set in ironic type. The world today is littered with tragic, broken figures, weighed down by remorse (though also sometimes by bulging wallets), who are paying the price for not having heeded that warning.

Leader
30 April 1988

21 October 1987

Their Cup runneth over

Nobody is too humble to win the FA Cup, no one is too grand to lose at Wembley, and in English football there is still no such thing as a Double indemnity.

Wimbledon re-established these truths when they defeated Liverpool in a final which will be remembered for the result long after all but one of the performances, that of their goalkeeper, Dave Beasant, have been forgotten. To this extent one of the biggest upsets in FA Cup history will be good for the game. Indeed the events which unfolded at Wembley on a hot, heavy, perspiring afternoon were only really bad for those preconceptions which had envisaged the Cup Final as a sort of Trooping the Colour in football boots; moves and countermoves from the men in red and, to finish, a triumphant march-past on the way back to Anfield.

Such thoughts had ignored one important difference: on the queen's birthday the Guards are not expected to fight anybody.

Wimbledon's victory is historic. In modern times no club has won such a major honour after so short a period of League membership. Wimbledon were voted into the Fourth Division 11 years ago, the same year that Liverpool were denied the Double by Manchester United. Had they known then what they know now, Liverpool might have led a campaign for Workington's re-election.

For shock value the result ranks with Sunderland's defeat of Leeds United in the 1973 final, Portsmouth's trouncing of Wolves in 1939, and Blackburn's victory over the then-mighty Huddersfield in 1928. In another sense it is unique because all these examples involved well-known clubs with long traditions in the game.

Wimbledon defeating Liverpool in an FA Cup Final does not sound right, any more than North Korea beating Italy or Algeria beating West Germany in the World Cup sounded right. When the Duchess of Kent watches Wimbledon from the Royal Box she is more accustomed to hearing the bink-bonk of racket on ball and players arguing with umpires.

Yet if the result sounds strange, the way it came about was entirely logical, so logical in fact that once Lawrie Sanchez had put Wimbledon ahead eight minutes before half-time you had the feeling that whatever Liverpool might muster by way of recovery – and in the event it did not amount to much – the Cup was heading for London SW19.

This was largely because Wimbledon planned it that way. Their triumph owed much to the pragmatic mind of Don Howe, ex-Arsenal, assistant to two England managers, who joined Bobby Gould at Plough Lane after turning down offers abroad.

Howe appreciated Liverpool's qualities but was not over-awed by them. He knew that Barnes and Beardsley, working in tandem on the left, presented the greatest threat, and he instructed Wise to support Goodyear, the Wimbledon right-back, by filling in the space in the right-half position and disrupting normal communications between the two England players.

What was also noticeable, and this had to be down to Howe, was the way Wimbledon worked hard to prevent Liverpool developing movements from the back as they had done, week in and week out, in winning their seventeenth League championship. Stopping Liverpool's passing game is like cutting off a regular flow of blood to the brain. Their movements became disjointed, their game lost its shape and balance, and for this Wimbledon's midfield players, especially Jones and Sanchez, and full-backs took a lot of credit.

Certainly Beasant's own private study of Liverpool penalties this season earned its reward. He had noted how Aldridge invariably put the ball to the goalkeeper's left when there was no movement on the line, 'so I just stood up straight and guessed right'.

It was the first penalty ever to be saved – or missed – in an FA Cup Final at Wembley (you have to go back to Crystal Palace in 1913 to find a precedent) and it was also one of the worst penalty decisions given by a referee. Goodyear pushed the ball back to the goalkeeper and the Liverpool forward simply fell over his outstretched leg. As Aldridge struck the ball Beasant was half off his line, but had Brian Hill ordered the kick to be retaken he would have been compounding a felony.

Mr Hill has had better afternoons. In the thirty-fifth minute a long free kick from Gillespie found Beardsley beating Thorn for pace, much as Stevens's prodigious pass to Lineker in the same area of the pitch had led to England's opening goal against Holland. Thorn tried to hold Beardsley back but he wriggled away and ran on to chip the ball past Beasant, only to find that Liverpool had been awarded a free kick.

It is always harsh to judge a referee from hindsight, but experience should have delayed the whistle by a fraction of a second. Had Liverpool scored then they would probably have won. In that moment, and in spite of the penalty given later, the referee made sure he would always be a Blue-remembered Hill.

Two minutes later, with Liverpool still cursing their luck, the match was lost and won. Nicol, surprised by Phelan's speed, held the little man back, Wise swung the free kick towards the near post and Cork, whose shrewd positional play had already caused problems for the Liverpool defence, leapt for it. He did not make contact but the well-practised ruse worked as Sanchez, moving in behind him, glanced a header beyond Grobbelaar.

After that prospects of the twentieth century's fourth League and Cup Double, and Liverpool's second in three seasons, steadily faded.

Perhaps Liverpool had won the League too early to sustain their appetite for the Double. At Wembley the old hunger was not there. 'They played to their potential, we didn't, and their goalkeeper was inspired,' said Kenny Dalglish afterwards in his flat way. True enough, but you

cannot reduce Wimbledon's achievement to such state-
ments of the obvious.

David Lacey
16 May 1988

Jesse in a King's mantle

It was after dark when Jesse Jackson went walkabout
through the black Northside neighbourhood of Milwaukee
where 20 years earlier, in the anguished hours after Dr
Martin Luther King was martyred in Memphis, veteran
mayor Henry Maier moved with Prussian-like efficiency to
crush a nascent race riot.

On this chilled Wisconsin night, with the appalling
images of 4 April 1968 and its aftermath flashing through
the mind, there was a sense of how little and how much has
changed for black America. The Jesse Jackson presidential
surge, which has revived the slumbering desire for economic justice and the morality of a nation, could not have
happened without King. But the awesome burden which
comes with black leadership, 'Bearing the cross', as King
biographer David J. Garrow called it, is as heavy for Mr
Jackson as it was for his slain predecessor.

The crush and chaos as Jackson progressed on the Northside clasping the arm of a white woman on one side and a
black on the other, made one fear for the assassin's bullet.
A democracy which would seek to exclude a black from the
ultimate prize of nomination, won at the ballot box, could
not expect to be immune from the fires which two decades
ago lit up the streets of Detroit and Watts, Milwaukee and
Cleveland, and still scar the urban landscape.

The decades have dealt kindly with the King legacy.
The ugliness of the death on the cheap motel balcony in
Memphis is long forgotten by most Americans, along with
much that preceded it: the vicious race riots, 'Bull' Connor
and his yelping dogs in Birmingham, the cattle prods on

the bridge at Selma, the firebombings and the grimy weeks in prison cells from Albany, Georgia to St Augustine, Florida.

It has been replaced with the more softly focused imagery which Americans find easier to deal with. Dr King is entombed like a pharoah in Atlanta, his powerful concrete memorial sitting in a blue reflecting pool adjacent to the Ebenezer Baptist church where the 'Daddy' King and MLK preached. Whites, tearful and humbled by his memory, pay homage solemnly alongside blacks, sobbing quietly before the memorial, soaking up the slide-show and the inspiration power of his 'I have a dream' address at the 1963 march on Washington.

Dr King and his causes have come a long way. He is the only American other than the father of the Republic, George Washington, who has his own full public holiday; his magnificent statue stands in the domed atrium of the US Senate and to American schoolchildren his reputation has reached mythical proportions. My own US-born seven-year-old son Justin tells the story of Rosa Parks and the 1955 Montgomery bus boycott which brought forth the civil rights movement with a fluidity and reverence which astounds.

There are those who have feared the sainthood of King, arguing that the crushing sentimentality will bury the radicalism of his ideas. Hosea Williams, among the small group closest to King, has remarked: 'There is a definite effort on the part of America to change Martin Luther King Jr from what he really was all about – to make him the Uncle Tom of the century. In my mind he was the militant of the century.'

The Reverend Williams need not despair. Whether the Atlanta leaders of the civil rights movement like it or not, Jesse Jackson, the illegitimate son of a Greenville, South Carolina, child mother, has inherited the kingdom left by Dr King – the plain-dressed scion of a Southern, brilliantly educated black élite. But any disdain they have for Jackson stems not from his modest slum beginnings but from the self-serving annointment in blood which took place at MLK's death scene.

Two minutes before he died at 6.01 p.m. on 4 April King came onto the upper motel walkway and called down to Jackson on the ground floor saying, 'I want you to come to dinner with me.' It was a gesture of forgiveness; the two men had quarrelled over tactics for Dr King's plans for a 'Poor People's' campaign.

When the shots rang out Jackson was a stairway below and it was King's sweetest friend and associate Dr Ralph Abernathy who cradled him, howling: 'Oh my God, Martin's been shot.' Jackson was asked to play his part by crossing the road to the temple where King had just spoken to calm the crowd but instead replied:

'Man, I am sick. I got to go to Chicago [his adopted home] and check into the hospital. This has shot my nerves.'

When the TV crews arrived on the scene half an hour later, though, the young Jackson boasted to them: 'Yes, I was the last man in the world King spoke to.' The next morning Jackson was on breakfast television in Chicago wearing the same brown turtleneck which he claimed was smeared in King's blood.

Jackson, blaming the racism of Mayor Daley of Chicago and others for what happened, said: 'This blood is on the hands and heads of those who would not have welcomed him [Dr King] here yesterday.' Author Gail Sheehy, who wrote a penetrating portrait of Jackson this year for *Vanity Fair*, speculates (using the witness of those present) that Jackson deliberately smeared himself in the pool of King's blood. This symbolic baptism by blood marked the first bold step of Jackson's long and difficult climb to his current pre-eminence. What is absolutely clear is that without the path blazed by Martin Luther King, a more cultured, better rounded and intellectually demanding man, Jackson would not have stood a chance. As King's stature has grown blacks have become increasingly comfortable with their right to vote and elect their own kind. Most of America's major cities (with the exception of New York) are now black controlled, from Philadelphia to Chicago, from Los Angeles to Atlanta, and no Democrat can count on election in the Old South without the black vote.

As important is the softening of King's image. Charges ranging from rebel rouser on Vietnam to softness on Communism have melted away with the course of time. Black leaders can now be accepted for what they are. There is none of the poetry of King in Jackson, but a simple rhyming pitched in his rat-a-tat can have the same effect. Here in Milwaukee he excited to cheers and Amens both whites and blacks with a piece of birthday card verse: 'Red, yellow, black and white, We are all precious in God's sight.'

Because King went before and blacks can now carry the cities of Detroit and Chicago and the states of Alabama and Mississippi through sheer voting power alone, Jackson no longer needs just address civil rights. His is a broader message and agenda. There are as many poor whites as blacks and Jesse Jackson has stood with them at the factory gates of Wisconsin where the corporate barracudas are 'merging and submerging' and cutting wages.

These are themes which after eight years of Reagan's America can resonate with whites in much the same way as his highly moral anti-drug, pro-family message does with black audiences. Jackson can lift the hearts in white Polish immigrant Catholic St Frederick's Church in Cudahy, Wisconsin, as he can in the black baptist pulpit. Jackson has become the incarnation of King's dream as expressed in the old Negro spiritual: 'Free at last, free at last; thank God Almighty, we are free at last.'

Alex Brummer
1 April 1988

Diary: Gun lore

The Quakers were as vigilant as ever yesterday. No sooner had a team of British riflewomen (with gun) appeared in the garden in front of the Friends Meeting House in London to have their picture taken by the press than a determined lady in grey emerged to tell them: 'This is a private garden and we are a pacifist organization. Go away.' So they moved to nearby Tavistock Square, where a memorial to Gandhi and a tree planted for Hiroshima failed to deter the snappers.

Stephen Cook
30 October 1987

A shipmate's shanty

'Britten's operas all have these dreadful, dubious themes,' I recall Dr Bernard Rose telling a group of us at Oxford in 1961. 'The only decent one is *The Rape of Lucretia*.' What he meant, of course, was the closet homo-eroticism which haunts *Peter Grimes*, *Billy Budd*, *The Turn of the Screw* and even the repressed *Albert Herring*. You might think *A Midsummer Night's Dream* was free of it, but the dashed composer went and cast the Fairy King as a counter-tenor, didn't he? Snigger, snigger.

No doubt Britten's sexuality was subversive. But what matters more than the subtext is the composer's predominant theme, which is not specifically to do with homosexuality. Britten's operas, it's often said, are about the alienation of the individual from society. Stating it like that puts the burden of guilt on the individual, whereas Britten was always showing people caught in a system that perverts their natural goodness and stops them being themselves. Behind his thick cloak of respectability, which extended to a peerage (Peter Pears received a knighthood), Britten was a classic relativist and liberal – deeply unfashionable today.

Britten's purpose is clearest, it seems to me, in *Billy Budd*, premièred in 1951 at Covent Garden, and only now for the first time entering the English National Opera repertoire. With no women to blur the message, offering romance as a surrogate for social change, the homosexual shipboard world of *Billy Budd* focuses unblinkingly on the nature of social guilt and responsibility. It was plainly about the politics of the forties, about bureaucrats who trampled on rights while deferring to the needs of the institution, about passing the buck for enormities committed. It also stirred E. M. Forster (joint librettist with Eric Crozier) to a last literary throw at his very finest. Forster and Britten, homosexuals who went in fear of persecution in that era of witchhunts, collaborated with more steely commitment than Forster alone ever showed. The great novelist sometimes softened with sentiment, but Britten here stayed almost sadistically resolute.

Tim Albery's ENO production, his first on the large scale of the Coliseum, uses the revised 1960 version in two acts although there was pressure to go back to the original four acts. The main difference between the versions is the reworking of the admiring chorus about the captain – 'Starry Vere' – which originally closed the first act in a conventional operatic climax.

'In our later version Vere is not on stage at that point, and the whole thing has a quasi-religious quality. "He cares for us, we are his sons." It's about an invisible captain, a presence they feed on in their despair,' says Albery. 'It's much more interesting to have Billy fall in love with an idea he's never met, than to have him sing along with a chorus addressed to this rather average man standing there.'

Forster's letters leave no doubt about the intended Christian symbolism, which Albery finds far less churchy than Ronald Duncan's in *The Rape of Lucretia*. 'Billy's last night as a prisoner is like Gethsemane. The wine-cup he is brought by Dansker is like the Last Supper, but also like the bitter cup of the Angel of the Agony. The flogging of the novice is like the Deposition of Christ from the cross. There are enough overt references on stage for those who want to read it that way to be able to. Billy is like Jesus, and Vere like God – though later the allegory shifts and Vere becomes a Pontius Pilate figure.'

Albery thinks the opera is better than Melville's story. 'Melville over-writes terribly. But Forster's libretto really got to the heart of things. I prefer Forster's stories that aren't about homosexuality, where he wasn't able to talk about what he really wanted to bring into the open. His stories about relationships between men that were published after his death are relentlessly self-indulgent. There's much more discipline when he's not writing about the theme that most involved him.'

The Albery production is not conceptual. He and his usual designers Tom Cairns and Antony McDonald considered – and rejected as irrelevant – updating to the U-boat era with officers in duffel coats waving binoculars. They also decided not to be more specific about the naval effects than was necessary to fulfil the narrative. 'If it says people have to haul ropes, then we have real ropes,' Albery says. 'But we took our cue much more from the constant descriptions of the ship as a "fragment of earth" or "floating monarchy". The ship is an allegory for the world, which one readily grasps in a movie. We've tried to make it feel as much like a planet as a ship. Reproducing naval life didn't strike me as remotely interesting. The key thing is the ship is hell on earth.'

Vere is 'a decent liberal human being who finds himself in charge of a structure he knows is deeply corrupt and wrong. The problem is heightened in the opera by the external French threat, which leads Vere to think it's not the right time to question the system.' He is not at peace with himself.

'What's more romantic than a beautiful man o' war, a multi-deck made of wood?' Albery asks. 'Ships like the *Cutty Sark* and *Victory* send people gooey with sentimentality. But John Masefield's book on Nelson's navy explains the lower decks were painted red because there was so much blood around. There's one moment when we give a glimpse of the kind of romantic production people might expect, and everybody sings fervently about "This is the moment, the moment we've been waiting for," before the French ship vanishes back into the mist. But it's really people putting all their unhappiness and aggression on to a distant enemy.'

The events of Melville's story took place in the US navy in 1842, though he transferred it all to the Royal Navy in 1797 after the Nore Mutiny. Budd and his mates are pressganged from a merchantman called *Rights o' Man*. But the systematic injustice of the story is a permanent state of affairs.

'The feel of our staging can be contemporary, but becomes period when that is a narrative guideline. Vere's "Centuries ago" at the end should make you think it's just like today.'

Perhaps, Albery agrees, the historical setting is part of Britten's characteristic evasiveness. The work speaks powerfully and simply, but it can be seen as a personal tragedy, a sad story about Vere, his bilious, bent and disciplinarian master-at-arms, Claggart, and the latest angelic recruit, Budd. Claggart describes Budd as a beauty. But Albery maintains: 'Britten's greatness as a composer lies in that evasiveness, that tight-arsed, unstated English prep school quality. What interests me is the tension between the repression and Vere's almost letting go – which naturally couldn't happen in the story without exploding it.'

Claggart's aria is no scream of hatred from a maniac, but a love declaration by a man who can't admit what would undermine his universe. The stern unfeeling face is simply hiding suffering. The final hanging of Budd will not be what people expect, Albery says. It is the epic it has become in Vere's memory, instead of just some poor bloke strung from the yardarm. 'What we do is a bit over the top, making the religious connection very explicity. For Vere, Billy has to be something more to keep him going. Billy is his angel of God, gives him his justification.' Which is the point of those 34 consecutive chords when Vere and Budd meet.

'The trouble is Vere is so unused to dealing with emotions,' says Albery. 'He imagines he can set Budd against Claggart, because he thinks Billy can deal with it. Vere can't recognize the reality of Billy as a human being, he's so carried away by the idea of him as his saviour. When Billy strikes and kills Claggart, Vere cannot spare his life without endorsing the revolutionary ideals he is commissioned to oppose. It's the classic liberal dilemma – unrealistic and romantic at the same time.'

Tom Sutcliffe
14 February 1988

At the crossroads in Kabul

The Russians are going, and as if to make the point six Soviet tanks came joyriding through the centre of Kabul the other morning. The first hot day of spring coincided with the public rally the government had called to celebrate the Geneva Accords. As cheerful crowds of secondary school children and office workers streamed towards the meeting, they met this unusual convoy going the opposite way.

Nowadays, Soviet military vehicles rarely enter the city centre, at least in daytime. The foray was all the more eloquent for being unscripted. The tank hatches were open and each crew had brought some friends along for the ride. On each vehicle lounged a dozen smiling conscripts, their tunics unbuttoned and sleeves rolled up, their wide-brimmed khaki hats, in direct line of sartorial descent from Baden-Powell, were raked at jaunty angles. With their blond hair and broad cheeks this was another European army glad to be leaving Afghanistan.

The Soviet contingent here is heavy on Ukrainians and Siberians and it is no longer these farmboys' concern whether the Afghans can make peace in their wake. That is someone else's problem.

Unexpected though it may be for the Soviet Union's conscripts, the withdrawal has been carefully prepared by the Soviet Union's political experts, who have been crafting the policy of Afghanization for the last two years. As they drive from their well-guarded embassy into town they pass a daily reminder of their success. Set up on a roof at the end of the street is a 15-foot-square portrait of King Amanullah, one of the heroes of modern Afghanistan. It has taken the place of Babrak Karmal, the Party leader installed by Soviet tanks in December 1979 and removed from power two years ago.

Karmal is one of Mr Gorbachev's political victims. Although the main point of the original Brezhnev-led invasion was to prop up a floundering revolution by giving it a more moderate and conciliatory face, the policy went stagnant, like so much of what the late Soviet leader and his elderly successors tried to do.

Overtures were made to the middle class and the clergy, but while these moves were able to consolidate the Party's rule in Kabul and some of the other cities, they were not enough to offer a real chance of ending the war. It was Gorbachev who decided that the only way to extricate his troops from the Afghan quagmire was to move the country sharply back into the 1920s.

King Amanullah, the idealistic reformer who tried to abolish the veil and start a modern education system, was the perfect symbol. Suspicious of the British, sympathetic to the Soviet Union, and the first crowned head to visit Moscow after the Revolution, he was a nationalist after the Kremlin's heart, aware enough of geography to believe that Afghanistan's non-alignment could be protected by polite relations with its giant neighbour.

To restore the king as a convincing emblem, it was first necessary to replace Karmal with a younger, more vigorous leader who would pursue a policy of 'national reconciliation' and make overtures to the Mojahedin resistance to join a broad-based coalition.

In his two years in office Dr Najib has been gradually dismantling most of the decrees announced ten years ago when the People's Democratic Party of Afghanistan (PDPA) took power in an army-led coup.

The maximum landholding of 15 acres was raised to 50 last spring and any landlord or property owner who fled abroad is being invited to return and claim back his expropriated property. A new constitution was adopted last autumn which enshrines a multi-party system and a mixed economy and which underwent significant changes from the originally published draft. The Democratic Republic of Afghanistan was renamed minus the word 'democratic' on the ground that it is a Marxist epithet. A clause was added that 'no law shall run counter to the sacred principles of Islam'.

Every day brings new efforts at change. The country's first Islamic university was opened last year, and last weekend, on the first day of Ramadan, PDPA members who are not practising Muslims were instructed not to eat anywhere in public during the daylight fasting hours. How much of all this is symbol and how much substance is a matter for debate. It has not impressed the Mojahedin leadership in Pakistan. But for the Russians it is one justification for withdrawal, as a taboo-breaking article in *Literaturnaya Gazeta* has put it.

Hinting for the first time in the Soviet media that the invasion had been a mistake, Alexander Prokhanov wrote: 'The goals which the PDPA originally announced have not been achieved and the revolutionary government themselves have abandoned them. As a result, the presence of Soviet troops in the country loses its point. Withdrawal is as inevitable as it is logical.'

Withdrawal is also a gamble, since Gorbachev is pulling his troops out without any guarantee of a ceasefire or a coalition government incorporating even the moderate elements of the resistance. But the Soviet leader is calculating that the Najib government is politically and militarily strong enough to stand on its own, if need be.

Whether he will be proved right is the talk of Kabul. Fascinatingly, in view of official Western scorn of the PDPA over the past eight years, the view today is much more respectful and many diplomats give it a good chance of surviving. The French are even muttering darkly that the Geneva Accords are a perfidious 'mini-Yalta' in which the Reagan administration has tacitly conceded Afghanistan to Moscow's sphere of influence.

The public American line rejects that. Robert Peck, the US deputy assistant secretary of state who monitored the Geneva negotiations, assured Congress a few weeks ago: 'We are confident that a PDPA-dominated regime cannot survive a Soviet withdrawal. Our estimate is that the government could splinter and fall even before the final Soviet pull-out. Once the Soviet protectors are gone, the regime will be unable to project power into the countryside, and its early demise will be inevitable.' No decent interval, Vietnam-style, here.

Other Western diplomats, who reject Peck's gung-ho analysis, pooh-pooh the Vietnam analogy from a different perspective. They argue that it took the North Vietnamese, even with their heavy armoured divisions and air power, as much as two years to defeat the South Vietnamese army of President Thieu. The Mojahedin have a divided leadership, fractured fighting units and nothing like that amount of weaponry.

While the Afghan army with its conscript base is claimed to be likely to desert en masse, Western analysts think manpower attrition could be just as much a problem for the Mojahedin. Once the main enemy, the Russians, pull out, how many Afghan peasants will want to carry on fighting to liberate distant Kabul rather than slip back to their villages which the infidel PDPA never bothered to enter anyway?

Unlike President Thieu, the Afghan government has abandoned any illusions of contesting every inch of the national territory. It concedes it controls only a quarter of the villages. There is less risk therefore of a psychological collapse with territory unravelling before an advancing army, as happened in Vietnam.

For the last two years, the Afghan military posture has been essentially defensive, designed to hold Kabul, the main towns, and two or three strategic roads which connect them. Even if the Afghan army folds up, the government now has at least 70,000 trained men in its professional police and state security forces.

What then of a political collapse in the centre – a kind

of Iranian or Philippine syndrome? No one knows how big the pro-Mojahedin fifth column in Kabul is. But given the splits in the Mojahedin ranks, the lack of a clear alternative government, and fear of the fundamentalists, who are an alien part of Afghan Muslim tradition, some observers put it at less than five per cent.

The PDPA has always been careful not to touch the urban traders and bazaar merchants. It has enlarged women's rights and subsidized education heavily. 'People also know,' as one Western diplomat put it, 'that the Russians provide every drop of oil used for transport and cooking, and have kept food supplies going all the time.' After the years of negativism, the change of tone is remarkable.

Jonathan Steele
23 April 1988

Country diary: Keswick

I have never seen the apple-blossom more lovely than it is now. Most of my remaining trees are old, over 50, and since they are grown on a dwarfing stock cannot last much longer. However, even if this should be their last spring they are seeing it out in a shine of glory, each leaf, each petal flying its own little flag in the face of time. Two small new trees were planted amongst them on a cold February day earlier in the year – an apple and a pear. I had the apple planted out of sheer pig-headedness for I was told it would not bear fruit in my lifetime, but I shall be happy either way. I shall be pleased if it produces even one apple but am quite content to 'wait on'. The infant apple tree has neat rosettes of blossom up each small branch, but the pear – never tidy flowerers – does as it pleases. Fruit-growing has altered a lot over recent years and it no longer seems to be said that you grow pears for your heirs. Apple-blossom time is always a bit nostalgic for me as I have no hive bees now, but I still remember all the hard work and the fun the local beekeepers had together on sunny Saturday afternoons in the summer. One small picture sticks in my mind especially. It was a hot day and my husband and I had been to a school Speech Day and were to meet our fellow beekeepers at Bassenthwaite. We had our bee hats with us so my best hat, a pretty thing, seldom worn, was parked on a hive roof to be joined by an old tweed hat and crowned with the village policeman's helmet – and very happy they looked all together and typical of any beekeeping 'do' up here. There are few bees out today but there are knots of Small White butterflies dancing over the lady's smocks (*Cardamine pratensis*), 'all silver and white' in the tall grass below the apple trees. A lovely sight but not to growers of brassicas.

Enid J. Wilson
4 June 1988

The medium's message

Comedian Les Dawson's stated intention of marrying blonde barmaid Tracey Roper (36) was warmly endorsed this week by an unexpected source: Mr Dawson's wife Meg. Mrs Dawson, who died 18 months ago, told the *Daily Star*: 'He is the sort of person who needs a woman as an earthly companion. Naturally I feel sorry for the girl's husband, but I know the magnetism that Les has.'

Mrs Dawson's views were made known through a medium, a Ms Meryllyn Seddon, who according to the newspaper has been commended for 'outstanding accuracy' by *Woman* magazine. The attractions of this new kind of celebrity interview are plain. In terms of chequebook journalism, the dead come cheap (though the medium no doubt sets you back a bit). They do not need, as living sources often do, to be spirited away, as it were, and installed with great armies of minders in exclusive hotels. And they rarely get in touch later, as the living do, to complain that you have distorted what they said – or even invented it.

"Through that gap in the ozone layer you can see Prince Charles making another speech."

24 March 1988

There has, for instance, been no known objection from the former Labour leader Keir Hardie to the interview which the *Sun* published during the election campaign in which he announced that if he still had the vote he would be giving it to the SDP. 'The great Labour dream is dead,' he warned the newspaper through the agency of medium Nella Jones (55). 'All fair people will lend their weight to the Social Democrats.' As they assess the lessons of the last campaign at Brighton next week, the Labour Party would do well to ponder Hardie's testimony, together with the fact that of eight distinguished dead people polled by Ms Jones on the *Sun*'s behalf, only Joseph Stalin was unequivocally backing Labour. That they came in for unreserved condemnation from Sir Winston Churchill, Lord Nelson and Benjamin Disraeli (though he confessed some fears that power was becoming excessively centralized) was perhaps predictable. But they would hardly have been prepared for the vehemence of Queen Boadicea, a patriotic heroine of truly cross-party appeal, who told the *Sun*: 'When I hear the words of Kinnock and his treacherous ilk I feel ashamed for England . . . When the Romans laid claim to the kingdom of the Iceni, would Kinnock have razed Camulodunum to the ground, as I did, and cut off the ears of their ninth legion? No!'

And it must have been disturbing for Labour to find that the one 'don't know' in the group, Genghis Khan, intended to withhold his vote until the emergence of 'a warrior king to crush Britain's enemies and lead her back to glory'. It would be a useful piece of journalistic enterprise if the *Sun* were now to recontact Genghis Khan and ask him whether Dr Owen's speech to the American Chamber of Commerce in London on Thursday had helped him clarify his views. And while they are at it, perhaps someone could have a word with Queen Boadicea about her unfortunate misuse of the word 'ilk'.

Leader
26 September 1987

Heartbreak motel

I always rather coveted the Old Chintz Sofa. This was in Meg Richardson's drawing room at Crossroads in the days when it was more a home than a hotel. How many knotty problems have we seen solved on the sofa.

Has yet another Crossroads chef been incinerated like toast? Is Jill trying to drown herself in the bijou pool ('Open to Non-Residents')? Have more long-lost illegitimate children turned up, pawing the ground? Is every mortal chalet infested with bigamists, kidnappers, arsonists and Amy Turtle? Don't say the fish has gone off *again*?

Noele sorted it all out on the Old Chintz Sofa with a consolatory pat on the hand and pale tea from a silver pot. Sure there was some magic in the sofa. The Old Chintz Sofa, 'Lot 209, three-piece lounge suite upholstered in a floral print fabric', turned out to be a rather aggressive tan with orange fritillaries unknown to horticulture and downright violent daisies. It was not as I remembered it.

All that was left of *Crossroads* was auctioned yesterday in Birmingham by nice Mr Biddle, who had a family feeling for it. His four children appeared in *Crossroads* off and on, one as a vandal, one as a choirboy. 'Three hundred lots of superior furnishings and effects' had the shabby pathos of household effects after a death. Someone's life, you feel, should have amounted to more than this. *Crossroads* jogged along gently for 24 years, the last couple of years jerking galvanically as though on a defibrillator. Noele Gordon was fired and died, Miss Diane's life support system was turned off, Benny climbed a Christmas tree to put the fairy on top and mysteriously has never been seen again. There was a shiny new cast who were, somehow, unloved as though viewers blamed them for the death of the old. And so, on Easter Monday, it ended.

It was hard to match the furniture to the memory. There was a sort of huge leather hat, 'Lot 81, a good quality conversation centre unit upholstered in brown hide', which used to stand in reception at Crossroads. Characters in hope of a job as a comic cleaner or in the throes of illicit love would meet there while, behind them, departing goldfish guests gaped because they had not been paid enough to speak. But what about 'Lot 363, circular white sunken bath', a clover-shaped job intended, one can only conjecture with a sharp indrawing of breath, for three people. No one ever shared a bath in *Crossroads*. For nearly a quarter of a century no one went to the bathroom for any reason whatsoever.

I am not a meticulous keeper of accounts but, nosing through Crossroads filing cabinets, diaries and account books, it was all too obvious why the hotel failed. The miracle was that it kept going so long.

Filed under invoices were audition slips for some show called *New Faces*. Cyril Purslow (tenor), Cyril Westcott (singer) . . . clearly a popular name among the musical . . . Mike Onions (Herbert Crump, character comedy), all marked with brutal brevity: 'No'. The appointment book seemed to indicate someone with severe physical and psychological disorders. It had entries for 9 a.m. hypnotist, 9.30 psychiatrist, 10.0 dentist, 10.30 plastic surgeon, 11.0 gynaecologist. Then a wild cry: 'What the hell is happening?' Then nothing.

Restaurant bookings suggested that no one ever ate there at all. There were only two entries in 24 years: 'Society of Motor Thingummies in Restaurant' and 'Rats in the kitchen!'

There were a number of letters from guests, all slightly odd in tone. Some claimed speciously to have stayed there: 'Dear Sir or Madam, I left an almost full bottle of Famous Grouse Whisky in my chalet. Please return it. Ys John St. John Bullivant Lt-Col (Rtd).' Some eagerly attempted to book rooms, making various stabs at spelling accommodation. Crossroads seems to have answered these in a rather spasmodic fashion. 'Thank you for your letter of the 18th. I would like to point out that all good things are not what they seem . . . the time has come for all good men . . . the time has come . . . now is the winter of our discontent . . .'

This sort of thing makes one wonder if Crossroads was recruiting the right kind of staff. Thank goodness for Mandy who, according to a memo, 'is quite happy to do evening shifts apart from her Morris dancing nights'.

If this had been *Dallas* or *Dynasty*, how it would have been hyped, but this was like walking into a ghostly Crossroads and calling self-consciously: 'Hello. Is anyone there?' No one. Nothing but the thing itself. Untouched, undusted, every stick and scrap preserved in a spell of neglect. A what-not made of three brass butterflies hovering menacingly, a tooled leather cover for *Radio Times*. Pampas grass going grey in a vase, a chipped Stilton dish, a pink Dralon pouffe, a bamboo jardinière, a dinner gong with horns like a Viking buried alive, a barometer without a pointer, a Crossroads Motel sign.

And, Lot 183, a framed print: 'Nostalgia'.

Nancy Banks-Smith
10 May 1988

Orphans of the storm

As Nicholas Ridley spoke in the House of Commons of the international disaster of Wakehurst Place, its 500 acres were abuzz with the noise of chainsaws. Fifty per cent of its trees have been destroyed or so mutilated they will not recover. Dumper trucks headed for the corner where, like a crematorium pyre, the smoke of burning trees climbed listlessly to the heavens which, six days before, had opened so mercilessly.

Wakehurst Place is – still is – the world's most remark-able arboretum. It stands in the high Weald of Sussex, the most heavily wooded of English counties, the arborial Koh-i-Noor in the Kew Gardens crown.

The analogy for once is not far-fetched. Its 500 acres are a legacy of Empire, irreplaceable on the old terms, visited by 160,000 people a year for its tree specimens. Like Ny-mans, Sheffield Park, Leonardslee and other National Trust areas of Sussex, Wakehurst Place, which is leased to Kew, derived from the tradition of colonial administrators and merchants bringing specimen trees and plants from all over the globe.

'A piece of swank, if you like, but quite unique,' said Tony Schilling, Kew's deputy curator, whose life Wakehurst

Place has been for 21 years. 'It's a tradition of Englishmen to grow plants. They like exotic plants, new plants, and Wakehurst is a prime example because it is so vast.

'We have everything here, from secluded wall gardens to botanical reserves of 125 acres or more. Its great strength is its natural beauty and diversity.

'The oldest trees are the native oaks and beeches because they predated it as the garden Sir Henry Price bequeathed, together with its fine house, in 1965.'

There was no pattern to the storm. Technically, it should never have come from the prevailing south-west quarter, bringing in the stinging, scorching salt of the Channel to wither leaves where it did not destroy.

Schilling, his face lined from lack of sleep, relived the night. 'The wind was doing such strange things. Such uncanny eddies and paths. Some places you've got 100 per cent devastation, others are miraculously untouched. There's no pattern. The redwoods behind us are almost untouched. Oak trees, funnily enough being native trees, have taken a bashing.

'The ground is incredibly well charged with water and many of the deciduous trees are still in leaf. The impact would be enormous with such a wind. But it's not as simple as that. The eye of the storm, I wouldn't mind betting – I wasn't out, thank God – was such that it all happened within a minute. The eye went through and the whole lot went down like soldiers.'

Wakehurst's public entrances, half a mile up from the Ardingly South of England show ground, are shut and guarded. It is an unsafe place to wander. Days after the storm it is still beleaguered, phone and power lines round its approaches ravelled like tangled knitting, a giant pine cutting in half the Fiesta outside a staff cottage. Central Sussex still has 25,000 clients without electricity. All around farmers face major loss or ruin. Calves have simply disappeared. Grain feed rots for lack of heat.

Yet Wakehurst's team of 30, including constables throwing off caps and capes to heave away sawn and shattered timber, slave to open up again. 'Were you in tears, people have asked me,' says Schilling. 'I was. At the incredible response of my staff. It moves me to talk about it. In three days we're making this place look like a garden. Give me another 10 days and I'll have it open again on a limited basis.'

Visitors who know the garden will find it cruelly re-landscaped, like so much of the high Weald. 'We've lost rare and unique specimens,' says Schilling, 'but the overall loss is of majesty and maturity. It's a loss of heritage. That's what is so sad.'

The cypresses lining the main entrance drive, ironically as a wind break for the rhododendron walk, were flattened like a pack of cards. The rhododendron walk is no more. Any saving is a gain. The Himalayan glade, deep and mysterious as a tropical ravine, has survived down in its belly. 'The shoulders have been hammered to hell,' says Schilling. Coats Wood, a canopied carpet of blue-bells in May, looks as if giant wrestlers have been at sport in it.

Darwinism? 'Yes, but pretty severe Darwinism. It wasn't natural selection really because it's taken out good growth as well as the weak. Yes, there are pluses. We are going to end up with views which even in our wildest management dreams we would not have the guts to do. We'd have been accused of being arboretum morons.

'It'll take two years to clear up all the damage, but we've got to think positively. It's no good damn well crying. A relative rang my home the other night and said a wonderful thing. "You know you must be one of the most privileged men in England." I said what the hell are you talking about. She said, "Look. You're in a unique position. You can create the same garden again in one professional life-time. You can do the same job twice." It's not the way I would have chosen to do it, and with seven and a half years to retirement all I can do is lay the foundations of the second attempt. But here goes.'

Out beyond the lawns and past the ornamental lake, mirroring sepia shrubs and felled beech and oak, they went and planted a Korean silver fir. It was three feet high, but sporting fine cones. 'It's our first tree back, a kick start,' said Schilling.

Its dedication? 'To the eternity of nature. You cannot stop her.'

John Samuel
24 October 1987

Index